AF652023

ZOHRA!

ZOHRA!

A Biography in Four Acts

RITU MENON

SPEAKING
TIGER

SPEAKING TIGER BOOKS LLP
125A, Ground floor, Shahpur Jat, near Asiad Village
New Delhi 110 049

Published by Speaking Tiger Books in hardback 2021

Copyright © Ritu Menon 2021

Front and back cover photos courtesy of Kiran Segal.
The front cover image is a detail from a still from
the Merchant-Ivory film *The Guru* (1969).

ISBN: 978-93-5447-079-0
eISBN: 978-93-5447-084-4

10 9 8 7 6 5 4 3 2 1

Typeset in Electra LT Std by SÜRYA, New Delhi
Printed at Chaman Enterprises, New Delhi

All rights reserved.
No part of this publication may be reproduced, transmitted,
or stored in a retrieval system, in any form or by any means, electronic,
mechanical, photocopying, recording or otherwise,
without the prior permission of the publisher.

This book is sold subject to the condition that it shall not,
by way of trade or otherwise, be lent, resold, hired out,
or otherwise circulated, without the publisher's prior
consent, in any form of binding or cover other
than that in which it is published.

Contents

FAMILY TREE

Father's line

Quais Abdul Radhid (Became a Muslim in c. 631 AD)
↓
Ibrahim, 'Satarban Khan'
↓
Khairrudin Khan
↓
Kund Khan
↓
Khashi Khan
↓
Maday Khan
↓
Yusuf Khan
↓
Malay Khan
↓
Daulat Khan
↓
Barka Khan
↓
Ibrahim Khan
↓
Maroof Khan
↓
Behram Khan
↓
Sarkeen Khan
↓
Hassan Ali Khan
↓
Sheroo Khan
↓
Pandoo Khan
↓
Daood Khan
↓
Maulvi Luqman Khan
↓
Maulvi Ghulam Jilani Khan (Came to India c. 1760)
↓
Risaldar Ghulam Hassan Khan
↓
Risaldar Ghulam Akbar Khan
↓
Risaldar Ghulam Inayatullah Khan
↓
Kamadan Ataullah Khan
↓

↓	↓	↓
Imadullah Khan	Maulvi Ziaullah Khan	Mohammad Mumtazullah Khan (Zohra's father)

FAMILY TREE

Mother's line

Omar Khan (Came to India c. 1760 and appointed Nawab of Najibabad)
↓
Nawab Zabtey Khan
↓

↓ Nawab Ghulan Quadir Khan

↓ Moinuddin Khan 'Bhamboo'
↓

↓ Nawab Jalaluddin (Shot in the Mutiny)
↓

↓ Nawab Mahmood Khan (Fled to Nepal)

↓ Jaffery Begum (Married Zohra's paternal grandfather Kamadan Ataullah Khan)

↓ Hamiduzzafar Khan
↓ ↓ ↓ ↓ ↓ ↓ ↓ ↓ ↓ ↓ ↓ ↓ ↓ ↓ ↓

↓ Aurang Begum

↓ Anwari Begum

↓ Batuli Begum

↓ Natiqua Begum
↓
(Zohra's mother)
↓ ↓ ↓

↓ Zakaullah Khan

↓ Hajrah Begum

↓ Zohra Begum
↓
(Married Dr. Kameshwar Segal)
↓

↓ Kiran Segal

↓ Pavan Segal

↓ Ikramullah Khan

↓ Uzra Begum

↓ Amina Begum

↓ Sabra Begum

↓ Kulsum Begum

↓ Massud-uzzafar

↓ Moin-uzzafar

↓ Rashid-uzzafar

↓ Said-uzzafar
↓ ↓

↓ Mahmud

↓ Hamida

↓ Gen. Azimuddin Khan
↓
Grand-daughter Askari Begum (Married Nawab Murtaza Ali Khan of Rampur)

Preface and Acknowledgements

Zohra Segal (1912-2014) spanned an Indian century that was politically, socially and culturally momentous. She lived through two world wars, albeit not at first hand, and was witness to the country's freedom from British rule. More importantly, for this biography, she spanned an Indian century of the arts, and in some ways, personified the innovation, exhilaration and sheer exuberance in the performing arts in the decades immediately preceding and following the Independence of India. Indeed, as the century unfolded, she became the only woman to have made her mark in all the performing arts, with the exception of music; Zohra Segal's accomplishments in dance, theatre, film and television both within the country and abroad remain unrivalled. She was, and still is, in a class by herself.

It is never easy to write a biography of a person so much in the public eye, and so beloved by it, that she becomes larger than life and her dazzling persona threatens to overshadow who she was as a person. The old conundrum presents itself—can one separate the dancer from the dance? In Zohra's case, she so completely inhabited the parts she played, the roles she assumed, the dances she danced, that performing became a way of being. How to see the face behind the mask?

Any decisions that one arrives at about how to write about a life risk being arbitrary, or whimsical or, at worst, misguided. For Zohra, I thought I could situate her remarkable life and the choices she made in the equally significant and transformative junctures she found, or placed herself in, whether in Dresden or Almora, Lahore or Bombay, London or Delhi. A great churning in the arts was taking place in all of them and she, having lived for a hundred years, witnessed, partook of, and wholeheartedly participated in it.

So many people gave so much of themselves, of their time, their memories and their insights, that I can never properly or adequately thank them. Still, I must do my poor best.

My first thanks are to Zohra's children, Kiran and Pavan Segal. I cannot count the many hours of interviews and conversations I have had with Kiran who never once demurred, or indicated in the slightest way that I was overstaying my welcome. Her frank and generous recall and detailed inputs have been invaluable; this telling would have been greatly diminished without them. In another register altogether was my meeting and conversation with Pavan in Kuala Lumpur; I was moved and disarmed by his openness and—rare for a man—his willingness to reveal his vulnerabilities. My deepest gratitude to both.

Salima Raza and Babar Mumtaz, and Kunwar Sinha, in Delhi, London and Bombay, revealed aspects of Zohra as aunt and dear friend, respectively, that only close relatives and associates can. In the same way, Jill Williams and Dolly Thakore, Zohra's agents in England and India, not only provided valuable documentary material and practical information, but offered a perspective on Zohra's singular attributes as a client—a client who became a friend.

Renu Setna, Madhav Sharma, Shelley King, Jamila Massey, Roshan Seth and Indira Joshi, who acted with her in London, in films and on television, were effusive, yet astute and judicious in their assessments, and always warmly affectionate in their reminiscences. I wish I could have spoken to Madhur and Saeed Jaffrey, Ismail Merchant, Art Malik, Rita Tushingham, Susan Wooldridge, Yul Brynner, Richard Gere, Michael York, Tilda Swinton, and… the many, many others she acted with in England; or to Amitabh Bachchan, Jennifer Kapoor, Govinda, Tabu in Bombay. Of course, I couldn't.

But among her directors, Waris Hussein, Lou Wakefield, Ken McMullen, and Gurinder Chadha were more than forthcoming, in particular about her distinctive qualities as an actress, and I owe much of my understanding of her as one to their critical appreciation.

I would not have been alerted to the changing theatrical scene in the UK in the late 1950s and 1960s, were it not for theatre critic Naseem Khan—for her detailed and close observation of the emergence of Asian, African and Caribbean artistes and their contribution to experimental theatre in that country. I cannot thank her enough, and my deep regret is that she did not live long enough for me to give her this book.

There are debts I can never repay, and among them is my debt to Jon, Jonathan Page, in London, whose diligent research, exceptional skills as an interviewer, professional interest in films and filming, and advice on how best to access archival material, have been enormously helpful. It will never be enough, but thank you, Jon, for your wonderful interviews, your unstinting, enthusiastic help—and your wisecracks!

Then, Seema. As I write in long-hand, it is no exaggeration

to say that this book owes its final shape to her uncomplaining, efficient retyping of successive drafts; she is, and always has been, my right arm.

Finally, the Raza Foundation and Ashok Vajpayee, most spontaneously generous supporters of the arts and of individuals in their pursuit. My sincerest gratitude to Ashok and to the Foundation for their support in the final stages of researching and writing this book.

And finally, finally, Ravi Singh, for being the kind of intelligent and firmly persuasive editor who only ever works in the best interest of the book. Thank you, Ravi.

It goes without saying that it was almost impossible to capture the fullness, the richness, of Zohra's life and times, and so despite all the help and valuable inputs I received, I know that this book offers only a glimpse. But then Zohra herself, looking back on her life, characteristically declared, 'Finita la comedia!'

Act 1, Scene 1: Dance, by Chance

Uday Shankar was her first love—as was dance. Zohra Mumtaz, all of twenty-three in 1935, couldn't believe her eyes when she received the following cable from Uday Shankar:

LEAVING FOR JAPAN TOUR ELEVENTH AUGUST STOP
CAN YOU JOIN IMMEDIATELY

She had met him briefly in Lahore earlier in the year, and before that in Dresden, Germany, while at Mary Wigman's famed dance school. She had even told him that she wanted to join his company. But to be invited to accompany him on a tour, without his ever having seen her perform?!

Well, there was no time to think, and anyway, what was there to think about? She wouldn't dream of turning down the offer. But she was in Pauri, Garhwal, visiting her father, and informing him that she was going to accept Uday Shankar's invitation and become a professional dancer was something that made even the impetuous Zohra pause. A young woman, born to privilege in an aristocratic, land-owning family in the heart of feudal India, embarking on a career in the performing arts—what on earth was she thinking of? It was one thing for her father to have indulged her whims as a teenager, quite another to have his daughter (who should actually have been thinking of marriage) take off on an international tour with a man she hardly knew! A brilliant dancer, no doubt, but an artiste who was an iconoclast, perpetually on the move, and also known to be something of a ladies' man.

But Zohra's father, Nawabzada Mohammad Mumtazullah Khan of the princely state of Rampur, was no ordinary parent. As she held her breath after he had read the telegram, expecting him to tell her off roundly, he took off his spectacles, left the room, and returned with a railway time-table.

'You had better take the 3:40 from Lansdowne,' he said, 'and change at Lucknow for the Howrah Mail.'

And so, without further ado, Zohra was on her way. To Calcutta first, then onward to Japan and Southeast Asia.

If there was one trait that Zohra happily admitted to and could be relied upon to demonstrate, it was acting on impulse. It was impulse and a spirit of adventure that had led to her accompanying her beloved uncle Memphis—Saiduzzafar Khan, her mother's brother—on a road trip from Dehradun all the way to Luxor in Egypt. It was 1930, she was just eighteen and had only recently finished studying at a purdah school in Lahore. While other girls of her age seldom left their homes without ample escort, Zohra used the purdah as her camouflage and journeyed in an open Dodge Tourer through Quetta, Baluchistan, Iran, Iraq, Syria, Turkey, Lebanon, and on to Cairo.

Zohra and Memphis travelled across Asia for three months, driving from 8 a.m. to 8 p.m. on most days, stopping briefly for a quick lunch, which they ate in the car. On the way they experienced blinding desert storms in Baluchistan that resulted in grit in every nook and cranny of the car, including their tightly packed sandwiches. They encountered abductresses and bandits and convoys of military and commercial trucks as they drove almost non-stop for two days and two nights across the Arabian desert, till they reached Damascus—a paradise after the deserts, with an abundance of luscious fruit and verdant greenery. Then Baalbek and Beirut, and on to Haifa, Tel Aviv, Jerusalem, the Dead Sea and Gaza, pausing to celebrate Christmas in Nazareth. In Baalbek, they were joined by her cousin Mahmud (Memphis' son) who was on vacation from Oxford. They stayed in inns and serais with no bathing facilities, so that when Zohra had her first experience of a real hamaam, she found the massage and hot baths heavenly. They entered Egypt from Port Said and went down the Nile to Luxor, returning to Alexandria, from where Zohra, Aunty Dicta—Benedicta Haslund, an old Norwegian friend of her uncle's, who had joined the group in Lebanon—and Mahmud took the boat to Dresden.

It was impulse, again, that had made Zohra declare in Beirut that she wanted to be an actress. Very well, responded her cousin Mahmud, let's see how you improvise: imagine your lover has sent you a letter saying he will not be able to meet you tonight. Before Zohra could arrange her expression to indicate dismay or disappointment—or even relief—she had changed her mind and decided that she wanted to be a dancer instead. She had been reading Isadora Duncan's autobiography and was suitably inspired. Then, walking to her room in the hotel one night, she heard strains of music wafting up from the ballroom, whereupon she snapped her fingers, clapped her hands, and began dancing a Punjabi folk dance. 'How wonderfully you move!' exclaimed Mahmud, who was walking with her, and so, as far as Zohra was concerned, the die was cast. She would be a dancer! And if it was dance she wanted, said Mahmud, then London was not the place for it; modern, experimental dance, of the Isadora Duncan kind, was happening in Germany, not England. Aunty Dicta agreed. The Dalcroze School of Eurhythmics in Geneva, set up by the pioneering Swiss composer and music educator Émile Jaques-Dalcroze, was also a possibility, but Aunty Dicta had friends in Dresden, so Germany it was.[1]

How was it that in 1930 a young woman who had grown up in an extremely protected environment decided to plunge into the unknown, in another country? How did a father, who kept his daughters in strict purdah when they were at home, agree to send one of them off, unchaperoned, so far from home for three long years? How did it happen that young Zohra, who had lived a fairly sheltered life (and in some respects a traditional one, despite an upbringing that was liberal for her time—meeting no men outside the family, for instance) found herself in Europe where she was left, more or less, to her own devices?

Part of the answer to this lies in Zohra's firm resolve not to get married after her matriculation. Her sister Hajrah had been married off unhappily at sixteen to her cousin Jamil, whom she divorced shortly after their son was born. Zohra herself could have married her cousin Mahmud, whom she liked (and to whom she had been betrothed as a child) or Jamil's younger brother, both matches that her father wholly approved of. But she had an absolute horror of child-bearing—her mother had died when she was just thirty as a consequence of too many births, too close together; so had her father's second wife, a young woman barely a few years older than the two elder Mumtaz siblings. Zohra was determined she wouldn't end up like them. Her uncle Memphis, a bit of a free spirit himself, played a major part in encouraging her when she expressed her interest in dance, and in persuading her father to let her go to Germany. But in the end, the answer must lie in Zohra's own impulse to find her way in the world and make of her life what she would, and in her intuitive realisation that this would only be possible away from her home and country.

Zohra, Mahmud and Aunty Dicta arrived in Dresden in January 1931, to look for a dance school for her. They visited several in Berlin and Dresden, deciding finally on the Mary Wigman Tanz Schule, because Zohra liked the atmosphere of the place. Of her interview with Wigman, Zohra recalled, '[T]he first question she asked me was, "Can you dance?" I told her that I hadn't learnt dance because my childhood was a sheltered one.' To a radical artiste like Wigman, who had rejected formal technique in favour of improvisation, this wasn't a disadvantage. Zohra was admitted to the school, and it was just the place she needed to be in.[2] A friend of Aunty Dicta's, the Baroness von Teufel, knew of an aristocratic family that took in paying guests—the Count and Countess Zedtwitz von Liebenstein, who had fallen on difficult times—and it was decided that Zohra stay with them for the next two years. She took to the Zedtwitzes immediately.

Every morning, after breakfast at the Zedtwitzes, Zohra took the train from Neustadt to Alstadt across the river Elbe. At the school she went straight to the changing room, removed her sari without removing her coat, and changed quickly into a long blouse and bloomers that the Zedtwitzes' tailor had made for her—it was a while before she felt bold enough to wear the halter and panties that the other girls did. The school was hard work. Not knowing German, Zohra was unable to attend lectures on theory, but she took courses in pedagogy and eurythmics, sometimes training for up to fourteen hours at a stretch. This enforced physical exertion built up her stamina, and would stand her in good stead for the rest of her life.

Classes began at about ten in the morning in a studio with glass windows, starting with limbering up exercises for the whole body, from fingertips and wrists to arms and shoulders, neck, head, back, chest, then hips and knees, legs and toes; splits and backbends, touching the back of your head with your foot. There were no mirrors, as part of the training was not to look at yourself while composing or dancing; Wigman believed that consciousness and awareness should proceed from within, rather than from an external image. The timetable was different every day. Composition, choreography, dramatic pieces—the last with masks. A mask, the teacher explained, speaks for itself, the features are still. Watching each other, said Zohra, 'we could see how the facial expression of the mask changed according to the inner being of the dancer'. A sad or lively effect could be portrayed with the same mask simply by changing the light.[3]

Although Zohra studied dance pedagogies at the Wigman school, the creative style of dance that the school taught was quite different from the grammar of classical dancing, Indian or western. The latter have fixed movement phrases which are learnt by heart; in the creative style, 'you have a thought, the body flows into that thought... then you create the emotion and try and recall the rhythm. You think, where does the beat come, where do I get my stresses, and then you harness it, fix it in your mind... you edit like a painter, eliminate unnecessary bits.'[4]

Zohra also took piano lessons at the Zedtwitzes, and was taught ballroom dancing by a tutor who brought along his own gramophone. She learned the waltz, foxtrot, quickstep, polka and tango—which she danced with flair at the Royal

Military Academy in Dehradun when she returned to India. 'As a dancer, I enjoyed a newfound freedom. I cut all my silk burqas and made them into petticoats and blouses. By the end of my third year at the dance school, I was in a bikini, nimble on my toes, and ready to touch the sky!'[5]

But the air was beginning to turn in Dresden, with Hitler hovering on the horizon; when a friend's son turned up at the Zedtwitzes in a brown shirt, everyone was taken aback. Still 1938 and Kristallnacht were in the future, and though there was talk of the Wigman school closing down, nothing happened while Zohra was there. And she loved being in Europe. Loved being free, being by herself, doing what she enjoyed, with enough money for food, clothes, fees—and holidays! It was like living in a fairy world—all of Europe was at her feet, and she travelled across the continent during the holidays, criss-crossing it by boat or, overland, by train or bus. A Bavarian trip with an English friend, Mary Hudson, also a paying guest at the Zedtwitzes; a walking trip with Patricia, her American friend, who had come to Germany to study dancing; trips to Norway, Austria, Hungary…

Zohra delighted in the adventure of travel, in discovering new places and people. She sought out travel agents, pored over brochures for package tours, travelled with groups by train or bus, went on walking tours with friends, rucksacks on their backs, sandwiches in their pockets. The prospect of holidays without travel was nightmarish, as she confessed to her uncle in a letter of August 1932:

> Lovely Memphis!
>
> That letter of yours arrived just in time to prevent my committing suicide! You see, I was in a dreadful state of mind. Here I was with my holidays having begun 3 weeks

ago, with no one and nowhere to go to, and with not enough money to take up something definite. I had been making many plans for spending these holidays, but all of them failed. The very first one was to go to Italy with a friend who plays the piano at our school. She could not go as early as July so I decided to wait for her till she got her holidays in August. In the meanwhile I tried to do something else—fly to Paris with a brother and sister and meet Uday Shankar, the Indian dancer. He was not in Paris just then and I never got a reply to my letter... Then there were some actors going to Russia and I thought of hooking myself onto their tail, but was rudely snatched back in my place by Graf Z., who said the journey would be dreadfully tiring and dull for me as the others would travel 3rd class for long nights and visit only picture galleries...[6]

Her two-and-a-half years at the dance school passed in a flash, and having got her diploma after submitting her thesis (in English), she graduated with distinction in June 1933. Darling Memphis got the breaking news first:

> There are three ways in which I could give you yesterday's news. I could say, 'Uncle, I have passed.' That would be keeping my little attic window shut. I could also say, 'Mamoosaheb!! Just fancy! There were *fifteen* of us who went in for the Diploma. All of them have been studying dancing for over *three* years. I, in spite of having been here *barely* more than two years and not knowing a *word* of German before I came, or ever having set eyes on this sort of dancing and only twice seen real Indian dancing, have passed, beating all of them but one, and stood second out of the whole lot!!'[7]

Shortly after, on July 8, 1933, Zohra left for a two-month trip by boat from Oslo to the North Cape, with Aunty Dicta and another Norwegian couple, Mr & Mrs Giertson. The first day on board, the weather was 'just perfect, sunny, cool-breezy, moonlighty, good-foody and jolly on the whole'.[8] There were about five hundred passengers on board, and Zohra was determined to make friends with at least half of them. Sure enough, she learnt that the young Swedish boy who sat opposite them at table was a good dancer, so she had found a readymade partner. Fancy-dress balls on board, short trips on land when they docked, impromptu parties that continued till the early hours—by the time they returned to Oslo at the end of August, Zohra had just one thought—sleep!

Time now to wind up in Dresden and return to India, but she had nothing definite planned for when she reached there. Take up Indian dance, perhaps? Write to Uday Shankar, whose performances she had seen in Dresden? Or should she go to Banaras to learn kathak from an ustad? Well, first she should book herself on a ship, the *Conte Verdi*, to Bombay, where she hoped Memphis would receive her when she arrived on September 20, 1933, exactly three years after she had left. Three years that she felt had been a lovely dream.

Like Zohra, Uday Shankar, too, came to dance by chance. In 1920, at the age of twenty, he arrived in London for an advance course in painting, which he had been studying at the J.J. School of Art in Bombay. His father, Shyam Shankar Chowdhury, a successful barrister and dewan (prime minister) of the princely state of Jhalawar in Rajputana, was in London to deal with a case that was to be heard in the Privy Council; through the good offices of the maharaja of Jhalawar, Rana Bhawani Singh, he not only arranged Uday Shankar's admission at the Royal College of Art, but also obtained a freeship for him. The Principal, Sir William Rothenstein, was a friend of the maharaja's, and Uday did not disappoint him. He proved to be a good student, and completed the five-year course in three.

If Bombay had opened up a heady new world of the arts for Uday, London was like a mecca, an endless journey of discovery. He studied all forms of painting—portraits, figurative drawings, still life—but was particularly attracted to the theme of dance. All his paintings centred on Krishna, one of them even winning a prize—*Dance in Moonlight*, which depicted Krishna with the gopis. London rekindled Uday's dormant interest in dance, which he had had little opportunity to indulge while in Bombay. His father, Shyam Shankar, had stayed back in London after losing Bhawani Singh's case in the Privy Council, supporting himself with lecturing and writing. He had also begun dabbling in and developing his interest in drama, music and dance, occasionally organising variety shows in the city, though not professionally. Now he inducted Uday into these shows. Uday's contribution was mostly 'magic'. Literally. He offered a mix of magic shows and performances, for which he improvised, devising his own movements and gestures. In effect, he was inventing a new vocabulary.

And then one day, in June of 1922, he performed for King George V at a Garden Party in Regent's Park. In a stunning display of originality, he appeared before the guests with a sword clenched between his teeth, a steely glint in his eyes but a shy grin on his face, and pirouetted again and again, effortlessly, before bowing out. There was an audible gasp from the audience. Breaking the spell, the king advanced towards him, and shaking his hand, said, 'Very good, very good, a good job!' Young Uday nearly passed out.[9]

At this time, the celebrated Russian ballerina Anna Pavlova was living and performing in London, and had just returned from her tour of the Orient, which included India. She had visited temples and seen monuments, watched folk dances performed at festivals and been struck by their vitality, and wanted very much to include some Indian dance in her own repertoire. But where were the dancers? India in the 1920s offered few possibilities and even fewer practitioners. Pavlova had seen the caves at Ajanta and inspired by them, was determined to choreograph ballets based on Indian subjects, even if she found no Indian dancers. She focussed on three themes: *Ajanta Frescoes, A Hindu Wedding* and *Krishna and Radha*. She commissioned Ivan Clustine, the Russian ballet master, for the choreography. Clustine had been premier danseur at the Bolshoi since 1886, and subsequently ballet master at the Paris Opera, before joining Pavlova in 1914.

A young Indian pianist, Comolata Banerji, daughter of Sir Albion and Lady Banerji, who taught and promoted Indian music in London, was summoned to Ivy House, Pavlova's residence in Hampstead, for an informal recital. She greatly impressed the assembled company with her playing and was promptly commissioned to write the score for *Krishna and Radha* and *A Hindu Wedding*. Pavlova now turned to her friend Mrs N.C. Sen, whose husband was an official in the India Office, for advice; she suggested that Pavlova meet Uday Shankar. She did, and invited him to her house, along with a few others. There were about ten people assembled in the room, including Pavlova's husband, ballet masters, leading dancers and the conductor. As soon as all were seated, Pavlova began by serving tea. Shankar later recalled, 'I could not help watching her all the time. The way she poured the tea, passed the sugar, moved her hands, it was so attractive, I could not take my eyes away. Every gesture of hers was full of life and energy and beauty. I felt she was dancing.'[10]

He then 'danced' for her, and was completely taken aback when she offered him a chance not only to perform in *A Hindu Wedding* and *Krishna and Radha*, but also to choreograph them for her! Pavlova's experienced eye knew a dancer when she saw one; she described Shankar as 'a born dancer with the finest dance body I have seen in men in any country'.[11] Although, as Shankar later confessed, he 'did not know what ballet meant,' he did know painting. He knew 'how to cover space, make group formations, create and blend movement', and after seeing Pavlova's troupe practising and rehearsing, he was able to understand what she had in mind for the two dances: 'It was no problem creating them.' Shankar had three months in which to produce the two dances; the decor and costumes were based on miniatures in the Victoria & Albert Museum, and the dancers' costumes were made with fabric that Pavlova had brought back from India.

Pavlova's season opened at the Royal Opera House in Covent Garden on September 10, 1923, with six new ballets: *Ajanta Frescoes*, *A Polish Wedding*, *Dionysius*, Oriental Impressions (*A Hindu Wedding* and *Krishna and Radha*), *Russian Folklore* and *La Fille Mal Gardee*. Pavlova danced with Shankar in *Krishna and Radha* in a performance marked by flowing, swaying movements and elaborate hand and arm gestures. Although, as Pavlova had remarked, Shankar's body was made for dance, not for painting or sculpture, his performance passed unnoticed by reviewers and critics. It was Pavlova who was applauded, and the costumes and decor that were appreciated.

Shankar wasn't the least bit bothered by the fact that he was 'invisible' to the critics, just as he hadn't been the least bit nervous about dancing with one of the greatest dancers in the world. After the season at the Royal Opera he joined Pavlova's Company, performed in many places in England and then in America in 1923, during a tour organised by the legendary New York impresario Sol Hurok. The Company toured in North America, including Canada, and in Mexico for nine months, travelling in a special train called the PAVLOVA EXPRESS. In New York, at least, Shan-kar (as he was billed) was more kindly received than he had been in England. *The Daily News* commented:

> Mr Shan-kar's *Krishna Dance* is a human thing, a sweet personification of something extremely touching and beautiful. What actually was seen could be described only in poetic symbols of the East and by means of very wonderful movements…[12]

As soon as the tour ended, however, Shankar fell out with Pavlova. He wanted to be included as a performer in the Company's 'western' pieces, but Pavlova wouldn't hear of it; she believed western ballet techniques would ruin his 'oriental' dancing. Unwittingly prophetic, she reprimanded him one day for wanting to perform as an extra in her ballets. 'You, if you want to learn our dancing, get out!' she shouted. 'You should go to India and bring something to show us.' Little did she, or he, know then that he would do just that. He left Pavlova's Company and for the next seven years wandered through Europe, half-starved and penurious, dancing or performing in cafés, nightclubs, seedy dens, wherever anyone would let him. In sickness or in health, he danced to keep body and soul together. 'There is no count,' he said, 'of the number of times I must have pawned anything I had for sheer survival.'[13]

It was only after he met Simone Barbierre, then only sixteen years old, in a chance encounter in Paris, that his fortune changed. Simone was an occasional pupil of the dancer Jeanne Ronsay, herself a 'student' of sorts of Uday Shankar and trained before that by the legendary Isadora Duncan. Simone, or Simkie as Shankar named her, was a pianist, and it was as his musician that she became part of his motley group. Other than playing the piano, she began to mimic Shankar's dance movements and was gradually inducted as a dancer, as his dance mate. She remained his principal dancer for twenty years, following him across Europe and the United States, and eventually to India in 1935. In Simkie, Shankar found his focus. She became his muse, his partner, his lover, the inspiration for his compositions.

But there were two developments before this that would prove transformative. At some point during the hard years following his parting from Pavlova, Shankar saw an illustration of Shiva as Nataraja, the 'lord of dance', in *The Mirror of Gesture,* Ananda Coomaraswamy's translation of *Abhinaya Darpana*, an ancient Sanskrit handbook of stage-craft and body movement. According to Shankar, he knew immediately that this was the kind of dance he had to do. Nataraja's tandava, he realised, was not simply a pose, but 'the centre of hundreds of movements that moved from one to another and finished with that pose... This idea of movements radiating from a source and merging back into it, I used in a number of my compositions.'[14]

Around the same time, Shankar met the successful Swiss painter and sculptor Alice Boner when he was performing at clubs in Zurich. An Indophile, she had harboured an interest in Indian arts since youth, and she discerned a quality in Shankar's dance that 'transcended its cabaret surroundings to convey a sense of authority and authenticity generally absent from the fanciful gyrations of his "exotic dance" counterparts.'[15] She invited him to model for her, and her sketches of him would help Shankar evolve a style entirely his own, inspired as much by the Nataraja image as by temple sculptures he had seen during an extended tour across central and southern India in 1927-28. He travelled to India again, in 1930, this time with Boner, and when he confided to her that what he really wanted was to bring a full-fledged Indian troupe of trained musicians and dancers to Europe, she endorsed the plan wholeheartedly and became his financial guarantor. Thus was born the Uday Shankar Company, and Boner remained his most loyal and staunch patron and supporter over the years, accompanying the troupe on many of their tours.

As Shankar and Simkie, the stars of the Company, danced across Europe, their performances were received rapturously by an audience ready to consume an exoticised, orientalised rendering that had little to do with either the classical or folk traditions of Indian dance. It offered, instead, romance, mystery, sensuousness wrapped up in myth and mysticism. Lavish praise now greeted this dancer from the East, who dazzled and astonished western audiences with his grace and energy. He and his dancers criss-crossed Europe, England and the US, performing close to nine hundred times over a three-year period. In Paris, *Le Miroir du Monde* wrote:

> The discovery of the dance and music of Uday Shan-kar will remain for us one of the most magnificent recollections we can record... the echoes, lights and thoughts of an entire world, an entire soul, an entire metaphysical system are projected into the performance...[16]

In Geneva, the music critic of *Il Lavoro* was mesmerised by the 'physical beauty', 'transcendental expression', 'grandness' and 'command of… muscles' of this 'rare, yet mysterious personality of Modern India'. Germany's Reichpost wrote of the 'infinitely beautiful and deep charm [that] emanates from these dances', and of Shankar that he 'ravishes the eye by the indescribable nobility of his dance and the transfigured, remote expression of his beautiful face'.[17]

Reginald Massey, a dance critic in London, summed it up well: 'Shankar, by his very presence on the stage, crystallised the popular image. His face and figure and the line of his hand and body movements seemed to be, in western eyes, the quintessence of the mysterious dance of India.'[18]

Uday Shankar had no formal training to speak of. Not only did he know nothing of classical or folk dance, he did not even know where to begin, till he found inspiration in the image of Nataraja—Shiva doing the tandava.

Zohra, on the other hand, had undergone a rigorous programme of training in eurhythmics and movement at the Mary Wigman school. When she first saw Uday Shankar perform in Dresden during his German tour in 1931-32, she wasn't particularly impressed. She thought Simkie was Kashmiri and Shankar's cousin Kanaklata was a real beauty, but of their performance, too, she didn't think much. When the other Wigman students went backstage to meet Shankar, she said disdainfully that she wasn't 'going to mix with a mere *nachkayya*'. She was less dismissive when she saw them perform a second time, yet even though Shankar asked her to 'look him up' when she returned to India, she thought little of it.

But that was then. Now, in Calcutta, with only eleven days to go before her first stage performance with his company on August 8, 1935, and only three days before their departure for Japan, Zohra's excitement was uncontainable. She had arrived from Pauri and been immediately taken under Simkie's wing. At the Wigman School she had learnt how to move gracefully, how to hold herself, how to discipline her body, rehearsing, rehearsing, rehearsing. As a dancer with Uday Shankar she had to, if not unlearn, then adapt her training to movement of another order altogether, for there were no 'rules' or theory in his dance practice. The pace was hectic. She learnt eleven dances in twelve days, including two duets with Simkie, and two with roles created specifically for her: *Shiva Parvati* and *Tandava Nrittya*.

There was also Calcutta to discover! Parties, restaurants, friends old and new, dinners with Huseyn Suhrawardy, then Governor of Bengal, meeting the Viceroy and his daughter, even dancing for the assembled company. Zohra lapped it all up. She and her Lahore school-friend Tazi (Mumtaz Shah Nawaz) went out together, 'driving in fast cars, going to ballroom dances and cabarets, and boating on Calcutta Lake. It was a mad crowd, everyone out to shock.'[19] Shankar had nothing but contempt for them, an effete bunch that represented everything he despised—lack of knowledge and an appreciation of one's own culture; flaunting of wealth; blind imitation of the West (a West which he too courted, but on his own terms); a reckless enjoyment of life. He mocked Zohra for her easy acceptance and enjoyment of it all. But he was also impressed by her nawabi lineage—'in the beginning,' she remembered years later, 'he always called me Begum Saheb'.

Calcutta was the rehearsal for what would be Zohra's first

professional tour, with performances in Rangoon, Singapore, Moulmein and Kuala Lumpur, when 'that stiff girl' (as Alice Boner referred to her) gradually became more fluent and at ease on stage. It wasn't just dance movements that she learnt, mainly from Simkie; from Dada (which was what she called Shankar) himself, she learnt how to apply western make-up on an Indian face, to highlight the facial expressions integral to Indian dance. 'Never make yourself too fair,' he advised, 'you should be the colour of the back of your hand when seen in the light.'[20]

On tour, mornings were taken up with rehearsing the difficult movements, with a break for lunch and short rest, and then preparing for the evening's performance. Shankar was a stickler for discipline—the discipline of the stage, its punctuality, and as Zohra recalled, 'its almost religious atmosphere during a performance'. Their training required them to be ready to catch a boat or train regardless of the time of day or night, and to arrive at the theatre an hour before the performance in order to shed all thoughts other than those of the dance, so that when they stepped onto the stage they were filled only with the spirit of the dance.

The tour was a great critical success; the reviews were full of praise. But as Zohra noted, 'the money wasn't coming in', and the troupe was forced to return to India earlier than planned.

Nevertheless, on tour with the Company, Zohra delighted in the happy combination of travelling and performing and of discovering the pleasure and camaraderie of both. Doing what she loved best without having to concern herself with the logistics—and what was more, getting paid for it! At the time, Shankar's was the only Indian company that regularly toured outside the country, and the glamour quotient of *that* was decidedly welcome.

The most powerful spell was cast by Shankar himself. In Dada, Zohra found the combination of physical beauty and creative iconoclasm that proved irresistible, and she succumbed happily to the seduction of both the dancer and the dance, Shankar and stage-lights. The more she saw of how Dada's dance imagination worked, the more she was struck by the potential it offered. No one then was experimenting with form or movement in the country, and no one was choreographing for an ensemble. Nor were they using the astonishing array of instruments that Shankar was—violin, piano, sarod, drums, gongs, cymbals, sitar. His musicians composed for the choreography, and the dancers adapted their movements to both. The sets and costumes glittered and dazzled on stage, transporting his audiences on a magical mystery tour of India.

Of the other pioneers of creative dance in India at the time, perhaps the most prominent was Rukmini Devi Arundale, and she established her academy, Kalakshetra, in Madras only in 1936, five years after the Uday Shankar Dance Company was founded. She herself owed her fascination with dance to Pavlova, whom she saw performing at Covent Garden in the 1920s, and then again in Bombay, the East Indies and Australia. Of Pavlova she wrote, 'I can never forget her, for she showed me the great possibilities in dance as an art form.'[21] Dance then, and especially in orthodox Madras, was the occupation of devadasis, dancers dedicated to the temple—respectable young women were not allowed anywhere near it. It was a taboo that Rukmini Devi defied when she chose to study dance, but when it came to reviving bharatanatyam, the classical dance form previously known as sadhir, she purged it of its sensual, erotic elements and its devadasi association, in order to make it acceptable to the upper-caste, often westernised, social elite of colonial India. Uday Shankar had no such inhibitions, in fact, he revelled in sensuality. He had no time for prudes or purists, nor should they have had any for him. But the classical dance purists, especially in south India, felt constrained to let it be known that they were unimpressed by Shankar's unorthodox approach to dance; one commentator declared tartly, '...appreciation from West is not everything, for the public there knows little about the genius and scope of our art forms. Uday Shankar is ambitious, and complete success in the dances he attempts is possible only if he equips himself with a thorough knowledge of the arts.'[22] But Shankar, unlike Arundale, was not looking for endorsement from the custodians of classical dance. His concept of dance was entirely different—and he had the world to conquer.

In January 1936, the Uday Shankar Company left for an extended four-month tour of the Middle East and Europe, performing in Palestine, Syria, Iraq, Egypt, Greece, the Balkan states, Czechoslovakia, Italy and Switzerland. This time they were joined by the sarod player Ustad Allauddin Khan, who remained with the Company during its two-year stint outside India, and then became part of the Almora Dance Centre when Shankar set it up in 1938. Also in the Company, besides Zohra, were Ravi, Uday Shankar's younger brother (who would become a great exponen of the sitar); Madhavan Nair, a Kathakali artiste from Kerala; Simkie, of course, and now Uzra, Zohra's younger sister. Uzra had just completed her teacher's training at Lady Irwin College in Delhi when Zohra wrote to her, asking her to join them in England. She did, taking the first available ship to the UK.[23] The highlight of the tour—and, as it later turned out, a turning point in the Company's future plans—was their stay at Dartington

Hall, a country estate in Devon. Dartington had a history of supporting the arts, and Uday Shankar and his troupe could not have entered a more hospitable environment.

In the late 1920s, the philanthropists Leonard and Dorothy Elmhirst set up Dartington Hall (with considerable help from Dorothy's independent wealth), a sprawling campus of many acres, for the promotion of a range of activities—agriculture, forestry, education and the arts, especially theatre. The Elmhirsts were friends of Rabindranath Tagore, and had financed the setting up of Sriniketan, a rural centre attached to Santiniketan in Bengal, in the early 1920s. Tagore introduced them to Uday Shankar, who performed at Dartington Hall as a soloist in 1933, and with his Company in the summer of 1934. Of the 1934 performance, Paula Morel, the then librarian at Dartington Hall, recalled: 'When the curtain went up, it was as though the gods had come to Devonshire. I shall never forget the experience... I have seen many dancers in my time, but none except Uday Shankar seemed to bring gods to the earth.'[24]

By 1936, when the Company arrived at Dartington Hall as part of its Grand European Tour, Dartington's drama department had already requisitioned the services of the acclaimed Russian actor Mikhail Chekhov, nephew of the writer and dramatist Anton Chekhov. Mikhail Chekhov was an alumnus of the Moscow Art Theatre trained in the Stanislavsky school of method acting, and had been brought to Dartington Hall by Beatrice Straight, Dorothy Elmhirst's daughter from her first marriage.[25] Shankar and his troupe were warmly welcomed by the Elmhirsts themselves and installed in the children's school on the estate; wrote Zohra, 'We felt like Goldilocks and the three bears, using their tiny beds, tables and chairs.'[26] England in May was lovely, and it was equally lovely to have Uzra with her in the Company. They could hang out together, occasionally go to tea at the Elmhirsts' house, which was next to the Great Hall. Beatrice was their contemporary, warm and generous, and with her they holidayed in Cornwall, staying with Uday Shankar at the Elmhirsts' cottage, 'Chalet'. They picnicked on the Moors, went for walks, drove down the coast to Plymouth or Exeter.[27]

But they worked hard, too. Rehearsals were held in the Barn Theatre, where they were trained by Mikhail Chekhov, from whom Zohra learnt a lot about the Stanislavsky school of acting, as well as by Kurt Jooss, the German ballet dancer of *The Green Table* fame. Jooss was training his dancers at Redworth, the house built by the millionaire Paris Singer—son of Isaac Singer, founder of Singer Sewing Machines—for Isadora Duncan (who bore him a son), and was now part of the Dartington estate. Zohra took to this bohemian life like a duck to water. A free-thinking, free-floating community of artists; no rules, other than the ones they made for themselves. Zohra found the freedom to develop her talent as part of a company that broke with convention at every level, working with a man who was revolutionising dance, infusing it with electric energy.

Before long, Mikhail Chekhov had 'more or less fallen in love' with Uzra—'sort of an open love', as Zohra put it—saying things like 'My god, this girl does things to me, and I go all soft and gooey... I just can't help it, it's in my make-up, for a girl of that beauty.'[28] However, Mikhail's attraction to Uzra apart, there seemed to be plenty of love going around then at Dartington Hall. Beatrice Straight had fallen headlong for Uday Shankar, Simkie was already in the picture, and soon, Zohra, too—'I was very much in love with Dada then,' she recalled. He, for his part, had just composed *Vilasa*, a love duet for the two of them—he and Zohra—to take on tour to the US. And as she danced with Uday, Zohra knew, with absolute conviction, that she had found her métier. There followed six months of rehearsals, a completely new repertoire, and then the S.S. *Lafayette* to the States in December 1936.

AMERICA!! Touring with Uday, dancing across the country in New York, Chicago, Boston, Philadelphia, performing on stages she had only ever heard of—Radio City Music Hall, the New Yorker Theatre—meeting celebrities like Margaret O'Sullivan, Basil Rathbone, Mickey Rooney, Walt Disney—could this be real? Could it be happening to her, to Zohra Mumtazullah of Rampur?? It could, it was, and there was nothing unreal about the applause and the bouquets and the photographs and receptions that greeted the Company wherever they performed. And on one such occasion, Pearl Buck presented Zohra and Uzra with a copy of her book, *The Good Earth*, inscribed, 'To the princesses, Zohra and Uzra.' Glamour attended their every performance, for Shankar was no stranger to America. He had already captivated audiences with his sinuous dancing, was rapturously received, especially by women, in much the same way as rockstars would be today. Their shows were jammed with admiring women, prompting Sol Hurok, Shankar's sponsor, to comment in 1934:

> He was beautifully proportioned, muscles smooth under a sleek golden skin. In those traditional costumes which subtly enhanced his height, the breadth of his shoulders, the slimness of his hips, he looked impressively virile. Sex appeal was one item with which I had not credited him—his audience is 75% women![29]

The Company performed *Vilasa*, of course, as well as *Snanum*, *Radha and Krishna*, *Tandava Nrittya* and *The Peasant Dance*, among other pieces. On one evening, Shankar's programme consisted of three musical interludes, eleven dances and one dance drama; 'to choose between them' said Mary Watkins of the *Herald Tribune*, 'for interest, fascination and optical delight is an embarrassment'.[30] Everywhere, they were billed as Shan-kar's Hindu dances ('The West Sees the Real Hindu Dance,' said *The Literary Digest*), with an emphasis on gods and goddesses and on the mythological, even though the repertoire contained several secular or everyday themes: *Rhythm of Life*, for instance, or *Labour and Machinery*.

Reviewers were dazzled by the sheer artistry of the dancers—'more plasticity of body would be hard to imagine,' marvelled the *Boston Evening Transcript*—but naturally, the most lavish praise was reserved for Shankar himself. Oscar Thompson of the *New York Evening Post* wrote: 'It has been said of him that each of the four hundred and fifty muscles of his body does exactly what he wills it to do... This arabesque is a sentence to be read. That counterpoint, a meeting, a parting, an interweaving of thought and mood. The language of dancing gods has become the language of dancing mortals.'[31]

In February 1937, the Company left America for London. Their eight-week tour was enormous fun, if tiring. It was Zohra's first experience 'of people going crazy over us... Worshipping the very ground we trod on—all because we were a tiny part of the dance god, SHANKAR!'

With each successive tour—Belgium, Holland, Denmark, Poland, Switzerland, Hungary, Italy, France—Zohra fell more and more under Shankar's spell. Now, after their US tour, with the troupe having disbanded and no performances scheduled in the near future, Shankar decided to visit Bali, a long-held dream, and wanted Zohra to accompany him. He rarely travelled alone. For Zohra, this would have been a first—alone on a trip with a man who was not family, who was known, moreover, for his several simultaneous liaisons. Simkie had peeled off in Paris to spend time with her mother, Uzra, who might have been his second choice, was in India, and so it was that Zohra, twenty-five and single, found herself on board the *S.S. Conte Rosso* with Uday, sailing from Italy to Jakarta, via Aden, Bombay, Colombo and Singapore. In Bali, 'island of happiness and beauty', Zohra and Shankar were by themselves, and Zohra, always adventurous, became even more so, happy to submit to Shankar's reckless charm. A chance encounter with a Miss Manx, a Scottish woman, in their hotel in Denpasar led to her offering them one of her bamboo shacks on Koeta Beach. Charmed by this unusual person who had spoken nothing but Malay or high and low Balinese for many years, they took her up on her offer and arrived at the beach to find that the shack had no doors! But it was spotlessly clean, the food was good, and the beach ran for miles and miles. They hired bicycles and rode along the beach, swam in the sea, drove from one village to another, seeing different dances, ritual ceremonies and plays. They were not performing themselves, but by the time they left Denpasar, they had been to 'two cremations, one tooth-filling ceremony, one temple feast and dance of virgins, two kris dances… a wyan klong (dance drama) of *Ramlila*, a wyan wong (shadow play), two monkey dances, three flirt dances, three jangyas, three solo dances…'[32]

Bali was a revelation. The grace and simplicity of the people, the artistry in their way of life, the richness of the arts—puppetry, shadow plays, masked dances, religious and ceremonial dances performed only by young virgins, male and female, and a most unusual *Ramayana*. Zohra was struck by the organic way in which music and dance were a natural part of everyday life, that young girls were initiated into dance almost as soon as they could walk, that a peasant could work in his paddy field by day and play an instrument in the village orchestra in the evening. Every ordinary movement became a dance, every festival an occasion for a performance.

Bali was also enchantment—for Zohra, a heady combination of romance and passionate discovery, not only of the many splendours of dance and music and drama on the island, but of her very being. Dada became the medium, the magnetic field, through which all her senses, her thrilling awareness of her body, were awakened to an intensity she had never experienced before.

She thought she could have stayed in Bali forever; but news of business problems with the Uday Shankar Company, registered in Paris, meant that they had to cut short their trip by a month. They returned to India on July 19, 1938, and Zohra detoured to Santiniketan to meet her younger sister, Amina, who was a student there, and to meet Rabindranath Tagore.

Two years of touring across the world, feted and lauded wherever they went, but the Company coffers were running dry. Alice Boner, their chief sponsor, had also decided to establish herself in Banaras and could no longer continue as Shankar's business partner. Shankar realised that he had to make a couple of decisions himself; a touring life was all very well, but the troupe needed a home. A space where the entire Company could live together, a studio where new dances could be created, a 'school' where students could be admitted and taught. In short, a Dartington Hall in India.

Following a tour of Europe in the spring and summer of 1937, Uday Shankar rented a large place in Hampstead, Bryan House, where the Company lived from August to November, when they were performing at the Savoy. They performed again at Dartington, and it was here that Uday announced that he wanted to start a school in India. Beatrice Straight, who by now had sort of set up house with Uday and the Company in London, was completely taken with the idea. Excited discussions were held between Uday, Beatrice, the Elmhirsts, and Beatrice's friend Deidre Hurst. Had it not been for Beatrice's increasing professional and emotional involvement with Shankar, the cultural centre that he would eventually set up in Almora might have had quite a different history. The Elmhirsts, concerned about Beatrice's future, decided to take a hand in it, by shaping Shankar's dream. A blueprint for the prospective centre was drawn up and a list of sponsors proposed. The final tally was nothing short of remarkable, and included Alice Boner, Mikhail Chekhov, the Elmhirsts, of course, and Jawaharlal Nehru, Sir Feroze Khan Noon, John Martin, Sir Chinubhai Madhavlal Ranchhodlal, Romain Rolland, Sir William Rothenstein (Shankar's erstwhile teacher at the London College of Art), Rabindranath Tagore, and Lady Daphne Straight, Beatrice's mother. The Elmhirsts provided seed money of £20,000 (roughly £1.3 million by today's calculation), with teachers' remuneration fixed at Rs. 30 per month (approx Rs. 6,270 today).[33]

Beatrice travelled with Uday to India to find the best location for the school. They considered various cities, including Banaras and Dehradun, Poona and even Bangalore, but settled finally for Almora, largely because of Boshi and Gertrude Sen, close friends of the Elmhirsts, who had set up the Vivekananda Laboratory there. Zohra was a tiny bit disappointed, for she and Uday had also seen several sites on the Rajpur slopes in Dehradun, even talked to the owners of various properties, but Beatrice was keen on Almora. And so they drove there, Zohra, Beatrice and Uday, along the Bareilly-Kathgodam road and up the slopes of Kumaon, via Ranikhet, and thence to Almora. As soon as she saw the idyllic environment, all of Zohra's disappointment vanished; 'It seemed to have no connection with the outside world, tucked miles away from civilisation, sparsely populated with a quaint, trusting people. We fell in love with the place.'[34] And so it was decided: the Uday Shankar Dance Academy would be set up in Almora.

Zohra was hugely excited at the prospect of the Academy and of putting her training at the Wigman school into practice, but first, a short break with her sisters in Dehradun, in the house their father had built at Majra, famous for its Basmati rice.

Act 1, Scene 2: The Almora Dance Academy

The Mumtazullah Khans were a close-knit family, and the five sisters were especially close, having lost their mother when the youngest, Sabra, was just over a month old. Zohra's mother, Natiqua Begum, had seven children, of whom Zohra was the third, born in Saharanpur on April 27, 1912. Zakaullah Khan, born in 1909, was the eldest, followed by Hajrah Begum, in 1910. Ikramullah was born in 1915, Uzra Begum in 1917, and Amina and Sabra in 1919 and 1920. Theirs was an aristocratic family, tracing its descent from the Rohilla Pathans of Afghanistan, with (as Zohra never forgot to add) a drop of Jewish blood, too. Her Jewish ancestor was called Quais, who travelled to Medina and converted to Islam—accepting the faith, according to family legend, 'at the hands of the Prophet Himself'—and returned as Quais Abdul Rasheed.

Zohra's father, Mohammed Mumtazullah Khan, was descended from Maulvi Ghulam Jilani Khan, a descendant of Abdul Rasheed. The warrior chieftain of a clan of the Yusuf Zai tribe and a religious scholar of repute, Khan came to the Mughal court in Delhi sometime in the middle of the eighteenth century. (In a book recording the family's history, a cousin of Zohra's writes that Khan came to the court of Ahmed Shah 'circa 1760', but Ahmed Shah was deposed in 1754, so Khan probably arrived in Delhi in or before 1754.) He was presented with 3,000 infantry and 1,000 cavalry, given the title of Khan Saheb and granted Chitargaon Pargana in Bihar. But as the British were taking over Bengal and Bihar, he fled to Rohilkhand, where he joined the Sardars Nawab Ali Mohammed Khan and Hafiz Rahmat Khan of Rampur, who however were killed in battle against the Nawab of Awadh. Khan Saheb then assembled all the Rohilla chieftains and made Rampur their capital. Originally risaldars, or squadron commanders, they subsequently gave themselves the title of Nawab.

Zohra's mother was descended from Najib-ud-Daulah, also a Rohilla Pathan, who had been in the service of Ahmed Shah Abdali and the Mughals. He founded Najibabad in the 1740s and received the hereditary title of Nawab, and by the early 1760s the tract of land he ruled included Dehradun, Najibabad, Meerut, Muzzafarnagar, Badayun, Bijnor and Bulandshahar. During the 1857 rebellion, his descendant, Mahmood Khan, joined the mutineers, appointing his brother Jallaluddin Khan as Nawab, whom the British executed when they captured Najibabad. Jallaluddin's widow escaped to Moradabad with her three daughters and two sons—Azimuddin Khan and Hamiduzzafar Khan. Azimuddin went on to become commander-in-chief of the Rampur army and was also put in charge, in 1887, of the regency council that looked after the affairs of the Nawabs. During this time he set up schools to teach English and impart western education and encouraged the education of girls, both revolutionary initiatives among the largely orthodox Rohilla Pathans. His younger brother Hamiduzzafar joined the British Provincial

Service in Moradabad, then the British Political Service, as chief officer in the princely states of Bikaner and Alwar. Zohra's mother was Hamiduzzafar's fourth child.

Like many members of India's Muslim royalty and the landed upper class, the Mumtazullahs were largely liberal, westernised, and mostly secular. Their daughters were educated in English-medium schools, and some, like Hamida Saiduzzafar, went on to become highly qualified professionals. Sons often went abroad for further studies, as did Zohra's cousin Mahmud, who was sent to school in England when he was twelve and later graduated from Oxford. Still, the Mumtazullahs were unusual in deciding to send their daughters to a boarding school in Lahore, a city so far from where they lived; and it was Zohra's mother, who left explicit instructions that any money from the sale of her properties be used to educate her children, especially her daughters, who was truly ahead of her time.

Zohra's parents were cousins from Rampur, but they lived in Dehradun and in Bulandshahar, where her father was posted; but Zohra herself grew up in Nainital and Lucknow, having been 'adopted' by her mother's brother, Saiduzzafar Khan (a professor of anatomy at the Lucknow Medical College) when she was five. He became her favourite Uncle Memphis, and an enormous influence in her life. When Zohra was seven, she and her elder sister, Hajrah, were sent to Lahore's Queen Mary's College (founded in 1908), where they studied as boarders. It was a purdah school for young girls from aristocratic families, and there Zohra remained till her matriculation in 1929. Unusually for schools then, Queen Mary's would pack up for three months in summer and move to Dalhousie, its summer campus, in much the same way as the government shifted from Delhi to Simla. In Dalhousie, classes were held in the open—under apricot trees, among fields of hydrangea, violets, larkspur, rhododendron and lily of the valley.

As with other children of privilege, Zohra's family life and her schooling were relatively secular and cosmopolitan. Zohra herself imbibed the broadminded values of her mostly British teachers in school, and of an education that placed an equal emphasis on sports. The school boasted four badminton courts, a hockey field and netball pitch.[1] It was at Queen Mary's that Zohra tried her hand at both art and acting—and had she not made a career of dance and theatre, she might well have been a gifted painter (uncannily, like Uday Shankar). The girls were encouraged to think for themselves and develop their talents, an encouragement that dovetailed neatly with Zohra's natural tendency to independence and boundless curiosity. 'It was Queen Mary's that gave me a career,' she has said. 'How would I have thought of it otherwise? I was good at two things—dancing and acting... I didn't want money; I was interested in fame, I wanted power.'[2] Notwithstanding this extravagant declaration, those ten years of imbibing a liberal, broad-based, secular education, that early experience of relative independence and active encouragement from the Misses Cox and Harvey at the school, socialised Zohra into developing skills that she would draw on later. Naturally gregarious, despite calling herself an 'anglicised snob', she learnt to swim with the tide, to get along, to keep her head and carry on.

The pivotal relationship in her life, however, was with her Uncle Memphis. Much as Zohra adored her father, it was Memphis she turned to for support. When, after matriculating, she decided to pursue her love of acting and informed her father that marriage was not for her—or at any rate, not yet—it was Memphis who thought nothing of taking his very young niece on an arduous, potentially hazardous, overland trip across Afghanistan, Iraq, Turkey and the Middle East. It was Memphis who enrolled her in the Mary Wigman Tanz Schule in Dresden, and it was to Memphis that she wrote her exuberant, chatty, newsy letters when she travelled all over Europe. And of course it was Memphis who financed the better part of her stay in Germany, to the extent of possibly forking out for a 'teeny weeny car, a second-hand one,' so that Sahebzadi Zohra Bi would not have to take the train from her lodgings to the Schule!

With Memphis she could discuss religion, her 'disturbing thoughts' about it, because he had been frank with her about his. Like all observing Muslims, she said her namaz five times a day and read the Quran, but all as a kind of exercise. Did she really believe? She couldn't be sure any more. She could also confide in Memphis her future plans, her opinions about mutual friends; ask him what he thought about her idea of 'combining Eastern and Western dancing' which she could only do after, and if, she trained with someone like Uday Shankar. And it was Memphis' friend from his college days in Edinburgh, Benedicta Haslund, an architect from Norway, who became Zohra's special friend and confidante when she was in Germany.

> 'I have opened my heart to her,' she wrote to Memphis from Dresden, 'and talked to her about things I would not think worthwhile to disclose to another ... I do not think any of my relatives or friends have so much understanding of my thoughts and deeds as Dicta... Both being women and having the same ideals of bodily strength and beauty helping the inner soul to achieve its goal, brings us together and closer to each other.'[3]

That Aunty Dicta was a very special friend of Memphis' was clear to Zohra. It was very likely that, but for his marriage that had already taken place, he and Dicta might have tied the knot. For her part, Aunty Dicta never married; she became one of their family, her home in Norway a home for Memphis' own children, as well as for Zohra, her brother Zakkan, and later, for Zohra's own children.[4]

In Memphis, Zohra found a kindred spirit. Strong-willed, independent, maverick. He had defied his father by insisting he wanted to study abroad and, when refused financial help, had sold his wedding ring to buy his passage to England, sending his father a cable from Aden to say that he was going to study medicine. 'He was my example,' said Zohra, and indeed it was Memphis who not only endorsed her every unconventional choice but helped her realise it, too. No surprise then that, later, when her own family was wary of her decision to marry Kameshwar Segal, it was Memphis who was unreservedly happy, and at whose house—*Nasreen*—in Dehradun the couple spent their honeymoon.

Nasreen (now the well-known Welham Girls' School) was a house Zohra knew well. Built by an Irishman, set in five acres of land, it had pointed roofs, gables and half-timbering, with extensive lawns, gravel pathways and exotic trees, including silver oak, only recently introduced in India. There was an artfully executed topiary, an aviary, even an artificial waterfall. It became a sort of refuge for Zohra, a place of repose and enveloping love, especially in times of lull between tours. Sarwat Rahman, a close friend of Memphis' daughter Hamida, chanced upon Zohra on one such occasion, which she described as follows:

> On a morning visit to *Nasreen*, after climbing the winding staircase, I came across her in the verandah overlooking the

> gardens. She was seated at a table, looking at photographs in an album. She showed them to me. Some were of her recent tour of Europe and America with the Uday Shankar troupe. The black-and-white photographs were fixed, here and there, on the thick, dark greenish-brown pages of the album. Around them, or close to them, Zohra had drawn little pen-pictures in white ink. The photographs about New York were surrounded by the glittering lights of the famous city to which Zohra Apa had just revealed classical Indian dancing for the first time. Other photographs of her recent tour of the villages of the then UP were adorned with drawings of bullock-carts, seen then, still seem to me to be moving slowly, across the years, towards their humble and unknown destination. The drawings, more than the photographs, evoked for me scenes of village life. Zohra Apa's gifts as an artist seemed to me as great as her accomplishments as a dancer. It was thus that I remembered her in later years, as she had appeared to me then, in the fresh light of a morning at *Nasreen*, a beautiful and youthful figure, surrounded by the aura of distant voyages and artistic creation.[5]

Hamida, the older cousin whom Zohra was very close to, would follow in her father's footsteps and study medicine, specifically ophthalmology, in England, and become one of the first practitioners of this specialisation in Lucknow. Hamida's brother Mahmud, Zohra's companion on her 1931 overland trip, who also accompanied her to Dresden when she joined the Mary Wigman School, would become a Communist, marry his comrade, the writer Rashid Jahan, and distribute all his land and inherited villages in Moradabad to the local peasantry, to become an ordinary worker of the Party.

Mahmud was not the only Communist in the family. His cousin Hajrah, Zohra's older sister, would become one too.

Married to her cousin, Jamil Khan, as was the custom, Hajrah soon realised that the life of a policeman's wife, kowtowing to the Brits, was not for her. She left Jamil, sold her jewellery, took her young son, Sami, and in 1933 left for England, where Mahmud and her brother Zakkan were already studying. She enrolled in a Montessori training programme, admitted Sami to a day school, and plunged into the life of a student activist as part of the Young India League in London. Already in India she had begun reading Left literature; now, together with her cousin, she was part of a Marxist study circle where she met Z.A. Ahmed, then a student at the London School of Economics. Not politically active then, Ahmed was subsequently recruited by Hajrah into the Left movement, and by the time they returned to India in the mid-1930s, and married, both were committed communists, active members of the Congress Socialist Party, organizing railway coolies, press workers and farmers, and also members of the underground Communist Party of India.

Hajrah, only a couple of years older than Zohra, remained an abiding sober influence on her; for her part Zohra held her in high regard and deep respect, even, according to Hajrah's daughter Salima, a certain formality. Uzra, born five years after Zohra, was the sister she was closest to, the sister who followed her first to Dartington Hall, then to the Uday Shankar Dance Academy, who preceded her in Prithvi Theatres, who became her confidante—and who was her complete opposite. Uzra was the beauty of the family, gentle and sweet-natured, with not a trace of ambition in her. 'We are poles apart,' Zohra said, 'I'm a vixen and she's an angel.' Circumstances and their choice of career meant the sisters led parallel lives, overlapping, sometimes, in unexpected ways.

The Uday Shankar Cultural Centre, modelled on Dartington Hall, opened for students on March 3, 1940, but the group of dancers and teachers had already been installed a year earlier. The Centre was beautifully sited. The provincial government, via the good offices of the Congress leader and former premier of the United Provinces, Govind Ballabh Pant, donated ninety-three acres of forested ridge land, known as Simtola, to the Centre, but its studio and residential complex of a few cottages (rented from the Pandes and Joshis of the area) were in Ranidhara. Things seemed to be falling nicely into place, but had it not been for the Elmhirsts' support, financial and material, and for Boshi Sen's administrative oversight, the Centre might not have had a fighting chance. Leonard Elmhirst had realised early in their discussions that while Shankar was the creative and inspirational magnet, he had neither the time nor the inclination to see to the day-to-day running of an institution.

When it opened, the Centre had only ten students, but as its repertoire and performances increased, its popularity grew. Among the students who joined later were Vijayalakshmi Pandit's daughters (and Nehru's nieces), Chandralekha and Nayantara; Guru Dutt (who would become a celebrated film-maker); Shanta Kirnan (later Shanta Gandhi, noted theatre director); Sundari Bhavnani (who became Sundari Shridharani, founder of Delhi's Triveni Kala Sangam); and Sheila Bharat Ram, who was then a student of the legendary Hindustani classical musician and guru Ustad Allauddin Khan.

Zohra threw herself into the Centre's regimen with her customary gusto. Before the day began at eight in the morning, she would emerge from the cottage to drink in the beauty of Nanda Devi and Nanga Parbat, and the brilliance of red rhododendrons and soft yellow mimosa in the morning sun. Classes began at 8:30, after breakfast, when Uday Shankar arrived at the studio for the general class, followed by a class in technique, and then classes in Kathakali, Bharatanatyam and Manipuri, conducted by the great practitioners Sankaran Namboodiri (Shankar's guru), Kandappa Pillai (the legendary Balasaraswati's teacher) and Amobi Singh. Allauddin Khan would provide musical accompaniment from time to time, assisted by his son Ali Akbar Khan and student Ravi Shankar. Senior to the latter two was Vishnudas Shirali, who had been with Uday Shankar since 1935 and joined the Centre as music director. Zohra was in charge of developing a five-year syllabus for the students, and, together with Simkie, she was also Uday Shankar's dance assistant. It was here that her training at the Wigman school came in handy, but she was also quick to see that Shankar's own genius lay elsewhere. Zohra knew and admired his extraordinary dancing, but it was his exceptionally inventive group formations that fascinated her. He was a master of innovation, skilfully coaxing Simkie, Uzra and Zohra to improvise exquisite and intricate movements. They became 'like putty in a sculptor's hands', moulded by his brilliant and questing imagination, performing to new and exciting rhythms. 'His own classes were fabulous', she said. 'It was as if years and years of an artists' vision had come to life, and he was able to explain his theories about his art, giving form and articulation to his dreams.'[6]

From Shankar, Zohra learnt the importance of being able to walk properly before learning to dance, and so for one hour every day, his students and the dancers walked around the huge studio hall to the beat of a gigantic drum made of rhinoceros hide. Then, simple dance steps, alone, in pairs or in groups, reverting to walking rhythmically. Shankar's exercises emphasised complete relaxation and suppleness, coupled with rigid control of the body. Facial expressions and moods were picked up from everyday life, poses derived from daily activities. Then there were the improvisation classes, including pure mime, in which students were required to improvise to musical themes.[7] Sometimes the music was there and Shankar created movements to go with it, at other times he first composed the dance and the music was then arranged. Movement had a melody of its own, he believed, the movement must express the spirit of the music and vice versa.[8]

'Shankar prepared the body as an instrument to reflect and obey and blossom into new dance forms,' Zohra said. 'His training evoked a consciousness in the dancer of a complete and complex human being.'[9] It was the evocation of this particular self-awareness that made his method unique.

Never in her wildest dreams, and certainly not when she was at Mary Wigman's school, had Zohra thought that she would be part of a Company that comprised the greatest names in Indian dance and music. Indeed, nowhere in the country was there a centre that broke away from the classical forms and experimented with movement and music, that performed secular pieces like *Rhythm of Life* and *Labour and Machinery*, or like *Grasscutters of Kumaon* that Zohra herself choreographed. Here, with Uday Shankar, she learnt to work with the body *as a whole*, in the process unlearning some of what she had been taught at Dresden. But only some; for Wigman's training was modern, based on eurhythmics, and while Shankar was seeking to incorporate the modern in his teaching and performance, 'modern' for him did not mean what was being taught and performed in the West; indeed, he had a 'great antipathy' to it. He told the dance critic Mohan

Khokar: 'When I first saw modern dance in Europe, it was shocking to me, I felt it was something being done just for the sake of doing something new… I did not learn or derive anything from it.' Nor was he impressed by Mary Wigman, Martha Graham or Ruth St. Denis.[10] What he learnt from the West was how to compose the body in space, and how the dancers' bodies formed patterns as they moved in it. Beyond that, his conception of movement and dance was uniquely his. So, from Shankar, Zohra imbibed that 'the body must be developed, not just for the dance, but as an element of intrinsic beauty'. The body beautiful was what Shankar sought to cultivate, what he wished to impart to his students: 'If I can teach the young to value the body, to perfect it, I will have done something for them.'[11]

As she danced with Uday, Uzra and Simkie in the vast, light-filled studio, the hills visible through the glass wall that formed one side of the building, Zohra felt a rare exhilaration. Shankar's focus on the body and the sheer boldness of his technique, combining the fluidity of movement with the discipline of yoga, was exceptional. 'Dada declared that once a dancer had been trained in his method, he or she would be able to follow any technique with ease, because his system provided the basic training for all actor-dancers. It was then that the realisation of his true genius dawned on me,' she said. For Shankar, too, this partnership was amazingly productive, as he maintained that he had 'never achieved the same creative satisfaction' as when he worked with Zohra, Simkie and Uzra at Almora.[12]

But Shankar did more than teach people, he claimed them whole. His magnetic, androgynous charm was hard to resist, and he ensnared all his dancers in the sensuous, gossamer web he spun. He broke the rules. Crossed all limits.

Encouraged transgression as essential to the creative impulse. He drove his dancers to an excess of emotional attachment. He became the quintessential bohemian lover. Of life. Of art. Of the body and of sensuality. His sexuality was on display in every gesture, every glance of his kohl-rimmed eyes, every rippling muscle, as he danced. His audiences swooned; no one could tell whether it was the dancer or the dance that held everyone in thrall.

And Zohra, too, was enthralled, dazzled by his brilliance. But she couldn't reconcile herself to his promiscuity. She saw what it was doing to the troupe, with jealousy and unhealthy competitiveness seething below the surface; and after Amala Nandi joined the company and made clear her evident interest in Shankar, the emotional and professional equation between Zohra, Simkie and Dada underwent a subtle change.

It was at this time that Kameshwar Segal joined the Centre. A beautiful Rossetti-like boy, 5'4", slim, fair, with thick curly hair and slender hands and feet. The great-grandson of one of the dewans, or prime ministers, of the princely state of Indore, Kameshwar was the fourth son among seven siblings, and his father, Ram Nath Segal, was manager of a small bank, first in Indore and later in Sanavat. Like many Punjabi upper-middle class families, the Segals were well-versed in Urdu, and their lifestyle, or rather, their household etiquette, was similar to that of UP gentry. Kameshwar was a rebel (like Zohra), and restless—a student of science but interested in art; studying art and craft at the Indore College of Art (where M.F. Husain was a fellow student), but attracted to dance. He wasn't a dancer yet, but he had seen Shankar perform during one of his tours in India and had fallen in love with the dancer, as well as the dance. Kameshwar now joined the Almora Centre as a dance student, but Uday Shankar, recognising his talent, soon put him to work as painter, set designer, handyman and mask-maker. He was talented and quick-witted, inventive with his hands, using papier maché and paint to great advantage. For *Ramayana*, a shadow play created by Uday Shankar, for instance, he cleverly devised light and flexible cardboard masks for the monkeys that worked wonderfully in shadow, replacing the heavy and unwieldy wooden masks used earlier.

Zohra and Kameshwar were thrown together during the mask-making sessions in the evenings, after classes, and during rehearsals. She admired his ingenuity and skill, and being fun-loving herself, responded to his humour and light-hearted banter. He was like quicksilver, and before she knew it, their evenings of mask-making extended into nights of long conversations. Soon, the conversations turned into confidences, as they talked about their families, their childhoods, their hopes for their careers and their future, and it dawned on Zohra that this charming man, whose beauty and energy she found so attractive, was falling in love with her. But Dada actively discouraged socialising between faculty and students, and so they met in secret. Zohra, no stranger to love and its many delights and seductions, was nevertheless only too mindful of the many odds against them. And then there was Shankar himself, not just her guru and mentor but so much more.

Involved though she was with Dada, Zohra was under no illusions about him. Shankar's affairs with his dancers, male and female, were known to all and he had proposed, in turn, to all the women in his Company. But Kameshwar? He was proposing marriage now, but that was mad! For a start, he was so much younger than her… In any case, she had no intention of getting married. She had turned down every marriage proposal that had come her way, defied every convention that a young woman of her background was bound by, in order to pursue her love of dance and to live as unconventionally as possible, on her own terms. She wasn't about to conform now.

And so they continued, Zohra as teacher and friend, Kameshwar as set designer and student, for close to two years, talking as before, sharing, on occasion even travelling together—to Ajanta and Ellora, living in a set of rooms carved out of the rock, under a mosque. Secretly going for moonlit walks along the ravines and hills of Almora, till one day Shankar chanced upon Kameshwar in Zohra's cottage, and that was that. They had broken the taboo.

When Kameshwar first proposed to her, she had refused. The very idea was absurd, she told him. Marriages in India were a family affair, how could she possibly expect hers to accept the fact that Kameshwar was so much younger than her, and of a different religion? They had accepted Uday, which was a big concession, she said, but Kameshwar wasn't famous; plus, he was a student. But Kameshwar wasn't about to be put off. 'How long will you go on like this?' he demanded, 'this' being the two years that she had prevaricated.

By now Zohra was thirty years old, and because Dada had discovered them together in her room, she succumbed. By now too, they had both met each others' families—his in Indore and hers in Dehradun—and so the decision was taken. But Abbajan, who had always stood by his unpredictable and self-willed daughter, was worried. Inter-faith marriages were uncommon, and even though Jamil, his former son-in-law, had married Shyam Kumari Nehru (Jawaharlal Nehru's cousin), Zohra's decision to marry a Hindu had upset him. It was all very well for some Progessives to marry their comrades or for writers like Krishan Chander and Vishwamitra Adil to marry Muslim women, but this match was different. Kameshwar's mother was uneducated, a strict vegetarian, and observed the ritual distance between Hindus and Muslims. Moreover, she was an orthodox Radha Soami. The Mumtazullah Khans, on the other hand, were nobility; westernised and highly educated. Kameshwar offered to convert, but Abbajan would have none of that. 'No!' he said emphatically, 'what would be my feelings if Zohra became a Hindu? Think of your parents,' he told Kameshwar. Zohra's happiness was clouded over for she adored her father and hated to displease him. Small comfort that Memphis was overjoyed at her news, and that Hajrah, her elder sister and her husband approved; it was Abbajan's consent that she wanted.[13] Kameshwar's family, by contrast, was more accommodating. Despite her orthodoxy, his mother welcomed Zohra into their home saying, 'If this is the girl Kameshwar has made the goddess of his heart, we will make her the goddess of our house.' As they customarily ate from thalis on the kitchen floor, she made Zohra sit with them and eat from her father-in-law's thali. There could be no greater acceptance than this.

Abbajan knew that once his daughter's mind was made up it remained made up, and so eventually, and somewhat reluctantly, he gave in. What he could not agree to, however, was to have the wedding in Dehradun—he would not be able to face his Muslim friends if he did. As Hajrah lived in Allahabad, it was decided that the wedding would take place there, under the recently introduced Special Marriages Act which enabled interfaith marriages. Zohra left her father's house with a heavy heart. Not only would the wedding not take place in his house, Abbajan would not even be present in Allahabad for it. The thought of her wedding without him brought bitter tears to her eyes; how was she to choose between Kameshwar and Abbajan? But having accepted Kameshwar in full knowledge of all the lines she was crossing, all the norms she was disregarding, there was no turning back now.[14]

August 14, 1942, the day of her wedding. Hajrah, whose husband, Z.A. Ahmed, was secretary to Jawaharlal Nehru, had requisitioned his friend Feroze Gandhi's mother's house for the baraat as it was large enough to accommodate a marriage party. A registrar would come to the house at noon, followed by lunch, and then dinner in the evening at Anand Bhawan with Pandit Nehru. The bride wore red, an outfit sewn by her elder sister-in-law, Khadija. Her jewellery was borrowed, her own share of the family jewels having been sold when she told her father she wasn't going to marry!

But this was 1942, World War II was raging, it was the height of non-cooperation with the British, and the inauguration of the Quit India Movement. Nehru was arrested on August 12, so there would be no dinner at Anand Bhawan (and no wedding present either, a pair of rugs that Nehru had planned to give them!). There was chaos in the country, with riots in several places as the British authorities cracked down on protestors. Train travel was hazardous, so no one from Kameshwar's family in Indore could make it to Allahabad—only one member, brave enough to venture forth, was present. Wedding photographs were taken but the photographer's shop was burned down during the riots, so none remained. The lavish reception planned at the Royal Hotel fell flat because hardly any guests showed up; and the few who did, hurried home before curfew at 7:00 p.m. The special cooks hired by Hajrah for Kameshwar's family and to feed the baraat sat idle most of the time. In fact, apart from Zohra and Kameshwar, the only family members at the wedding were Uzra, Hajrah and her husband, their daughter Salima (who was three), and Khadija. As Zohra said later, 'Only a mad couple like us could have chosen a time like this for our wedding!'[15] Still, they spent their wedding night in splendour, in Hajrah's gorgeously decorated cottage, with them as its sole occupants.

Zohra and Kameshwar's was not the only union forged in Almora, however, for romance was in the air they breathed. Uday Shankar married Amala Nandi; Simkie married Prabhat Ganguli; Rajendra Shankar married Lakshmi Shastri; and Ravi Shankar married Annapurna, Ustad Allauddin's daughter.

But romance apart, things were beginning to unravel at the Centre.

Uzra had already left. Within a year of joining she realised that she couldn't cope with the difficult training of Bharatnatyam and Kathakali. 'I came to the conclusion that these two dance forms require very strict discipline, and a dancer should start learning them at a very early stage when the limbs are supple and tender,' she wrote to her sister.[16] She left Almora and went to Calcutta to learn Manipuri, which attracted her very much. She stayed with their brother Zakkan, found a Manipuri guru, but 'just as I was able to get to know the A, B, C of Manipuri', the threat of war loomed. A 'Japan scare' gripped the city and Uzra was despatched to her father in Dehradun. While in Calcutta, however, she had met and fallen in love with her future husband, Hameed Butt, an aspiring writer and actor; he followed her to Dehradun and they were married in 1942, the same year as Zohra and Kameshwar.

At the Dance Academy, discontent had been simmering for a while. Indiscipline and moral laxity apart, the students went on strike in 1942, protesting Shankar's authoritarianism and arbitrary choice of dancers for performances. In the winter of 1943-44, the troupe was on tour with *Ram Leela*, a shadow play, when Shankar declared that, henceforth, he would focus on making films, specifically his dream project, *Kalpana*—and that the students would have to work with him on that. They revolted. The Centre had offered them a five-year diploma course and here was Shankar, terminating it after three-and-a-half. What would become of their diplomas? Unmoved, Shankar replied, 'Join me on *Kalpana* or leave.' But the students would have none of this, and in protest refused to perform the play that evening. Shankar carried on regardless. Apologising to the audience, he performed a selection of pieces from his repertoire without the students, but with his group; paid the students their railway fare and allowances, and bid them goodbye. All was over in the blink of an eye.[17]

Shankar, emotionally, sexually and financially profligate, was singularly unsuited to sustaining and administering an institution. As long as Boshi Sen was around cheques were signed, salaries were paid, and expenses met. Shankar had never saved a penny, didn't even have a bank account. After his marriage to Amala, however, he began to draw money from the Trust Fund for all sorts of expenses, including cinema tickets for the students.[18] Financing the Centre became difficult; appeals to the government went unheard; in fact, the UP government withdrew its gift of Simtola, and Dartington Hall withdrew its support. The initial donation of £20,000 had long been exhausted. When Shankar returned from the tour of 1943-44, Gertrude Sen recalled:

> He stayed two days to pack his personal possessions and left us to do the rest. We felt very sad that he needlessly spoiled his own bright dream, and let down those who financed him. When we went to say goodbye to him, my husband

> broke down and wept... But Uday failed to recognise that certain aspects of his own character contributed to his final disastrous failure.[19]

With the Centre's closure the entire group disbanded. Simkie gave up performing altogether, unsuccessfully tried dance direction in Bombay cinema, then left India, never to return. Kanaklata and three others went to Kerala to learn Kathakali with Sankaran Namboodiri. Of the other faculty and students, Narendra Sharma set up his own outfit, Bhoomika; Sundari Bhavnani (now Shridharani) established Triveni Kala Sangam in Delhi; and Sachin Shankar started his independent ballet unit in Bombay. Reminiscing with Mohan Khokar in his twilight years, Shankar himself said:

> Wonderful work was done at the Centre, no doubt. But of course, like any institution, when you run a place like that, there are all kinds of people to cope with. Naturally, there are problems. I was very free with everybody. I loved them all. But some people took advantage of this. Gossip started: they knew Dada inside out. There were many problems. I knew, and even today I strongly feel, every institution has to face that sort of thing. Where there are many human beings together, such things do happen. But the real bad luck was that the war came. That spoiled the whole thing. Food scarcity, transport problems. The £20,000 was spent. We were trying to get money from different sources.
>
> The upheaval was unfortunate. Some, who were behind it, were right; some were wrong. But young children—you can't blame them, you know. When I decided to close down, it was very painful for me. But I realised that if I had gone on, I would have been a hypocrite. Keeping the undesirable element alive there and continuing—I did not want that. That money which I had got was sacred for me,

> and for the people on whom it was spent. The manner of its use was holy to me. I felt sure this could not go on. I must stop the whole thing and start again. The experience of shutting it down was painful, but it had to be done. I had to stop.[20]

The winding down of the Almora Centre presented Zohra with what became her first real challenge—where to go and what to do next. For some time, it had been clear to her that things couldn't continue the way they were: she as teacher and Kameshwar as student during the day, but a married couple the rest of the time. Awkwardness apart, Kameshwar's personality—independent and unconventional—would have begun to chafe at the bit. He wanted a place of his own, a school where he could decide what should be done, and equally important, where he could right the creative balance in his relationship with Zohra.

In June 1943, Zohra and Kameshwar left Almora and the Uday Shankar Academy to set up a dance school of their own. The decision was not without its sadness—at leaving Dada, at distress about the rift between him and the students, and real sorrow at the end of an extraordinary experiment, of daring to dream another kind of dance. Thinking back to that time, Zohra would write:

> The closing of this institution was the greatest tragedy for modern Indian ballet. A new technique and dance grammar, which were on the threshold of being formulated, were lost forever; whatever Shankar had contributed to the art of modern Indian dancing fizzled out, and the training was wasted, as it did not have time to mature and become a tradition. So great is the loss that young dancers today have hardly heard of Uday Shankar and are unaware of his genius.[21]

After they had decided on setting up the school, Kameshwar said, 'I will be the director.' This came as a little shock to Zohra, who had assumed that the role was hers. But, 'Look at you,' Kameshwar said to her unkindly, 'you have had such an opportunity and what have you done with your life?'

Starting the school was only the first of many decisions that Kameshwar would take regarding their life together, although they both knew that their implementation depended critically on Zohra, for she was the sensible one, disciplined and pragmatic. The choice of Lahore as location for the school was primarily because Zohra had been educated there and knew people who would publicise the school. Its initial finance was provided by her father, who gave them Rs. 2500 so that they could begin, but clearly they would need to supplement this. The Zoresh Dance Institute came into being in October 1943, in a rented house on Empress Road, the school in its front rooms, their living quarters at the back. But it would be a while before they got their first students, and so Zohra returned to her old school, Queen Mary's, to teach eurhythmics, slowly expanding her reach to other schools and colleges.

The great tragedy of the Bengal Famine gave them their first real break, albeit in sad circumstances. The School organised a music and dance show in aid of the Bengal Relief Fund at the Open Air Theatre in Lawrence Gardens, and managed to raise the considerable sum of Rs. 42,000 (about Rs. 25,00,000 today). Suddenly, to their surprise and delight, the school was inundated with students. But then, as suddenly, Kameshwar prevailed upon Zohra to take another crucial decision—start a family. Zohra demurred. This was not the time, not when they had just begun a new venture that would require all their energy and imagination and organising ability. There were the students, an all-India tour in the offing, rehearsals and performances—and their own finances were precarious. But Kameshwar was adamant and Zohra was overruled. Was it simply waywardness on his part or a desire to establish a kind of hierarchy in their relationship, both personal and professional? With Zohra preoccupied with pregnancy and a baby, Kameshwar would naturally be in sole charge of their school. Setting her misgivings aside, Zohra plunged into preparing for their next show, performing a ballet, *Shiva Parvati*, again at the Open Air Theatre. Except, she was now two months pregnant. Zohra left Lahore to go to Dehradun for her confinement, and their daughter, Kiran, was born on November 17, 1944, at the Dufferin Hospital. Her older sister Hajrah was with her, but Kameshwar remained in Lahore. Zohra returned in January 1945, and before she could catch her breath, she was back in the saddle. Or rather, onstage.

Kiran was only two months old, but the all-India tour that had seemed like a dream scenario earlier was now actually happening, and preparations were in full swing. An anonymous benefactor took charge of the finances, but musicians and dancers had to be found and trained, dances had to be choreographed, a music director engaged. As a new school with no dancers attached to it, they decided to use their own students; Zohra inducted her younger sister, Sabra, and Laj Bedi from their Almora days, plus Mohan Khokar, a current student, as dancers, and Timir Baran, also from Almora, as music director.

Two months later, in March 1945, the motley troupe set out to conquer the country, complete with costumes and jewellery, instruments in specially padded boxes, stage curtains, and the rest of the paraphernalia that accompanied them for four months as they performed—in Lahore, Amritsar,

Moradabad, Bareilly, Meerut, Lucknow, Allahabad, Patna, Asansol, Dehradun and Calcutta. The tour was exhausting, a huge success artistically, but financially, a hefty loss. Expenses amounted to Rs. 15,000 (about Rs. 9,00,000 in today's terms), including salaries to dancers, but their coffers were dry.

Money worries were not the only worries Zohra and Kameshwar were confronted with on their return to Lahore. It was July 1945 and the War had ended; Britain may have been victorious but could no longer rule the waves, and India was restive. It was clear to both ruler and ruled that the countdown to independence had begun, and gradually it was also becoming clear that the simmering political tension between the Congress and the Muslim League was coming to a boil. In Punjab, relations between Hindus and Muslims acquired a sharp edge. Lahore might have been a Hindu majority city, but Punjab was seething with unrest. And so, what also became clear to Zohra was that, in the circumstances, she and Kameshwar were particularly vulnerable.

> Our erstwhile Muslim friends began to look upon us with certain misgivings, and an unspoken and hostile unease pervaded our circle of acquaintances. There would be no room for a Hindu-Muslim couple in the future country of Pakistan, and we felt we should move away from the danger before it overtook us.[22]

They would have to leave. Close down the Zoresh Dance Institute. Find another city, put down roots there. And so, after just two years of striking out on their own, they were on the move again, this time to Bombay at Uzra's urging, but with no idea about what to expect when they got there, or what the future held.

Zohra never danced again—or, rather, she didn't perform

on stage as a dancer in India, after she left Lahore. Bombay had never been a city for dance, nor was there an innovative practitioner like Uday Shankar there whom she could join. Setting up another school in a city where she had few contacts or associates was difficult, and moreover, Bombay had always been more inclined towards theatre and film than dance.

In Shankar, Zohra had found a perfect match—her training and strength lay in movement, not in classical dance. Shankar's experimental style allowed her to adapt what she had learnt at the Wigman school to his intuitive understanding of the body, and to his genius for sculpting it in space. Dance remained her first love, her vocation lay in teaching and choreographing, but it became less and less a part of her life as a performer. Years later she would tell her daughter Kiran, 'My one regret is that I never became a guru.'

Important though he had been for Zohra, in time even Shankar began to recede into the background. After his experiment with *Kalpana* he relocated temporarily to Calcutta, then returned to dance with a US tour in 1949, sponsored by the reliable Sol Hurok. By now the country had been partitioned, Zohra was in Bombay and working as dance choreographer in Prithvi Theatres. Might Shankar have invited her to join his troupe again and tour with them? Possibly, for all his dancers were new—even Amala was performing with him for the first time—but Zohra did not accompany them. Yet, the question remains: did she sever her ties with Shankar completely? In an unguarded moment she confided that she had destroyed all his letters to her. When I asked her why, she replied: '*Dada ne kaha, jala do, toh maine jala diye.*' (Dada said, burn them, so that's what I did.)

Eight years with Dada, and with dance. In Germany she had thought the world was her oyster, but with Uday

Shankar it was as if the world was at her feet. She couldn't remember the number of cities she had danced in, and so she started a journal, writing down every place she had been to in alphabetical order! She loved to dance, but she also loved the applause, the lights, the attention, the rapturous reception they received. She realised that she loved performing.

She had no idea now when she would perform again. Or with whom.

Act 2, Scene 1: In the Wings

'We found a big, rambling, tumble-down bungalow on Pali Hill in Bandra, No. 41, surrounded by mango groves,' wrote Uma Anand in a book on her then husband, the film-maker Chetan Anand. 'We could see distant hills and woods from the windows.'[1] It was this rambling bungalow that Zohra and Kameshwar made their home in Bombay.

Pali Hill, now one of Bombay's most affluent neighbourhoods, is spread across rolling hillocks, still dotted with large banyan, neem, mango and laburnum trees and wild jasmine and bougainvillea bushes. Until the 1950s, the area was densely forested, and hidden in the little valleys and crests were old cottages and bungalows where mainly British, Parsi and Catholic families lived. In the late 1940s and early '50s, some actors and film-makers who later became Bollywood's royalty also began to buy homes or land here: Meena Kumari, Dilip Kumar, the Kapoors. The Anands, not quite royalty in the mid-1940s (Dev Anand was still some years from stardom), were among the first film people to come to this quiet, green suburb.

The old bungalow that the Anands took on rent was perched on a little hill, its three floors sloping up and down the hillside. It was owned by an Anglo-Indian couple, the

Vernon Corkes, who lived on the top floor. Uma and Chetan, and Chetan's two brothers, Dev and Vijay (Goldie) lived on the second, and Zohra and Kameshwar Segal, with their daughter Kiran, lived on the ground floor. The house being on more than one level meant that the Segals' flat had two levels, the upper half with two bedrooms and a bathroom, and the lower with a huge hall, small bedroom, storeroom and second bathroom. A couple of verandahs, a servant's room, and a kitchen looked out onto a dilapidated tennis court and an overgrown garden. A creaking wooden staircase connected the three floors from the inside, but because the house was on a hill, each family had their own entrance. The rent was Rs. 50 a month, with all the occupants contributing, 'but even this was difficult for us to meet,' admitted Uma, and so the house became a kind of commune for actors and artistes, with each of them pitching in in whichever way they could, whenever they could.

The Segals were introduced to the Anands by Uzra and Hameed Butt, friends of Uma and Chetan, who had moved from Poona to Bombay shortly before Zohra and Kameshwar arrived there with Kiran. The actor Balraj Sahni and his wife Damayanti were already at No. 41, sharing one of the floors, and before long were joined by Balraj's younger brother Bhisham and his wife Sheela, who were in Bombay for their honeymoon. And then there were those who were not living in the house but spent so much time in it that they may as well have moved in. There were Guru Dutt, Raj Khosla and Mohan Segal, all aspiring filmmakers; Dilip Kumar's brothers, Ayub and Nasir Khan, both actors; Geeta Roy (later Dutt, who had only recently been launched as a playback singer); the actors Hima Devi, Krishan Dhavan and Rashid Khan; the writers Raja Rao, Ahmed Ali and Hayatullah Ansari (editor of

Qaumi Awaz); the young film critic Amita Malik; poets and lyricists Sahir Ludhianvi, Ali Sardar Jafri and Vishwamitra Adil; and composers S.D. Burman and Ravi Shankar. Many of them had relocated from Lahore, not yet as a reaction to the possibility of Partition, but drawn, perhaps, by the ferment that the freedom movement had created in the arts. 'Life at 41 Pali Hill resounded with ideas; scripts being discussed; Kameshwar painting; Zohra dancing; everybody arguing, enquiring, reading and discussing,' recalled Uma Anand. 'Ideas were what we lived off; theatre was what we worked at; films were what we dreamt of. It was such an exciting time.'[2]

And Bombay, it seemed, was *the* exciting city to be in, abuzz with creative energy and experiment in the visual arts, literature, cinema and theatre. The Sri Lankan architect Minette de Silva, who was studying and living in Bombay at the time with her older sister Anil, an art critic and political activist, recalled some half a century later, 'It was such a mixed world of the political Left and Right, industrialists, army generals, executives, struggling artists, writers, filmmakers, dancers, actors—a cosmopolitan world.'[3]

Many of India's most talented Urdu writers were in Bombay in the forties, drawn there by the possibility of finding work in Hindustani cinema. The Bombay branch of the Progressive Writers' Association (PWA)—which had been set up in Calcutta in 1936 (Zohra's cousin Mahmud was a founding member) and had expanded quickly with branches in the rest of the country—would meet in the Silverfish Club on top of the famous Taraporevala Sons bookstore in Fort. Primarily an Urdu writers' group at first, it soon included all the other major languages of Bombay—Hindi, Marathi, Gujarati and Sindhi. The Urdu group met frequently 'in the proletarian flat of Sajjad Zaheer on Walkeshwar Road,' recounts K.A.

Abbas, one of its first members, 'and it was there that I met and befriended the leading lights of progressive literature: Zaheer, Saadat Hasan Manto, Ismat Apa [Ismat Chughtai] and her husband Shahid Lateef, and Razia Sajjad Zaheer... the daughter of a great friend of my father and a worker-writer, Yusuf Mannaan, who was called the Gorky of India.'[4] Zaheer, Jafri and Sibtay Hasan were members of the Communist Party of India, and although less than half the members of the PWA were communists, their political biases and writings were decidedly Left, leading many to believe that the PWA was a 'front' organisation for the party.

On May 25, 1943, the Indian Peoples' Theatre Association (IPTA) was formed during the national conference of theatre artistes, held at the Marwari School, Bombay, in response to a call to theatre artistes to participate in the freedom struggle. Its origins lay in the first PWA Conference held in 1936; the establishment of the Youth Cultural Institute in Calcutta in 1940; and the setting up, by Anil de Silva (Minette's sister), of the Peoples Theatre in Bangalore in 1941. Its initial members consisted of various cultural troupes, theatre groups and cultural activists, with the name Peoples' Theatre suggested by the scientist Homi Bhabha. Prominent among its members were the thespians Prithviraj Kapoor, Balraj Sahni, Utpal Dutt, Khwaja Ahmad Abbas, Ravi Shankar, Safdar Mir, Ritwik Ghatak, Salil Chowdhry and others, who pledged to represent—and present—the crises of the times through the medium of theatre.

The formal launch of the Association took place with a performance of a Marathi play, *Dada*, by T.K. Sarmalkar. 'Six hundred mill workers rubbed shoulders with a hundred intellectuals, journalists, art critics,' recalls Abbas. Whether or not Sarmalkar himself was a mill worker was not known then, but, wrote Abbas, '... he certainly knows proletarian life as perhaps no professional writer does. Out of the stuff of chawl life, he drew out humour as well as pathos, degeneration as well as glory, individual servility and collective strength.'[5]

Over time, IPTA became an all-India movement, with units in every province. It performed hundreds of shows, revived and revitalised many art forms—tamasha in Maharashtra; burra katha in Andhra Pradesh; jatra in Bengal—and drew thousands of people as audiences. It played a defining role in the lives of hundreds of artistes whose careers were maturing or just beginning in the late thirties and through the forties—Zohra being one of them.

Meanwhile, English theatre in Bombay was represented by the Theatre Group, set up in 1941 by Sultan—Bobby—Padamsee to present 'an Indian perspective of the human experience'. Hamid Sayani, the great actor and radio personality, was part of it, as were Deryck Jeffries, technician and lighting wizard, and theatre legend Ebrahim Alkazi.

And then, of course, there was cinema. The 1940s were the glory days for studios and actors. Bombay Talkies had already made stars of Devika Rani and Ashok Kumar in 1936 with the reformist film *Acchut Kanya*, the love story of a Dalit girl and a Brahmin boy. *Kangan* (1939), *Bandhan* (1940) and *Jhoola* (1941) would do that for Leela Chitnis and Sohrab Modi's *Sikander* (1941), an epic based on the life of Alexander, for Prithviraj Kapoor. Meanwhile, the Punjabis from Lahore had begun arriving in the city some years before Partition, and among them were the singer K.L. Saigal, the actor Jagdish Sethi, the prospective film producers B.R. Chopra and F.C. Mehra, all of whom would transform Bombay's Hindustani cinema.

It is true that most movie studios from Poona to Kolhapur

and Bombay were churning out mythological and historical romances, but gradually, realism and unconventional themes and techniques began to enter the films, especially towards the end of the 1940s, when independent filmmakers entered the fray. K.A. Abbas, supported by IPTA, made the immortal *Dharti ke Lal*, based on the Bengal famine, in 1946, with noted theatre personalities Tripti and Sombhu Mitra, Balraj Sahni and Damayanti Sahni (Zohra had a bit of a part, too). Uday Shankar made the boldly experimental *Kalpana* (with a scenario by Guru Dutt) in 1947; the previous year, Chetan Anand's *Neecha Nagar*, a film about the class divide in Indian society, financed by the brothers Rashid and Rafiq Anwar, and scripted by K.A. Abbas—with Uma Anand, Kamini Kaushal, Hameed Butt and Zohra in the cast—had won the Grand Prix at the first International Cannes Film Festival. 'We were the voice of an emerging nation,' said Uma Anand, resolutely moving away from costume drama to neo-realism, 'facing the daunting reality of freedom. We were the pioneers of independent India.'

But whether the films were studio-financed or independently produced, actors like Prithviraj, Dilip Kumar, Dev Anand and Balraj Sahni moved between them with pragmatism—to the former for the money they needed, and to the latter for professional, political or aesthetic satisfaction. Their camaraderie and shared sense of purpose is captured by Abbas:

> Actually, *Neecha Nagar* and *Dharti ke Lal* were produced in Bombay, almost on parallel lines, with several artistes in common. The direction was also assigned to me but I chose three associate directors to assist me—and they were Shombhu Mitra (a very talented actor and director from the Calcutta IPTA, playing the identical role in *Nav-Anna*),

> Balraj Sahni, and P.K. Gupta, a Marathi stage director of repute. We had decided to take only non-professionals in the cast. I thought back of the play *Nav-Anna* and chose Tripti Bhaduri as the younger daughter-in-law. Damayanti Sahni (Balraj's first wife) was to be the elder daughter-in-law. Usha Mehta, a young girl, also from the Bengal IPTA, was to act the old wife of Samudder Pradhan, playing an identical role in *Nav-Anna*. The great Ravi Shankar, then composer for our IPTA's central squad, was to be our music director, and the late Shanti Bardhan, the dance director. We were producing a totally different kind of film in India.[6]

This was the artistic environment that Zohra encountered in Bombay, and although she had small roles—dance numbers or walk-on parts—in some path-breaking films of the time, it was in theatre, with IPTA and then with Prithviraj Kapoor's travelling company, that she came into her own.

Never having lived in Bombay (or anywhere else in the country other than the north) Zohra was glad to have a readymade 'home' to come to, especially as Uzra and Hameed were already at 41 Pali Hill. Kiran had plenty of company, what with Uma and Chetan's children, Kuki and Gunnu; and Chetan's sister's children, three girls and three boys, of whom the youngest two, Munni and Baba, were Kiran's special friends. 'Among us kids we never had the feeling *ke yeh mera ghar hai, woh tumhara ghar hai* (that this is my home, and that is yours),' recalls Kiran, 'we were perpetually running up and down, into each other's flats.' The novelty of this camp life was enhanced for Kiran by Kameshwar's unconventional response to normal situations. When she asked him what she should call him, he replied, '*Main tum bachhon ka dost hun, to dost bulao*. (I'm a friend to you children, so call me Friend.)' And so he became Dost, not just for Kiran but for all her friends, too. When she saw him light up a cigarette, she insisted that she also wanted one. '*Main bhi piyungi* (I will also have one),' she said, and wouldn't take no for an answer. So he put the cigarette in her mouth and said, '*Zor se sans lo*.' (Take a deep breath.) 'My god, I saw hell! And my mother was so angry with him. '*Chhoti si bachchi hai, yeh bhi koi cheez hai* (She's just a child)', but he replied, '*Zidd kar rahi thi* (She was insisting), so she has to learn.' Such 'lessons' notwithstanding, Dost was the kind of father who would cook jacket potatoes, or grill fish stuffed with green masala on a tava for her; not mind if she returned late from school, not fuss if her hair was uncombed for days. Unlike Zohra, who was the disciplinarian, 'Dost was *great* fun!'[7]

The house, though crowded, was located on a wide, leafy street, it was safe, and Bandra itself was a microcosm of Bombay society—cosmopolitan, growing and changing organically. An area originally dominated by the Koli (fishing) community, it was colonised by the Portuguese, who set up Catholic missions and schools, which meant that an Anglo-Indian, Christian population soon displaced the fisherfolk. There was also a smattering of Muslim and Parsi professionals, as well as, of course, Hindus of different backgrounds. Anyone, therefore, could fit in here and find their feet in a location of their choice.

And then, at 41 Pali Hill, was the kind of bohemian community that Zohra had known at Almora, sort of missed in Lahore, and now, quite by chance, found again in Bombay. But what could she *do* in Bombay? How were she and Kameshwar to support themselves? Bombay had always been about cinema and theatre, and everyone at 41 Pali Hill was also into films. Even Hima Devi, the only other dancer in the group, performed mainly on screen. Should Zohra and Kameshwar start a school in the city, as they had in Lahore? But where? Unlike Lahore, they had few contacts here, and everyone they knew was also a migrant.

Kameshwar, ever the optimist, refused to let this uncertain state of affairs get him down. He bought an ancient broken-down Opel (like Prithviraj Kapoor, though unbeknownst to him!) which was parked in the garden, and in it the family went on picnics and long drives, getting to know the city, as it were. Chetan and Uma always had actors and directors over, organised impromptu musical soirées, and hosted large bring-your-own-food parties. For Zohra, who had never lived in a large city, it was both new and exhilarating.

> 'Like any big city', she remarked, 'its inhabitants are not bothered about each and every individual and consequently, one leads a more or less un-interfered-with life. As a result, Kameshwar and I were just another couple striving and struggling like similar young men and women, who had come here with high hopes of making their fortunes.'[8]

More than a few of these strugglers, gifted lyricists and musicians, as well as writers, drawn to cinema, coalesced around the Anands and Sahnis at Pali Hill. Bombay's film industry was by now the second largest in the world, and opened up immense possibilities not only for actors, directors, musicians, scriptwriters and producers in the hundreds, but also thousands of ancillaries like set and costume designers, make-up artists, extras, and so on. For Kameshwar, artistic and with eclectic interests and skills, it should have been easy to find employment, even satisfaction, in the film world, but he was not in a hurry to do so. It was left to Zohra, ever the pragmatist, to look for ways to support the family.

In Hindi cinema, generally, the dancer's role was that of the 'naachnewali' (the dancing woman) or the 'gaanewali' (singing woman); the former was almost an euphemism for tawaif or prostitute, and the relationship between the tawaif and reel life/real life was ambivalent. She could be the cultured and cultivated courtesan, well versed in literature and politics, and in the arts, and of course, able to hold her own with worldly men who sought her out; but at the same time, because she was sexually available, she was located at the fringes of polite society, not a complete outsider but by no means an insider either.[9] At best, she could be seen or presented as an interlocutor of social mores, but more often than not, she was simply what came to be known later as an 'item girl', albeit an accomplished one, and a necessary foil for the heroine—or hero.

Because she was a dancer, Zohra, too, was offered 'strange and exotic roles, all of them making me shudder at the emphasis on "sex" and the "box office".' She was Menaka, the apsara, in V. Shantaram's *Shakuntala* (1943), a fleeting role only a little less routine and unimaginatively conceived than the others that she was offered. Her training with Uday Shankar had been the polar opposite of this crude commodification, and she was 'nauseated by this debasement of art. And yet the fault was mine,' she admitted candidly, 'else why had I come to a city like Bombay?'[10]

Perhaps theatre would provide an alternative. The Anands, of course, were members of IPTA, and Zohra had joined the organisation, too, almost as soon as she arrived in Bombay. By 1944, IPTA's membership read like a Who's Who of theatre, film and literary personalities of the time, and as Zohra remarked, every artist who lived in Bombay between 1940 and 1950 was connected with IPTA in one capacity or another. As Zohra herself was to be, for at least two years, acting in many of the plays that IPTA performed, at street corners, in neighbourhoods, in public halls or schools, occasionally even in theatres. IPTA's production of Clifford Odets' *Waiting for Lefty*, for example, was produced by Mulk Raj Anand; had Anil de Silva as stage manager; and included Romesh Thapar, Zohra Segal, Hameed Butt, Bakul Khote, Zaka Rahmatullah and many others as actors. The very idea of a peoples' theatre fascinated Zohra; with India in the last stages of the freedom struggle, the impact that a radical theatre with political content could have on ordinary people was not lost on her. IPTA's reach expanded exponentially, with branches in cities and towns across the country, and in 1947, Zohra was appointed vice president of the organisation.

The Cultural Squad (of which IPTA was a part) was supported by the Communist Party of India, and Zohra was asked by P.C. Joshi, secretary of the CPI, to take charge of the troupe, but she declined. She was an actor, she decided, not a purveyor of political messages. But more importantly, she had already begun her association with Prithviraj Kapoor and his Prithvi Theatres, via Uzra, who herself was on a detour from K.A. Abbas' production, *Zubeida*, for IPTA.

Theatre had always been Prithviraj Kapoor's first love. He had been performing on the stage in Lyallpur and Peshawar, while still a teenager, for some years before he moved to Bombay in 1928 and joined the Imperial Film Company. After playing the male lead in a number of silent movies (including *Cinema*

Girl, *Sher-e-Arab* and *Prince Vijay Kumar*), he went on to star in the early talkies, his biggest success being the sweeping historical epic *Sikander* (1941; remade in colour in 1951).

In 1930, an English actor-manager named Grant Anderson came to India with a few actors and technicians from England, with the intention of forming an amateur group, the Grant Anderson Theatre Company. It was a touring company (like Shakespearana in the 1950s), and had among its members Durga Khote (who was also starting her remarkable career in Marathi and Hindi cinema at the time), David (a popular character actor from Hindi films) and Prithviraj Kapoor, who was beginning to tire of acting only in films. With Grant Anderson he acted in *Hamlet* and *Julius Caesar*, in *Romeo and Juliet*, in an English adaptation of the Sanskrit play *Mrichhakatika*, but it was hard times on the road—very little money, of course, but also irregular food, with sometimes only parched gram to eat. By the time the company reached Calcutta in 1932, its coffers were completely dry, and Anderson disbanded it.[11]

Prithviraj stayed on in Calcutta for another seven years, acting in films produced by the socially committed directors of the time—Debaki Bose, P.C. Barua, Hemchandra and others like Birendra Nath Sircar of New Theatres. By 1939, however, he was back in Bombay and acting in films again.

But his heart was in theatre, and in January 1944, a year before Zohra arrived in the city, he set up Prithvi Theatres. In time, Prithvi became the leading repertory for Hindi theatre in India, till the curtain came down on it in 1959. Whereas Bengali, Marathi, Gujarati and English theatre had been active for some time and were slowly articulating a modern sensibility, Hindi theatre was far behind. Prithviraj, larger than life in all his endeavours, had a larger-than-life vision for Prithvi—an all-India presence for a form and a medium that was far more than what had hitherto been performed on a stage. '*Theatre har shahar mein hona chahiye*,' he said. '*Masjidon aur mandiron ke ban-ne mein ab adhik paisa nahin lagana chahiye... Uski jagah jan mandiron ka nirman hona chahiye, aur in mandiron ko hamari sanskritik shiksha ka kendra ban-na hoga*.' (There must be a space for theatre in every town. We should not spend too much money on building mosques and temples... instead, we should inaugurate temples for the proletariat which should become centres for cultural education.)

Theatre was a wonderful thing, he maintained all his life, it was the greatest temple on earth. In his maiden speech as a Rajya Sabha member, to which he was nominated in 1952, he would say:

> In that temple, Hindu, Muslim, Christian, Jew, Sikh and Parsee all get together. Nobody comes and asks who is in the next chair. A Pandit sits with a Mulla. A Communist friend may sit with a socialist friend. A Congressite may sit with those people who are very much communal minded. All sit together. That is a beautiful way of bringing people together and teaching them how to behave. They would laugh together, cry together. It is the biggest temple that could be built for the benefit of the nation.

Zohra joined Prithvi Theatres in 1945, and spent fourteen years with the company; Prithviraj—his personality and work ethic—became a defining influence. 'If you like my work today or praise my work, it's all thanks to Papaji [Prithviraj Kapoor],' she has said. But the association might never have come about, had it not been for Zohra's perseverance.

The rehearsal room that IPTA used was the basement hall in the Deodhar School of Music, located at Charni Road, Girgaon, and made available to it after 6:00 p.m. every day. It was here, recalled K.A. Abbas, that, sitting on the floor, he read out the draft of his first full-length play, *Zubeida*, about a young Muslim girl who discards purdah and goes out to do social work. Listening to him were Balraj Sahni and his wife Damayanti; Chetan and Dev Anand; Uzra and Hameed Butt. Balraj Sahni, recently returned from London, was enthusiastic in his praise, and Abbas asked him to direct the play. He agreed. Chetan Anand was offered the hero's role, Uzra was Zubeida, Hameed, the old Mirza Sahib, one of the town's busybodies, and Abbas himself was the reactionary Meer Saheb. Cast and director in place, daily rehearsals followed for two months, after which the play was staged at the Cowasjee Jehangir Hall like a pageant, with audience participation.[12]

At about the same time, Prithviraj Kapoor was working on the very first Prithvi Theatres production, Narayan Prasad Betaab's rendering of *Shakuntala*. Betaab, who had written several film scripts for Ranjit Movietone (the studio that Prithviraj had also worked for) was a name to reckon with in the film world: to produce a play written by him would be the perfect launch for Prithvi Theatres. And so, paying him an advance of Rs. 1001, Prithviraj acquired both Betaab and *Shakuntala*. On January 15, 1944, a havan was performed at Dhuru Hall in Dadar to formally inaugurate the theatre and begin work on its first production. Raj Kapoor, Prithviraj's eldest son, then all of nineteen, was made stage manager; sets were constructed in Dhuru Hall, and costumes were stitched on the terrace of the Kapoor residence in Parsi Colony, Matunga. People came from Hyderabad to audition for the play, and from Calcutta, as musicians. Rehearsals began with film actresses Vanmala and Swarnalata as possible Shakuntalas, but they didn't survive for more than one day.

Prithviraj, who had heard of an actress called Damayanti Sahni, was in the audience at Cowasjee Jehangir Hall to watch *Zubeida*, and to see if Damayanti might be right for his Shakuntala. He saw Uzra instead, and knew immediately that he had found his heroine. He kept returning to see the performance, captivated by Uzra's stage presence, and by her acting. Uzra herself was surprised. 'I can't say what attracted Prithviraj Kapoor to me or why he preferred me for the role of Shakuntala. He didn't say anything. After landing up a few times at the hall where we were rehearsing, he would send me the car and say, 'Please come and watch my rehearsals.'[13]

He offered, or rather, insisted that she take the role. But Chaiji (as his wife, Rama, was known) who was tangentially involved with the company, wouldn't allow it. She put her foot down; under no circumstances was Uzra to play opposite her husband's Dushyant. Prithviraj, that lion among men, had no choice but to comply. Uzra would be the original Shakuntala Indumati's understudy, but he told her she should sit in the front row in the auditorium when the play was performed. She did.

Shakuntala opened on March 9, 1945. When Prithviraj as Dushyant delivered an impassioned speech declaring his love for Shakuntala, he looked out across the stage at Uzra, and addressed her directly. Tears poured down her cheeks. Eventually, Uzra did replace Indumati, and appeared with Prithviraj in the 112 performances of the play, saying, 'What a difference, watching him on the stage and then on the film sets. I told him it was like having seen a lion in a jungle, and then watching him perform tricks in a circus.'[14]

Zohra accompanied Uzra on and off while she was

rehearsing for the play, and also saw its first performance, but she didn't think much of the production. The sets were atrocious and the overall effect, dated and laboured. 'The only redeeming feature,' she said, 'was Uzra's dignified grace and beauty, which stood out.' Prithviraj himself was impressive and dominated the stage as well as the performance, but the production left much to be desired. Why, she wondered, when India had produced an exhaustive treatise on drama centuries before any other country, did it have so little to offer? When had it lost its rich heritage? Was cinema to blame for theatre's decline? 'Apart from translations and adaptations of western plays performed by amateur societies or schools and colleges, or a crude form of folk opera during religious festivals, it was almost impossible to see a good theatrical performance anywhere in the country... Except for the regional plays of Bengal and Maharashtra, professional theatre was non-existent.'[15]

But then, later the same year, she saw Prithvi Theatres' second production, *Deewar*, and was forced to change her mind. Here was a play that was original in its subject matter, thoroughly contemporary in its politics, and communicated its message in a language that could be understood by everyone. Its impact, she felt, was stunning and instantaneous. It dealt with the partition of India, symbolised by two brothers who insisted on dividing their ancestral home, egged on by the foreign wife of one brother. A wall would be erected between the two halves. The parallels were unmistakable, and the wall represented the barrier to Hindu-Muslim unity in the country. In August-September 1945, when demands for the partition of India were gathering force, the storyline couldn't have been more relevant. Written by Inder Raj Anand as an original script, it interpolated speeches by Gandhi, Jinnah and

Macaulay into the script, and represented Prithviraj Kapoor's unequivocal rejection of the two-nation theory. In the play, a united revolt by peasants succeeds in breaking down the walls; sadly for Prithviraj (whose play was a warning to politicians and others) and for the country, the story played out very differently and tragically, two years later.

So prescient was the play's message that it was refused permission to be staged. The British government said it would not allow a performance without a green signal from the Muslim League. At a secret meeting in Bhendi Bazaar, Prithviraj pleaded his case before League representatives, but to no avail. He then asked if they could hold a private performance for Jinnah, so that he could see it for himself—his request was denied. Many years later, Prithviraj informed the Rajya Sabha of the sequence of events:

> The local Muslim leaders of Bombay honoured me by visiting my house. The Vice-President and the General Secretary said, 'You are an artist. Why are you dabbling in politics?' I replied, 'Sir, you are going to turn me out of Peshawar, and leave my unfortunate Muslim brethren here in the lurch, with their roots uprooted from the soil.'[16]

Deewar was both a personal and a political statement for Prithviraj, and he argued passionately for freedom of expression with the British. When permission was finally granted, he remarked, 'My law studies were finally of some use.'[17]

Within days of its opening at the Royal Opera House, however, protests broke out, with some Urdu papers saying the play was anti-Muslim and anti-Jinnah. *The Daily Inquilab* of August 20, 1945 declared: 'The feelings of Muslims are inflaming day by day against "Diwar". Particularly when the Hindu audience shout out remarks in dirty filthy language against Quaid-e-Azam and Pakistan.'[18] The then Superintendent of Police, CID, was obliged to clarify that the play had been 'reviewed by S.J Anand of the [Home] Branch and passed as unobjectionable on 14.4.1945'. He continued, 'So far, the *Daily Inquilab* is the only Muslim paper that has criticised the play.'

On August 20, 1945, *The Muslim Times*, a Gujarati daily, reported that Prithviraj had suspended performances for three days. On August 23, he invited members of the Muslim League and editors of some Urdu papers to see the play and give him their responses. In his report regarding the meeting, the Inspector of Police, Lamington Road Police Station recorded that 'Mr Prithviraj also told me that if Muslim leaders objected, he would revise the play.'[19]

In the event, and despite demands that scenes be deleted and dialogues changed, the play was performed regularly right up till 1947, after which it was exempted from entertainment tax for a period of one year.

For Zohra, *Deewar* would be a turning point. Unlike IPTA productions—also political and, often, original—which were more in the nature of street theatre, Prithviraj's repertory company only performed original plays, in auditoria, for urban audiences, and its shows were ticketed. Every person in the company was paid, whether they performed or not, a remarkable fact, given that it had more than 60 people—actors, actresses, dancers, musicians, singers, make-up men, tailors, carpenters and technicians—on its rolls. Like the Almora Dance Centre, here was a group of professionals (albeit without formal training as actors) Zohra could relate to, and a towering theatrical figure like Prithviraj Kapoor from whom she believed she could learn a great deal. She begged him to include her in his company. He demurred. He could not afford another female actor. And as a dancer, what sort of opening could he offer her? She would do anything, she said, take any role she was offered, accept any responsibility. She was desperate to join. 'I was shattered when Papaji refused to give me work. He revealed to Kameshwar that he was not sure whether I could work as a character actress for a group in which my younger sister was the leading lady... Though I love and admire Uzra, I now realise that there was a tinge of jealously. I knew I was not beautiful enough to be a leading lady. Being short, plump and ordinary[.]'[20] Then one day Kameshwar went to see Prithviraj and said, 'Zohra will not let me rest in peace till you take her in.' And because Prithviraj could not ever refuse anyone who pleaded with him, he relented. Zohra could be the dance director at Prithvi Theatres.[21]

Was it just the power of *Deewar* that decided Zohra, or the realisation that she should avail of an opportunity—even if it didn't actually exist—while she could still change course? She was not trained as an actor, true, but then no one at Prithvi Theatres was; they were all amateurs, learning as they went along. She, at least, was a trained dancer.

Zohra joined the company in October 1945, and stayed with it till 1959 when it ceased operating. Her first role was as the foreign woman in *Deewar* (replacing Damayanti Sahni). The play went on to become one of Prithvi Theatres' most successful productions, performed 712 times between 1945 and 1959.

The Royal Opera House on Charni Road, home to Prithvi Theatres for sixteen years, is an imposing three-storeyed building built in the baroque style. Jehangir Framji Karaka, a Parsi businessman who headed a coal brokerage, and Maurice Bandmann, a Calcutta theatre artiste, collaborated on its design in 1908; its foundation stone was laid in 1909 and it was inaugurated by King George in 1911, either before or after the grand Delhi Durbar that same year. Its marble foyer, complete with the requisite Greek statuary, great chandeliers, gold stucco on the ceiling, painted doors to the private boxes and opulent maroon velvet curtains, were reminiscent of European opera houses, and for at least the first twenty or more years of its life, it staged only operas. Its acoustics were designed specifically for opera, but as the years went by, the expense of keeping it in trim forced the management to offer more diverse fare and hire out the great stage for other performances. By 1935, it had become more of a cinema hall than an opera house, screening films every afternoon and evening, but it did also have the odd theatrical performance, albeit only in the morning.

Every day during Kiran's holidays, Zohra and Kiran would take the bus from Pali Hill to the Bandra Railway Station, from where they would travel by local train to Charni Road and walk to the Royal Opera House. Kiran would sit in the auditorium while rehearsals were on (in the front row, so that her mother could keep an eye on her), hating every minute of being cooped up in a dim hall while all the other children at Pali Hill were running wild after school. But Zohra was adamant—Kiran could not be left alone at No. 41, as Dost was sometimes at home, but often not.

Rehearsals began with Zohra getting the entire cast (Kiran included) to do some exercises; shoulders, hips, arms, again and again. 'She was very strict,' said Kiran, 'we used to call her Hitler at home, and at the Royal Opera, everyone would get into a panic: *Zohra bi bula rahin hain, Zohra bi bula rahin hain!* (Zohra Bi has summoned us!)' When the Company was on tour, daily meetings began at ten in the morning, with an hour of singing and voice production, another hour of dance practice, followed by an hour of classes in Hindi and Urdu. Voice production was handled by Prithviraj himself, while Ram Gangoli, the music director, rehearsed the songs that were part of their repertory with the entire cast. Base tones were practised by singing 'Allah Hu!' and high pitches by intoning 'Ram, Ram.' The actual play rehearsals, which lasted for a couple of hours, came last, but before rehearsals began each play was read out to the full cast and Papaji (as Prithviraj was referred to by all) would invite suggestions from everyone, including the technicians. After the rehearsals were over, Papaji would come onstage; '*Unke liye ek takhta jaisa rakha hota tha* (There was a sort of wooden bench reserved for him), he would sit on that and everyone would sit around him, facing him,' recalled Kiran. His back would be to the auditorium, and the whole play would be revised. If something new was to be added, the roles would be redistributed.

Prithviraj never 'trained' anyone. He always said, 'I am not a teacher, don't treat me like a guru.'[22] As far as acting was concerned, he was not being unduly modest—never having trained as an actor himself, he would not have presumed to tell others how to act; what was more, he believed that one needed several rebirths to master the art of acting. 'Rather than teach,' said Zohra, 'he related anecdotes and stories, and by his sheer presence and example, one learned.' Recounting her experience with Papaji, the actress Shaukat Kaifi (who, with her husband, the poet Kaifi Azmi, was also associated with IPTA) remarked:

> Prithviraj Kapoor taught us that human behaviour was the best window for an actor...one has to consistently and consciously observe people... His tips on acting came at the oddest of moments. At picnics, in between plays, he would point out faces, body postures, hand movements, of people passing by... I learned to observe, imbibe, store away and then recall what I had seen, whenever required to.[23]

Zohra found she had to jettison many of her own preconceptions about theatre, as far as play-writing and characterisation were concerned, but in other matters, her own training and experience with Uday Shankar informed her assessment of what was performed. 'I disagreed with the length of the plays, thinking some too long. Up to a point improvisation is all right and our improvised dialogue was incorporated in the text of the play, but sometimes I felt that Prithviraj himself would go on for hours and hours, so that the play stretched from two-and-a-half to four hours!'[24]

She herself brought to the company the discipline and punctuality that had been instilled in her by Mary Wigman and Uday Shankar, together with her strongly grounded understanding of the body and of movement. The professionalism and seriousness of purpose that was inculcated in her then, became second nature now—attributes she hoped to encourage in her colleagues by example.

On actual performance days, the entire company would assemble in the theatre and repair to the green rooms allotted to the cast. There were three on the ground and first floors, and one, Prithviraj's, on the top floor. Leading off from his green room was a magnificent cast iron spiral staircase, down which he would descend to make his grand entrance on stage. Shaukat Kaifi recalls:

> Shows always began on Sunday morning. Before the performance, the atmosphere backstage would be quite special. Dim lights, the sweet sound of the shehnai, the scent of agarbatti wafting through created a temple-like ambience. From the make-up room, in the half-light, the soft laughter of women. Before the show began, all the artistes would assemble onstage and recite a Sanskrit shloka in praise of theatre. Then a brief arti. By the time the curtain rose, the magic of theatre completely enveloped us...we felt we had become part of the play's reality.[25]

After *Shakuntala*, every Prithvi Theatres play was an original, with Prithviraj collaborating on ideas, plots and dialogues with his scriptwriters. The first draft itself took several sittings. Writing and rewriting or rearranging could well take a year or more, followed by reading sessions. There were no deadlines for production, nor any certainty about a play being staged at all if it was unsatisfactory. Prithviraj's emphasis on using an everyday language, and on realism and authenticity, distinguished him from both prevalent Parsi theatre, with its spectacular effects and highly stylised presentation, as well as from the few adaptations of western plays that passed for modern theatre then. Audiences, he insisted, must be transported to the scene of the action, whether a street in Peshawar, a Muslim mohalla, or a village in the hills; no trapdoors, fly-wires, mirrors or technical wizardry found their way into the plays, only a full-blooded realism, as true to life as possible.

It was serendipitous that the very first play Zohra acted in was *Deewar*. Damayanti Sahni, who played the foreign woman, had been snapped up by Bombay cinema, so Zohra was inducted to play her part. Kameshwar, moved to tears by the performance, photographed it with his Roliflex camera, but he himself never took part in any Prithvi Theatres production, in any capacity.

In Bombay Zohra was breathing a different air, an air heady with the promise of fulfilment, of stretching herself creatively, of living and working with the best and the brightest in film and theatre. At home, on Pali Hill, there was no telling who would alight when, which film or play was being discussed, which writer celebrating his story being made into a film by one of the big studios. Guru Dutt might wander in to talk about film, or play chess. Writers Raja Rao and Mulk Raj Anand, painters M.F. Husain and Krishen Khanna were regulars, and there was never an evening when ideas and opinions were not animatedly discussed.[26] Everyone was passionate about their art, and everyone was mostly penniless. Sometimes, one of them would sell a film script, or work in All India Radio (AIR), or as an extra in a film, or paint a movie poster, in order to meet their immediate needs. Dev Anand worked in the censor office, Hindi & Urdu department of AIR Bombay; Uma Anand wrote for India's first women's magazine, *Woman and Beauty Spectator*, 'practically writing the magazine from cover to cover', for which she was paid Rs. 200. They would pool their cash, meet in a coffee house where they would be served peanuts with coffee, and would pocket the nuts to eat at home. Or, returning home after midnight from wherever they had gone, by the late milk train, they would eat channa for dinner, and when they could afford to, bananas or oranges.[27]

The city was alive with cultural activity. Exhibitions at the Artists' Aid Centre at Kala Ghoda, film shows organised by Friends of the Soviet Union Society, poetry readings at the Silverfish Club… And, of course, their own plays, both by Prithvi Theatres and IPTA.

Politically, too, the tide was turning; for the Raj, certainly, but also for the nationalists. The Naval Mutiny broke out in 1946 and the streets of Bombay were flooded with protestors. Army tanks were paraded through the same streets, and shoot-at-sight orders issued. Strikers at sea took possession of twenty-two Royal Indian Navy ships, pulling down the Union Jack and hoisting the flags of the Indian National Congress and the Muslim League. '[In a] rather ramshackle building on Walkeshwar Road,' writes Uma Anand, 'where Raja Rao lived on the first floor and actor Moti Lal on the top floor, unknown to all but a few of us, was housed a cell from where a secret radio station kept the country in touch with imprisoned Congress freedom fighters. Such centres operated throughout the country.'[28]

Six months later, in August, Jinnah issued a call for Direct Action Day, having rejected the Cabinet Mission Plan for an Interim Government in India. 'If you want peace,' he declared, 'we do not want war. If you want war, we accept your offer unhesitatingly. We will either have a divided India or a destroyed India.' On August 16, violent clashes broke out in Calcutta, with rioting, arson, looting and killings leaving close to 5,000 people dead, 15,000 rendered homeless, charred shells of automobiles and dead cattle, and the acrid smell of smoke rising from funeral pyres. Communal violence spread across north India, engulfing Noakhali, Punjab and Bombay. Police opened fire nineteen times in Bombay in March 1947; curfew was imposed, and troops asked to stand by. Of that time, Zohra later recalled: 'During the riots Papaji wanted to present a secular front, so he would drive through the streets in an open truck, Uzra on one side of him and I on the other. It was a display of Hindu-Muslim amity, but I don't think it went down well with everyone, and we received death threats.'[29]

The turbulence on the street found an echo at home. For some reason, Kameshwar found himself adrift in Bombay. In the early days, he and Zohra set up Segal Ballet, not a school as in Lahore, just a troupe, taught young students and performed on weekends. But this was short-lived. He tried his hand at acting, had a small part in the film *Neecha Nagar*, for which he also did the art direction (Zohra was the dance director)—'but', said his daughter, 'he was hopeless in it, really bad'. Given that he was a physically beautiful man, he should have been much in demand in cinema city, but Kameshwar, it turned out, was not employee material, and at the time movie studios employed their actors; even the stars, almost without exception, were employees of big studios. As Zohra became more involved with theatre, the tension between them began to surface, and Kameshwar became more and more eccentric. His room in Pali Hill had an aquarium, a radiogram, and a huge table with an ultraviolet lamp on which he would lie, tanning himself. He dabbled in homeopathy, decided to manufacture some soap, and when that failed, some oil. He began drinking, a Segal family trait, and soon it became a habit. Kiran remembered Dost grinding bhang (cannabis) in a bowl: '*Holi pe to sab chadhate the* (Everyone would take it on Holi), Ammi too, but with Dost it was a regular thing... this introduced a lot of discord in the family.'[30]

Kameshwar was also an outrageous flirt—'Women would come and go from his room,' said Kiran, 'my parents had always had separate bedrooms'—and it could be that he thought Zohra was involved with someone in Prithvi. The strong attraction between Uzra and Prithviraj was already a well-known fact, and as Kiran admitted, 'I wouldn't be surprised if Ammi was also involved, after all it's only human nature.' Whether or not this was the case, Zohra herself confessed that 'our family was definitely disrupted when our tours began, and Kameshwar was not at all happy about it. As a result there was constant tension in the house.'[31] Although she put the discord down to her being away from Bombay for long stretches, there was no getting away from the fact that part of the reason was also that Kameshwar had not been able to find his feet, either in film or in theatre—or indeed, in any of the arts. Zohra tried to put a positive cast on their circumstances, but the reality was that she was the only earning member of the family. '*Dost ka paisa kabhi aata tha, kabhi nahin* (Dost's income would bring in something at times, and at other times there would be nothing),' said Kiran, 'and shopkeepers, people who had given us credit, would come to the house, asking to be paid.' This would upset Zohra, not only because she abhorred being indebted to anyone, but because it deeply offended her sense of herself as an honourable and honest individual, who held strongly to her principles.

Working at Prithvi Theatres had meant shedding many of the privileges and comforts she had taken for granted, growing up as a member of the aristocracy and, later, as part of Uday Shankar's company which had wealthy patrons bankrolling it. She had never known want, indeed had been indulged in ways that few young women of her background would have been; yet she adapted to the difficulties of touring with the company with grace and pragmatism, both of which would stand her in good stead throughout her career. 'A lot of snobbish nonsense fell off me during this period,' she wrote. 'With Uday Shankar I was treated like a star, always travelling first class in India, staying in the best hotels. All this ended when I joined Prithvi Theatres. Everyone travelled in the third-class compartments booked for the troupe… We slept in dormitories on the floor, either in rented accommodation just above the theatre, or in a rented house. All our food was cooked together and everyone ate the same thing'.[32]

And so, for the next fourteen years, Zohra's acting life was lived with Prithvi Theatres.

Act 2, Scene 2: Onstage with Prithvi

On January 6, 1947, the All India Congress Committee accepted the Partition Plan by a majority of 99 in favour of, and 52 against, the resolution. With this, the partition of India on religious lines became a certainty. Muslims, Hindus and Sikhs who had lived together for generations, often claiming descent from the same original ancestor, who were sometimes even members of the same tribe, were now caught in the vice of suspicion, mistrust and animosity. 'Propaganda with its ghastly brood—mutilation, massacre and rape—' wrote Malcolm Darling, 'has turned Jinnah's two-nation creed in the village from a theory into a bloody fact.'[1]

Prithviraj, passionately and implacably opposed to the division of the country, responded by producing what came to be known as his Partition Quartet, four plays, beginning with *Deewar*, that dealt with the politics of the time, and with the terrible consequences of Partition. Within three months of the All India Congress Committee resolution, Prithviraj's second play, *Pathan*, written by Lal Chand Bismil, opened at the Royal Opera House on April 13, 1947. It was a paean to Hindu-Muslim unity, an attempt to halt the seething hatred by emphasising their shared values of love, loyalty and honour. The Muslim Pathan and Hindu Diwan are sworn friends, their two sons like brothers. When Tarachand, the Diwan, dies, Sher Khan promises to look after his son, Vazir, as his own. Local rivalries and feuds result in a revenge killing, in which Vazir is implicated. Tribal custom demands an eye for an eye, and the opposing chief insists on Vazir's head as compensation. Sher Khan refuses, offering his own head instead. But no—one young man's death requires another young man's head, and so the Khan sacrifices his own son, Bahadur.

The Pathan was Prithviraj, in the lead role, as always. Zohra was his wife, Khairunissa, and Uzra, the Diwan's wife, Kaki. Prithviraj's eldest son, Raj Kapoor, played Bahadur, but so, in later productions, did his other sons, Shammi and Shashi Kapoor, and members of the extended family—Premnath, Shriram, Vishi Kapoor and others—for apart from Prithviraj himself there was no permanent leading lady or man. Everyone could be cast in many roles, and so both Zohra and Indumati were Khairunissa; Rani Azad, Indumati and Uzra could be Kaki; and so on. Rehearsals for the play were in full swing, but so was rioting in towns and cities across north India. After rehearsals, Prithviraj, together with his cast and colleagues, would visit riot-affected mohallas in Bombay and hold peace processions. Major film and theatre personalities participated, with Prithviraj, his wife Rama, and his troupe leading from the front.

Raj Kapoor, all of twenty-three then, was Prithviraj's art director. For *Pathan* he travelled to Peshawar to research the environment, painstakingly designing and redesigning the single set for the play. Pathan jewellery, the mud of the fort wall, the majesty of the terrain were breathtakingly lit, and the sound of the muezzin at dawn drew admiring gasps from the audience. Zohra loved being Khairunissa. A Pathan herself, she was totally immersed in the role, but in retrospect, was honest enough to admit that she hadn't done justice to the final scene, when a grieving mother tells her son to learn from his bride's forbearance. It was a beautifully timed speech, carrying the force of heightened but controlled emotion, yet 'only occasionally was I successful in bringing a certain quality to the speech, to engage the audience in the exact pitch and rhythm'.[2] Indeed, it was only after she saw Indumati playing Khairunissa that Zohra fully appreciated her own inadequacy, for Indumati received thunderous applause each time she performed.

Prithviraj, of course, was splendid as Sher Khan, a towering presence on stage, his performance a tour de force. When he is mocked for sacrificing his own son, he roars:

> Do you want that Hindus should sacrifice their lives for Muslims, but when the time comes, Muslims should not sacrifice their lives for them, when both have always sacrificed their lives for each other? And why should they not when they know they belong to one country, eat the same food, drink the same water, and what is more, the air which they breathe is the same. I am surprised that knowing all this you should have raised this hateful question of Hindu-Muslim.[3]

Zohra recalled that 'every time in the climax of *Pathan*, when Sher Khan [Prithviraj] handed over his young son to the enemies, honouring the creed of an eye for an eye, there was not a dry eye in the house'.[4]

K.A. Abbas remarked, 'Whenever Prithvi achieves the desired balance between conviction and its expression, the result is histrionic greatness, unsurpassed on the Indian stage or screen… If I was asked what I regard as the masterpiece of

Prithvi's career, I would unhesitatingly point to his title role in *Pathan*. It is rare that an actor, by memory, by feeling, and by conviction, can become so completely identified with a character.'[5] Between 1947 and 1960 *Pathan* was performed 558 times; and according to Shashi Kapoor, 'It was the best production that we had, it was superb.'

August 14, 1947 was declared a holiday at Prithvi Theatres. The entire company gathered in the compound and Prithviraj unfurled the Indian flag. 'We sang Vande Mataram,' recalled Zohra, 'and hymns dedicated to theatre. And then we took out a procession. August 14 was a day of processions—workers, trade unionists, IPTA, painters...the whole of Bombay seemed to be out on the streets, overjoyed at Independence.'[6] Much to Kameshwar's annoyance Zohra herself danced with abandon in the middle of Bombay. But the delirious happiness of August 14 would soon be snuffed out by the death and destruction that followed Partition, as the whole of north India was engulfed by untold, horrific violence.

Prithviraj, who had anticipated but hoped to avert Partition—portrayed as the partition between brothers in *Deewar*—was devastated, now that the division had become a reality, but he refused to accept that violence was inevitable. '*Mera vishwas hai ki dharm kabhi jhagda nahin karta* (It is my belief that religion does not allow conflict),' he said. It was only when religion was abused, he believed, that it became the handmaiden of vandals and opportunists. 'It is the responsibility of art to present the true aspect of reality to society. Bapu recognised this truth; my goal is to follow in his footsteps. Artists and writers cannot be neutral in politics, in the struggle between the forces of war and those of peace.' And so Prithvi Theatres' next production was the ground-breaking and unequivocally critical *Ghaddar* (Traitor) that premiered on August 15, 1948, at the Royal Opera House. With a cast of only nine characters, *Ghaddar* was Prithvi Theatres' smallest production; it covered the period from the Khilafat Movement to 1947, and dealt with the question of those four million Muslims who had chosen to remain in India, and were called traitors—whether to Islam or to Pakistan, is open to interpretation. Mohammad Ashraf (Prithviraj) is a young Muslim who, with his wife (Uzra), joins the Muslim League but remains a staunch nationalist, disappointing his wife who assumed that they would move to Pakistan. Ashraf is appalled by the violence in Punjab after August 15, 1947; shattered, he vows to serve his motherland. Labelled a traitor by those Leaguers who fought for Pakistan, he is shot dead by an erstwhile 'friend'.

Zohra played an old maidservant in the play, Bari Bi, who is opposed to Partition from the very beginning. At the end of the final act she tells the Begum that she will not accompany her to Pakistan, will remain in India. Although a minor role, it was beautifully written, and she believed that its simple dialogue and patriotic sentiments immediately endeared the maidservant to the audience. Zohra was surprised by the success of her portrayal, but concluded that Bari Bi's homely comments came as a relief after the political harangues and party intrigues in the rest of the play. It helped that she added her own extempore dialogues to the script! The difficulty, she said, was 'trying to feel old from within'. Since the play covered a span of some thirty years, she had to transform herself from a middle-aged woman to a very old one, despite being young and exuberant at the time, and had to keep saying, 'Kill it! Kill it!' to herself, meaning she had to suppress the great surge of energy she always experienced on stage. Her own contribution notwithstanding, she thought the real reason for the success of her character was the scriptwriter, Inder Raj Anand, 'who created the role of that darling old mother-figure'.[7]

We cannot know what dialogues Zohra added to the script, but it is quite possible that they were modelled on the speech of the old retainers and servants she had heard as a child in her mother's home; it is also quite likely that her portrayal was deeply felt and came from her own unhappiness at the division of the country and the impending break-up of her family. She herself, married to a Hindu, could not think of living anywhere else; but even had that not been the case she, like her father, was opposed to the very idea of two nations based on religious separation. Kameshwar, who photographed the production one day, was so moved by her performance that his tears fell on the camera's viewfinder.

As with *Deewar*, censor board clearance for *Ghaddar* became a problem. The chief minister of Bombay asked Prithviraj to approach the central government for permission. Sardar Patel introduced Prithviraj to Nehru, who asked him to meet Maulana Azad, then minister for education and culture. Azad heard him out for forty-five minutes, smoking one cigarette after another. Soon after their meeting, Prithviraj received an official letter granting permission, not only for *Ghaddar* but for all future Prithvi productions! Also attached was a copy of a directive to the railway ministry, granting 50% reduction in train fare for all cultural troupes.[8]

Film India, in its review of the play in October 1948, wrote that it was 'a truthful exposition of Muslim political activities during the last 27 years, without any exaggeration or even equivocation. There is nothing in it to hurt a single sensible Muslim', and went on to say that the play sought to once again instil in Muslims 'love for the land they were born in'.

As a result of this kind of opinionated endorsement, coupled with the title of the play (*Ghaddar*), there was an almost total boycott of the play by Bombay Muslims. According to Shashi Kapoor, there were those who wanted to shoot Prithviraj, 'they said he was making a mockery of Islam. But he would say, "Come and see the play".' And so, about thirty Muslims arrived from Bhendi Bazaar to see it. Trouble was brewing, the entire cast and the company were tense with worry. After the performance, however, the band of thirty hugged Prithviraj Kapoor and said, 'You have called Muslims ghaddar, but they are those Muslims who *should* be called ghaddar, they *are* ghaddar.'[9]

The play was performed 262 times, but did especially well only in UP, Bihar and Hyderabad. South India, removed from the devastation caused by Partition and remote from the politics of the north, responded to it not at all; and in Cochin, Muslim Leaguers threatened to burn down the theatre if the play was performed there.

Meanwhile, the aftershocks of Partition were being felt across the whole of north and east India as waves of refugees, fearing for their lives, crossed both new borders. Who could have imagined that whole populations, entire villages, would be uprooted? And who even knew what the border represented? Your world was your village and your community; your family and your neighbours were your solace and your society. Both—or rather, all—were now at terrible risk. Thousands were faced with what was a Hobsons Choice—to go or to stay? Why leave? Or then, why remain? And whether you left or stayed, how would you describe yourself—Pakistani or Indian? Muslim-not-Pakistani? Neither Indian nor Pakistani? What, after all, was your country?

And so, many whose lives had been lived on one soil,

in one city, were forced to relinquish a way of life, to forego friendships, and relocate to a place that could never be home. Many of Prithviraj Kapoor's friends and colleagues in film had left—the writer Saadat Hasan Manto; the actresses Noorjehan, Beena and Swarnalata; the actor Nazir. So many families were being divided before their very eyes. And among those that were divided, was Zohra's. Her two brothers, Zakkan and Ikram, were already in Karachi and decided to stay on. Sabra, who was living in Lahore, married to an Afghan, also decided to remain, and Amina followed soon after Independence. Zohra's father refused to leave, as did her older sister, Hajrah, for they were against the division of the country, but in 1949 Uzra and Hamid also left for Pakistan, so that overnight, Zohra's family was reduced by half.

Hamid was Kashmiri, and his parents had already left India for Pakistan. Together with Subodh Mukherji, Hamid had financed a film, *Heer Ranjha*, which unfortunately failed at the box office, following which Hamid suffered a heart attack. Advised by doctors to move to a place with a better climate than Bombay, he decided to join his parents in Rawalpindi.

The same year the Anands moved out of 41 Pali Hill to a place of their own, The Shack, in Juhu. With the Anands gone, the almost constant flurry of activity in the house on the hill shifted to Juhu; and with Uzra and Hamid's departure, both of Zohra's families—her social one and her biological one—were no longer within easy reach.

Away from the distractions and camaraderie of Pali Hill, the strains in her relationship with Kameshwar became more apparent. Zohra worried about him and about the growing distance between them. He was not violent, not ever; there were no public outbursts of frustration or dissatisfaction, but she knew that he was withdrawing into himself. Mealtimes were silent, with the children acting as intermediaries. Zohra, tense, watched as Kameshwar's behaviour became more unpredictable. She would return from touring to find Kiran more or less unsupervised, with Kameshwar distracted and vague about her whereabouts. His unhappiness at Zohra's frequent absences while on tour was obvious. Family life was disrupted, with the household left to the management of cooks and ayahs. From the family's point of view, what would have been ideal was for Zohra to stay home and look after husband and children—although Kameshwar clearly couldn't support the family. Zohra was up against the old, impossible-to-reconcile demands of domesticity and career that few women can avoid. Simpler by far for her to have a privileged marriage and motherhood over a life before the footlights, but she had found what she called her 'real love', which in some ways also became her calling; and so what may have been simpler for some (as indeed, it would be for Uzra later) was difficult for her, as acting slowly became second nature.

Ahooti (Sacrifice), the fourth and final play in Prithvi Theatres' Partition Quartet, is the story of Janki, a woman who is abducted and raped on the eve of her wedding. She is rescued by Mahomed Shaffi and reunited with her father in a relief camp. The family moves to Bombay, Janki is the subject of terrible slander, and although her fiancé is willing to marry her, her father-in-law-to-be refuses to acknowledge her. She commits suicide. Janki's story mirrored the real-life experience of thousands of women, Hindu and Muslim, who were abducted in the aftermath of Partition.

Published estimates of the number of women abducted put out by the governments of India and Pakistan were 50,000 Muslim women in India, and 33,000 non-Muslim women in Pakistan, but unofficial estimates were much higher for both. The scale and enormity of the problem was so huge that both governments entered into an agreement to locate, recover and restore all such women to their respective families—and countries. *Ahooti* was Prithviraj's response to their predicament. But overwhelmed by appearances in films and in his own theatre's productions, he decided to sit out *Ahooti*, which in its original script was a mother-daughter story. Uzra was to play the mother, with Pushpa in the role of her daughter, Janki. Zohra was cast as the hero's mother, Visheshran. But with Uzra no longer in the country the play had to be rewritten. Uzra's role of the mother was now replaced by Janki's blind father played, naturally, by Prithviraj.

Without Uzra, Zohra lost interest in the play, and so she opted for a minor character in *Ahooti*, never having warmed to the subject, anyway. What was it about the play that hadn't appealed to her? Was it the subject matter or the fact that her original role had been dropped altogether? Was it Prithviraj's self-indulgence that she recognised, even as she admired his versatility? Whatever the reason, she thought it the least compelling of his four Partition plays. Written by Lal Chand Bismil, it opened on September 30, 1949, and was met with tepid, if not outright negative, reviews. *Film India*, in its review of December that year, called *Ahooti* 'a dull, boring and ineffective production, mainly because of Prithviraj's irrepressible enthusiasm to talk a person's head off on almost every problem under the sun'.

Other reviewers were as caustic, but reviews

notwithstanding, Bombay's director-general of police saw the play and was greatly moved by the girl's plight. He met Prithviraj and offered him his services, promising to help in whatever way he could; Prithviraj introduced him to an old gentleman, a refugee, whose daughter had been separated from him in the chaos of fleeing. Within days, she was found and restored to him. This was a gratifying outcome, but although the play was performed 339 times it could not be called a success.

Prithviraj's Partition Quartet, political to the core, was one man's attempt to take the tragic fact of that division and confront the devastation it caused, with compassion and humility. At the end of the shows, when the curtain came down, this larger-than-life theatre and film personality would stand with bowed head, his shawl open, seeking donations for Partition relief work. When he stood at the exit after the show with his jholi open, asking for donations, many in the audience, especially women, would get very emotional. They would take off their jewellery—necklaces, earrings, bangles—and throw them into the shawl. But their gesture presented him with a dilemma. Money could be used, but what was he to do with the jewellery? And so Prithviraj would make an announcement at the end of the shows asking women not to donate their ornaments.[10]

No one in film or theatre before or since has dealt with that horrific, tragic period in our history, and with its impact on ordinary people, Hindus and Muslims, with the same sustained passion and commitment. Prithviraj was the first to see where the rhetoric of religious difference might lead, what the contest over territory would entail, and the violence and violations that would ensue. Long before Manto's disturbing story '*Khol Do*', Prithviraj spoke the unspeakable in *Ahooti*; he took on both the Muslim League (which created a furore when *Ahooti* was staged) as well as the RSS, telling M.S. Golwalkar, after Gandhi's assassination, to keep his men under control; and he addressed nationalist leaders via speeches that he delivered before or after his plays were performed. More often than not, all four plays in the Quartet met with resistance and protest, came up against the censor board, and faced a hostile press. The plays were performed only for a few years, but as Salma Siddique remarks, 'They provoked debate in drawing rooms, affected political discourse, and infuriated bigots.'[11] All the Partition films now considered classics followed Prithviraj's plays—Ritwik Ghatak's *Meghe Dhaka Tara* was made in 1960, *Komal Gandhar* in 1961 and *Subarnarekha* in 1965; the Hindi film *Dharmputra* was released in 1961 and M.S. Sathyu's masterpiece, *Garm Hawa*, as late as 1974. It is an irony that Prithviraj's trailblazing Partition Quartet has been more or less forgotten, even as Partition nostalgia continues to find expression in diverse media.

Prithvi Theatres' next new production was two years away, but the touring kept up a brisk pace. Roughly four months of every year were spent touring, for Prithviraj was determined to take theatre to the people. In 1941, speaking to *Film India*, he said:

> I would like to start a caravan theatre company and tour the villages. Through my plays I will let people see what life is like and what it should be like. I do not believe in preaching. My plays, I hope, will guide the people better than any preaching could.[12]

Between 1945 and 1960, about two million people across the country would have seen Prithvi's productions, a record for any company at the time—and perhaps, ever since. Venues could be palaces, cinema halls, schools, municipal buildings or makeshift stages outdoors. The Company's carpenters and technicians went ahead to prepare the space, and all the lighting equipment was carried with them. At site, the dressing rooms were basic, and bathrooms were either appalling or non-existent. No proper beds, your trunk at the foot of the mattress, washing your own clothes, sleeping on durries, but the one luxury Zohra couldn't do without was a daily hot bath!

Being on tour might have had its discomforts, but there was no denying the excitement that everyone felt. At the end of the long lines of wagons were the third-class compartments where the entire company was ensconced, 'some fast asleep, some holed up in a corner playing cards; some huddled together whispering into one another's ears…' In a diary that he maintained, Shammi Kapoor wrote:

> The journey may be long or short according to the destination, but it is never tiresome or weary or dull… we are some 80 members, one big family, very clannish. We are performers, artistes. Actors and actresses… collars up, flying high… we may look like coolies in the morning (hauling luggage and unloading sets from the brake vans) but at night, we are the stars.

'The entire procession of Prithvi Theatres was like a circus,' wrote Zohra, with board and lodging thrown in, even for those who were not on the salary register. Artistes' children would be paid a nominal Rs. 1 for every month on tour.

The company travelled to Delhi, Saurashtra, Sangli, Bilaspur, Jabalpur, Calcutta, Hyderabad, Poona, Ratlam,

Jodhpur, Kolhapur… In Kolhapur, they performed in a venue that sat 1,000 comfortably. The theatre's upper gallery opened onto an open-air stage, a wrestling arena, and an amphitheatre, with high walls all around. As if this were not plenty, there was also an arena for elephants! The enclosure was dug to a depth of fifteen feet, with four circular bastions and four small gates into which mahouts could dash for safety from the fury of the elephants.[13] In Ahmednagar, although the theatre had good dressing rooms and bathrooms, the audience brought their own cushions and sat on the ground—tickets were therefore priced at only Rs. 1.50. In Hubli, the company played to a packed house but there was a hitch in the performance: 'Speak louder!' shouted a member of the audience. Prithviraj stopped mid-sentence, demanded pin-drop silence, and told the man who had interrupted him that he had no manners.

In Sangli, the company was housed in a cowshed, in Jabalpur, in MLA quarters, in Delhi in Constitution House. And Zohra reported that there were times when they were buffeted by hail, wind and rain during open-air shows; held up by electricity failures; delayed because the wagons carrying their sets failed to arrive; devastated by lightning that struck a brand new set, smashing it to bits. To top it all, during a rehearsal of *Deewar*, the sari of one of the actresses caught fire as they were acting out the last scene![14] In short, 'every conceivable calamity and mishap' befell the company, but the show went on—Prithviraj's caravan never halted.

In May 1951, an All India Peace Convention was held in Bombay, with over 400 delegates and representatives from all over the country attending. *Unity* reported that the Sunderbai Hall resounded with a 'multitude of voices, speaking in Malayalam and Hindi, English and Bengali, Marathi and Urdu'. The Convention collected over eleven million signatures in response to the Berlin Peace Appeal made to the Five Superpowers, following the US/Soviet Cold War. Their draft pledge declared:

> We, writers and artists,
> Singers and musicians,
> Scientists and dancers,
> Playwrights and poets,
> Painters and sculptors,
> And all who love culture
> … answer with clamorous songs
> The resounding voices of peace in the world
> So that there shall be no war
> So that there shall be peace.[15]

Zohra, part of the milling throng at the convention, felt her heart swell with pride as Prithviraj rose to address the gathering, calling on the people of India to turn the movement for peace 'into a mighty mobilisation of men and women'. Through Papaji, Zohra found herself in the company of people she would have had little to do with had she remained within the social and economic milieu she was born into. Not even Zohra, who was given to adventure, could have imagined performing for prisoners in Punjab's Ferozepur jail in 1952, who sat in an open compound, handcuffed and with their feet in chains.

There was more to come. The governor of Punjab asked Prithviraj if he would like to witness a hanging scheduled for the following day. Women were barred from watching but Zohra, being Zohra and not to be deterred, begged to be allowed to see it, too. The experience, she recounted, was 'unforgettable'. In the presence of the doctor, the executioner, the governor and others, they heard the distant but rousing slogan, 'Boley so nihal!' from the condemned man's cell, and an answering call from all the other cells, 'Sat Sri Akal!' The rhythmic litany became louder as the prisoner passed through the jail; when he reached the small courtyard where he was to be executed, he was blindfolded, a black hood was dropped over his head, his chains were removed, and he was hanged. The man, a poor peasant, had hacked his wife and her lover to death.

Other experiences, however, were less dramatic, but together they changed Zohra. Being with Prithviraj, working with him, altered her life in a fundamental way. Here was a man, already famous as a film star, an actor to reckon with on stage, a man with a mission and an uncommon vision for the arts in his country—a man who, for example, was also president of the National Railway Workers' Union (Central Railway) for four years, working for the real welfare of the railway worker. From his example, Zohra learnt to shed her arrogance, to recognise and respect the dignity of everyone she worked with, however humble or talented. Through him, too, she understood the transformative potential of theatre, of which she had received a glimpse with IPTA; but it was only after the experience of touring with Prithvi Theatres to villages and qasbahs, small towns and big cities, that she began to appreciate the enormity of what they were trying to do.

Much to Zohra's relief and joy, Uzra and Hamid Butt returned to India and Bombay in 1950-51 after a short lived stay in Pakistan. Uzra was welcomed back to Prithvi Theatres with open arms, and her own happiness at returning was evident. The sisters were reunited professionally as well as personally, and Kiran spent many afternoons and weekends at Soona Mahal on Marine Drive with her aunt, developing a close bond with her.

Prithviraj's next production, *Kalakar*, which opened on September 8, 1951, was a complete departure from all his earlier plays, with an artist in search of himself as its hero. The original script was by Ramanand Sagar, but its entire third act was rewritten by Prithviraj himself, turning what he thought was a 'hackneyed' representation of the artist as dissolute playboy into a sympathetic figure. Sagar had promised to write a play for Prithviraj, a romantic one, but said he could only do so after a couple of months because he was busy with his novel, *Ek Aur Insaan*.

> But one day the artist Sajjan just came and took me to Malad. We went by train, third-class. It cost one and a half paise, and we walked the rest of the way. He put the bedding in the veranda and gave me the agreement. Papaji had typed it and kept it ready. There were four lines: 'You will write a play for Prithvi Theatres. You will complete it whenever you want. You don't have to attend office. You will be paid three thousand rupees.' The next morning, I went to him. His staff was not happy: other writers had taken money and not written anything. I asked Papaji to give me three hundred rupees [a month] for ten months. I sent two hundred rupees home and kept hundred for myself.[16]

As usual, Uzra played the heroine, Papaji the artist, and Zohra, for the first time with Prithvi, appeared in a masked dance-duet, depicting the spirits of mountain deities. Although she agreed with Papaji's rewriting of the play she was dissatisfied with the result. She thought the artist's words sounded false, and although well-written, the third act seemed a quite separate piece. Papaji himself called it his 'weakest child', but the question remains: did Zohra ever communicate her misgivings to him? Did her disagreements lead her to try and influence his decisions, or was she ever the obedient director's actor?

While on a break from touring in Jalandhar and Kashmir, Zohra was in Bombay busy with dance direction for a couple of films, among them Guru Dutt's *C.I.D* (1956) and Navketan's *Nau Do Gyarah* (1957; co-directed by Vijay Anand, with Dev Anand in the lead). Then, out of the blue, Kameshwar informed her that he thought it was time for a second child. Unsure about a second pregnancy because of her age, Zohra nevertheless conceived, but completed her tour of Kashmir. She then left for her father's farm in Dhakka, near Rampur, for the rest of her pregnancy. She took Kiran, now eight years old, with her, and the better part of 1952 and 1953 were spent on family matters.

It was January, and after close to ten years in Bombay, Zohra was back in the crisp, sunny winters of north India. The farm at Dhakka consisted of acres of wheat fields and was miles away from civilisation, peaceful and rustic. On early morning walks with her father, Zohra drew close to him again, found she was able to confide in him her worries about Kameshwar, about leaving Kiran for long periods while on tour, even about having a baby at her advanced age—who was due in May 1953, by which time she would be forty-one years old. Her peripatetic life meant she had spent little real time with Abbajan, but during the five months of her pregnancy in Dehradun, Dhakka and Nainital, she discovered again his innate kindness and wisdom.

In April that year, the family went up to Nainital, where

Zohra's father had booked a suite of rooms for the season at the Metropole. The old-world hotel was comfort itself, and despite the fifty-seven steps that she had to climb every day to get to their rooms, Zohra was back in the lap of luxury that she had known as a young girl. She revelled in the serenity of the landscape and the still beauty of the lake, around which she walked every day, savouring the quiet pleasures of a routine as remote from the hectic pace of her Bombay-and-touring life as could be. So much so, that she even found herself sewing some baby clothes!

Pavan was born in Ramsay Hospital at 4:45 a.m. on May 20, 1953, just as the early morning sun was beginning to turn the snowy peaks of the Himalayas to gold. It was an easy delivery. The baby, though tiny at five-and-a-half pounds, was perfectly healthy, and although Kameshwar didn't come to Nainital for her delivery he was overjoyed. Dhakka, Nainital, the baby and Abbajan had been a lovely interlude, but by July Zohra was back in Bombay and on the road again—and Pavan accompanied her, cutting his baby teeth on theatre, with his first stage appearance at eight months old! On the tenth anniversary of Prithvi Theatres, January 15, 1954, the curtain rose on a chubby little Pavan sitting centre stage, swaying to a tabla in the wings, and inaugurating the celebrations.

Soon after Pavan's birth, Zohra and Kameshwar moved to 37A Carter Road, a huge bungalow, now in the actor Aamir Khan's family. The landlord lived on the first floor, and various parts of the ground were rented out: the Segals on one side, and Talat Mahmud's family on the other. At the back lived a Bengali family with whom Kiran would sometimes have her meals. For a short while it seemed that Kameshwar's equilibrium had been restored, and Zohra felt happier than she had been for some time. She and Kameshwar spent time together, talking, he taught her how to use a sewing machine, fashioned jewellery for her with everyday objects, and of course, produced wonderful meals for her and the children. He made his own pickles, distilled his own liquor from oranges and potatoes. He had studied homeopathy on his own and obtained a doctor's degree in it, and now treated friends and relatives and all the fisherfolk in the area. And he continued to create oddly beautiful vases, plates, pots and pans, decorated with intricate designs and painted in bright colours.

Mercurial by temperament, Kameshwar could be kind and compassionate, yet quick to experience jealousy and possessiveness. He was talented and resourceful, but given to self-destructive impulses and extended bouts of alcoholism. He acknowledged Zohra's skill as an actress, but in a fit of pique, destroyed an album full of photographs of her tours with Uday Shankar. The fact remained that while Zohra was steadily achieving success, he had not made it in the film world of Bombay. He was inventive with materials, could produce dazzling effects with meagre resources and should have been much in demand by producers with limited budgets. He experimented with filmscripts, but never found a producer for them. His experimenting then turned to drugs and other substances using his own body as his laboratory, taking small doses of arsenic and other poisons just to see if he could immunise his system to them. As a result he came close to dying on two occasions. It was almost inevitable, then, that he turned to tantra and mysticism, spending long hours locked in his room, first while in Pali Hill, later at Carter Road, too. Concentrated and intense meditation, aided no doubt by the psychotropic effects of cannabis, induced in him a state in which he believed he heard the snarl of the goddess Durga's tiger, which both frightened and thrilled him. Often, he would go out to sea with the fishermen in Bandra, and was invited to attend their magical funeral rites as a favoured spectator.

Zohra worried about him, about his pendulum mood swings which oscillated between euphoria when he managed to sell a story idea, and extreme dejection when things took a turn for the worse. But someone had to bring in the money and keep the house running, and so she resumed her touring with Prithvi's next production, *Paisa,* which opened on September 4, 1953. The play was a simple tale of greed and avariciousness, with little subtlety or character development, but appropriately enough, it opened in Ahmedabad, India's financial centre at the time. Zohra, who played a social butterfly in it, thought it a mediocre play, not one of Bismil's better scripts, but it was popular and ran to packed houses, perhaps because it reflected the creeping commercialisation and corruption that afflicted society. Its popularity prompted Prithviraj Kapoor into turning it into film, hoping partly to recoup some money for the theatre company. His sons Raj and Shammi Kapoor, the former already a very successful film actor and the latter beginning to make a mark, were willing to act in the film as were Nargis and Geeta Bali, but Prithviraj insisted on using only his repertory actors. Zohra had her reservations about the suitability of the play for film, mainly because it lacked variety in locations and sets, but Papaji was adamant. The film was a resounding flop. A stage play did not adapt to film, Prithviraj was not a film director. *Film India* described it as 'a crude, noisy and muddled affair…[that] makes precious little sense and provides less entertainment.' In its harshest review yet of Prithviraj's productions, the magazine continued, 'It deserves to be remembered as a torture to be avoided.' (October, 1957) Zohra was right—Papaji should have adapted *Pathan* or *Kalakar* instead.

The real worry, however, was the financial health of the

company, and the failing health of its mainstay, Prithviraj. For years the theatre had been supported and sustained by his film income, most of which went towards new productions, salaries and fees to writers. But now, although he was barely fifty, his energy was waning and a cyst on his larynx affected the great voice that had held audiences spellbound for so long. For a while, Raj and Shammi Kapoor, now almost wholly in films (with Raj in his own production company, R.K. Studios) helped out financially, but after a while the laryngitis overwhelmed even Prithviraj's iron constitution. Soon, he was stricken with a heart problem, painful varicose veins and a persistent eczema, all of which more or less brought the curtain down on his acting career.

Prithvi Theatres' last production was *Kisan*, which opened on October 26, 1956, in which Zohra played a bad-tempered, loud-mouthed vixen, Gajmukhi Bua, and also directed a dance sequence which comprised an entire scene—a group of villagers celebrating the arrival of the monsoon. Zohra herself danced briefly, with her face veiled. Audiences broke into spontaneous applause at the end of the sequence—'which always pleased me greatly,' she said, till one day, just by chance, she looked up to see Prithviraj, as the hero, and Uzra, as his wife, doing 'the most exquisitely naïve dance movements... swaying to the rhythm of the drum'. They owned the stage, achieving beauty almost without effort; she worked hard, but her best could only bring her close. Still, she enjoyed her role hugely (a character type she would later play to the hilt), fighting, cursing, and slapping people around.

Kisan, written at the suggestion of Dr. Rajendra Prasad, then the President of India, focussed on the feudal hierarchy prevalent in India's villages. It was performed 120 times, and although the company continued touring and performing till 1959, no new plays were added to its repertoire.

Prithvi Theatres closed down in May 1960. In a letter to Norah Richards, the remarkable theatre practitioner who had settled in Punjab and was his mentor and staunch supporter, Prithviraj said, 'It is true—I had to cry halt and declare "The party is over".'[17] To others, he is reported to have said, 'Sherpa Tenzing stayed on the peak of Everest for ten minutes only. I cannot grumble as I have been lucky to stay at the top for sixteen years.'[18]

The original playscripts published by Prithvi Theatres carried the following message from Prithviraj:

> My Patrons, My Friends,
>
> Since March 1945, I have been performing my stage plays SHAKUNTALA, DEEWAR, PATHAN, GHADDAR, AHOOTI and KALAKAR in the mornings only, and that too under great handicaps. Still you have been patronising them. You are very kind. Morning is no time for theatre. Give me a theatre and I promise to give you shows that will be worthy of *Our Culture, Our Traditions, Our Country*. Shows that will go a long way in making our *Secular State* the healthiest nation in the world both in body and in mind.
>
> *The Theatre will be the*
>
> 1. NATION'S PROPERTY
> 2. DONATED BY THE NATION
> 3. FOR THE BENEFIT OF THE NATION
>
> Will you rise to the occasion? I know you will. If you have faith in me and my work then kindly send your contributions to PRITHVI THEATRES (Building Fund), Royal Opera House, Bombay 4.
>
> Soliciting Your Patronage,
>
> Your most humbly,
> PRITHVIRAJ KAPOOR[19]

Unfortunately, neither patrons nor well-wishers or governments rose to the occasion. Prithviraj had told Zohra, when she asked why his company was called 'Theatres', that he wanted a theatre in every town in India, but this remained a dream, unfulfilled.

'Are We Burying the Great?' asked *Film India* in August 1960.

> To the lovers of the Indian stage, the saddest news of the year is the closing of Prithvi Theatres... After giving sixteen best years of his life to the stage, this great producer-director is virtually unemployed—beaten by the inherent indifference of our people and the almost wicked apathy of the State. It is no disgrace to the man. But his failure is a disgrace to our people and the State.[20]

In 1960, Som Benegal, then Editor of the journal, *Natya*, wrote:

> Farewell, Fair Thespian.
>
> It would not be inaccurate to say that, despite the steadfast efforts of other groups in Bombay, Calcutta and Madras, Prithvi Theatres brought the promise of theatrical resurgence and advancement and added a new dimension to the movement in India.
>
> There was never anything nearly like it in Indian drama. What social comment there was mainly took the form of satire. Of political comment there was none. Even Maharashtra and Bengal could not wholly plunge into incisive, hard-hitting social and political analysis of contemporary society. The burning issues of the day hardly touched these theatres.
>
> It was, perhaps, too much to expect that one dedicated man with a dedicated band could forever hope to carry on alone.

> In mourning the collapse of this fine theatre one must pause to ask why, when the State can lavish munificence on mediocre or esoteric projects and productions, it cannot support and sustain worthy institutions; why when dubious efforts merit such felicitous aid, noble purposes should come to so paltry an end.[21]

May 1959, exactly one year before the closing of Prithvi Theatres, would forever be etched in Zohra's mind. For some time now, Kameshwar had been sinking deeper and deeper into depression; try as he might, nothing was working out for him and no recognition was coming his way. He retreated further into himself, avoiding the company of others but drinking heavily. Only the children seemed to draw him out of this terrible apathy. The children, and his fisher-folk friends. With some of the latter he delved deeper into the black arts, spending long hours locked in his room, chanting mantras, burning incense.

For the most part, Zohra left him to himself when he was particularly uncommunicative, and so it was on May 11, 1959. She woke up in the morning to find a notice pinned on his door, saying, 'DO NOT DISTURB. I AM HIBERNATING.' She left for the Bandra Gymkhana where the Company was rehearsing that day, and came home for lunch with Uzra. In the evening she and Kiran went to see a play, and returned home to find Kameshwar's door locked, the fan rotating, and the light burning. Alarmed, Zohra called out to him asking him to open the door, but there was no reply. She moved quickly to the bathroom, opened the window, and through it, unlocked his door. Kameshwar was lying on the floor, bare to the waist, one arm flung out—quite dead. Next to him, a note which read: 'I have seen the world, I have done what I had to. Now I must explore further. I hear the roar of the lion, of Ma Durga, I feel the fire in my belly. I must go.'

Zohra snatched up the note, turned swiftly, and closed the door. There was only one thought in her mind: the children must not see this. She called Kiran and walked quickly with her to her embroidery teacher's house, around the corner. Then she called Prithviraj, who came immediately. She would have to inform Kameshwar's brothers Lilanath and Triloknath, but how to tell them? Kameshwar, not yet forty, and dead, by his own hand. What black despair had led him to end his life? What other reality or fantasy world had enticed him? Could it have been an accident, an experiment gone horribly wrong? Could he have been saved?

There followed for Zohra what she called 'a period of dying'. 'I was walking in a strange world of emptiness which had lost its meaning,' she said. She left the Bandra flat with the children and moved in with Uzra and Hamid, her mind in turmoil. How was she to explain what had happened to the children? Pavan was not yet six years old, Kiran just a teenager. What could she tell them about what Dost had done? One week after his death when Pavan asked why Dost was not with them to celebrate his sixth birthday, she had to make up an elaborate story about Kameshwar's absence in order to reassure him. In the days that followed she was wracked with grief and guilt, alternating between despair and the need to keep up a semblance of normality for the children. Could she have prevented Kameshwar's suicide, foreseen the depth of his depression and sought help for him? Should she not have focussed so single-mindedly on her career? Would he have been better able to cope with his lack of success if she had been less successful herself? And again and again, the gnawing doubt: what if he had married someone else, someone who would have helped him retain his equilibrium? Someone whose devotion and fidelity he could take for granted.

They never returned to the flat in Bandra, that flat filled with memories of Kameshwar's eccentricities, yes, but also his humour, his cooking, his teasing ways, his creativity and crazy experiments, his boundless love for Kiran and Pavan. Zohra took off the little jewellery she wore, and never put it on again.

Zohra and the children lived with Uzra and Hamid in their maisonette in Soona Mahal. It was a relief that the sibling closest to her was in the same city and could look after them. Kiran was sent to Aligarh, to Zohra's cousin, the ophthalmologist Hamida Saiduzzafar (Memphis' daughter), to complete her schooling at the Muslim Girls High School, but Pavan's education was more of a problem—who would look after him while Zohra and Uzra were on tour? Fortunately, Hamida came to the rescue again and arranged to admit Pavan into Welham Preparatory School in Dehradun, her father being a good friend of Ms. Oliphant, the Principal. Pavan was taken in immediately on compassionate grounds.

The children settled, Zohra went back to Prithvi and to touring but it was not the same any more. Her heart was not in it. Not in Bombay, not in trying to come to terms with staying on and rebuilding her life there without Kameshwar. Theirs may not have been an ideal marriage, perhaps not even a happy one, but it was her emotional anchor and it had enabled her to pursue her career more or less without hindrance. After Prithvi closed down, it would have been the easiest thing for her to join any of the other repertory companies that were now very active in the city. The vast open spaces of Bhulabhai Institute reverberated with Ebrahim Alkazi's Theatre Unit, with Alaknanda Samarth and Kusum Bahl, and the institute itself was a place that started a cultural explosion—'like lightning, it lit fires everywhere in India,' said Bahl. The enfant terrible of modern Indian theatre, Satyadev Dubey, was waiting in the wings, and actresses like Dina Pathak, Shanta Gandhi, Sulabha Deshpande, dissatisfied with commercial Marathi and Gujarati theatre, would find roles that challenged their skill in plays written by a crop of younger playwrights—Girish Karnad, Mahesh Elkunchwar, Dubey himself, Shreeram Lagoo; Badal Sircar in Calcutta and Mohan Rakesh in Delhi.

Zohra would have fitted right into this scene, but she had already decided. As she told Papaji, 'Everything in Bombay reminded me of the tragedy... until I felt I must escape this constant reverberation or else lose my mind.'[22] She did not know then, in October 1959, that only a few months later, Prithvi Theatres itself would cease to be.

Coincidentally, Uzra and Hamid also decided to leave Bombay for Pakistan, this time for good. With both Kameshwar and Uzra absent and Papaji increasingly reclusive in Janki Kutir, the modest cottage, his 'jhonpda' that he had built for himself at Juhu, it seemed that Zohra's last links with the city had dissolved. Like Uday Shankar, Prithviraj Kapoor had been an enormous and formative influence on her, and she would carry that experience with her wherever she went. But for the time being, she needed a complete break.

{FIRST INTERMISSION}

The decision to move to Delhi almost made itself. It was not a city Zohra knew, nor really did it offer any real opportunities in theatre or dance, but where else was she to go? At least there was some family in Delhi—her sister Hajrah, whose husband was a member of Parliament, had a home on North Avenue where they could stay, if only temporarily. As important, perhaps, it was a city that carried no shared memories with Kameshwar. But she still had to find something to do.

Not one to wait for fortune to come knocking at her door, Zohra sent off letters to Pandit Nehru, Kamaladevi Chattopadhyay, both of whom she knew, although not well, and others whom she did not, asking if there was an opportunity available. And sure enough, she was invited by Kamaladevi to take charge of the Natya Academy for Dance and Drama to be set up in Delhi, under the auspices of the Natya Sangh. Coincidentally, she was also asked by Begum Zaidi of Hindustani Theatre to train its members in movement and dance.

Zohra was not an administrator, had never run an institution, but she looked upon this new assignment as a challenge. However, she was not about to make a fool of herself by making mistakes born of inexperience, and so she asked for a month's preparatory leave from Begum Zaidi and Kamaladevi, to return to Bombay and familiarise herself with the management of the Bombay Natya Academy under its Director Herbert Marshall. But the Academy only occasionally staged plays or performances, so more useful for her was her stint with Ebrahim Alkazi (later the legendary director of the National School of Drama in Delhi) whose deep knowledge of theatre and of the various schools of acting were most instructive.

They met in Alkazi's flat at Kemps Corner for short sessions, in which he discussed Stanislavsky's method acting and gave her all his notes on dramaturgy to look through. Alkazi had trained at the Royal Academy for Dramatic Art in London; Zohra had been exposed only to Prithviraj Kapoor's sink-or-swim style of acting, and she realised now that she would have to shed much of what she had imbibed then if she was going to teach new students.

The Natya Academy had no office, no address. The then minister for public works, a Mr Subrahmanyam, offered her an outhouse in his official residence for use as a makeshift office; but she used her own room in her sister's house on North Avenue for correspondence, drawing up the academy's curriculum, and so on, with the help of a typist who came in every morning. Classes were to be held at 34 Shankar Market, above the shops.

This was all very well, but how was she to begin? Her teaching experience was limited to Uday Shankar's Dance Academy, and to the improvised movement classes at Prithvi Theatres, which was hardly enough for a formal course. Necessity being the mother of invention, she put together an innovative and eclectic course for her students over the next three months, combining her German training at the

Wigman school; Uday Shankar's experimental techniques; Michel Chekov's acting style from Dartington Hall; Prithviraj Kapoor and Alkazi's methods; and what she had gleaned of Indian classical traditions from reading the *Natya Shastra*. Realising that her own education in the performing arts had only just begun, she took a deep breath, crossed her fingers, and opened the doors of the Natya Academy to students on February 3, 1960.

A year earlier, the Sangeet Natak Akademi had set up the National School of Drama (NSD) as one of its constituent units, and began offering courses the same year. The Natya Academy's students were generally those who had been unable to find a place either at NSD or in any of the amateur theatre companies in existence at the time. It wasn't a large number. Even so, Zohra could not carry out all the work herself and so, to her delight and relief, she was joined by Joy Michael, the talented actress and director who later set up the repertory company Yatrik; and by the highly regarded Khayal exponent, Pandit Amar Nath.

It was hard work. Seeing to all the administrative details as well as the creative content required all Zohra's abilities and disciplined way of working, with records meticulously maintained and submitted to Kamaladevi Chattopadhyay. When despondent or in doubt, she turned to Prithviraj who encouraged her, reminding her that her experience of eight years with Uday Shankar and fourteen years with Prithvi Theatres was more valuable than any textbook learning. Nevertheless, it was with a sense of relief that, as part of her other assignment, she participated in Begum Zaidi's Hindustani Theatre, happy to be in the company of thespians Habib Tanvir, M.S. Sathyu, Mohan Upreti, Salima Raza, Uma Sharma, Pandit Amar Nath, Kusum Bahl and Shama Zaidi.

Begum Qudsia Zaidi had set up Hindustani Theatre in 1955 as a professional theatre that could perform the classics as well as experiment with modern plays. She inducted the young Habib Tanvir, recently returned from a three-year stint abroad, as her director and set about recruiting members, actors, technicians, musicians, and a host of others, with the Begum of Pataudi as president, Mulk Raj Anand as vice president, and Sardar Bhai Mohan Singh as treasurer. She herself was the secretary. The Theatre's patrons were Indira Gandhi, Morarji Desai and Dr. Zakir Hussain.

When Zohra joined, the Theatre's strength was 150+, just slightly lower than what Prithvi Theatres had been at its peak. Almost as soon as she became a member, Zohra choreographed the dance sequences for *Vasant Sena* (a revised version of Tanvir's initial production of *Mitti ki Gaadi* in 1958-59) which had eighteen shows; and then for *Amrapali*, directed by M.S. Sathyu, which had twenty-one shows.

Other fledgling theatre activity was also beginning in Delhi. The Triveni Kala Sangam, set up in 1950 by Zohra's old colleague, Sundari Shridharani at the Almora Dance Academy, began operating near what was then the city's cultural hub: Bahawalpur House, Rabindra Bhawan, Mandi House and Sangeet Bharati, all near Bengali Market. Triveni was unique for its time, the first non-government centre for all the arts—dance, music, contemporary painting and sculpture, photography, glass and ceramics—with classrooms, studios, open air theatre, café, bookshop and galleries. It became a cultural oasis, a mecca for artists, students, theatre buffs and writers. Zohra was a frequent visitor.

Slowly she picked up the reins of her acting again, appearing in various productions put up by amateur companies in the city. At the time, the Amateur Dramatic Club of the British

Council was also active in Delhi, and she appeared in some of their productions along with Marcus Murch, Aftab Seth, Barry John and other young actors, all of whom would go on to act professionally. Alongside, Zohra began writing reviews for *Shankar's Weekly* as their theatre critic, at the suggestion of the journalist Amita Malik, then a columnist with *The Statesman*.

But things were not going well at the Natya Academy, and Zohra was not popular with the bosses at the Delhi Natya Sangh. According to them she had no academic qualifications and was not equipped to run courses or put up full-length plays with the students. They lost no opportunity to place obstacles in her path. To make matters worse, Begum Zaidi, her staunch supporter, died suddenly in December 1961, depriving Zohra of her one reliable and vocal ally. With no stomach for intrigue and unwilling to compromise on what she believed was best for the Academy, Zohra knew that her time there would be finite.

For some time, her brother-in-law, Z.A. Ahmed, had been encouraging Zohra to think of an overseas tour, revisiting Europe on what today would be called a lec-dem programme. But how was this to be done? She had no idea of how to go about it. Write to different embassies, suggested Hajrah; so with their help and their network of contacts in the communist bloc, Zohra received invitations from Russia, Czechoslovakia and East Germany to speak on Indian dance and drama in their countries; they would provide her with hospitality and travel within their countries if she was able to finance her ticket to get there.

Excited at the prospect of travelling abroad again, Zohra seized the opportunity and wrote to the British Drama League in London, asking if she could apply for admission to their ten-week course in acting. She was accepted, and decided that she would proceed straight to London after her tour in Russia and East Europe. But how was this Grand Tour to be financed? Who would buy her tickets and how was she to support herself in London? Who could she turn to for help? Should she ask the Elmhirsts at Dartington Hall if they could assist in some way? They replied promptly, and immediately deposited £100 for her in a bank close to the British Drama League in Fitzroy Square, to cover her fees and expenses for ten weeks. That left the tickets. With some hesitation, but in the spirit of in for a penny, in for a pound, she wrote to Vijayalakshmi Pandit, explaining her situation. Mrs Pandit had been a close acquaintance ever since her daughters had enrolled at the Almora Dance Academy, and she spoke to her brother, the Prime Minister, who asked Zohra to meet Humayun Kabir, minister for cultural and scientific affairs at the time. Not only did Kabir support her travel to East Europe and Moscow, he offered her a return ticket to and from London!

Within three months, Zohra planned her lecture tour; got letters of introduction to the relevant people in the British Council in London; arranged for Joy Michael to replace her as officiating principal at the Natya Academy in her absence; and applied for and obtained leave for herself for the next three or more months. Then, a fortnight of excited, feverish packing, goodbyes to Kiran, Pavan, Hajrah and Z.A. Ahmed—and she was off!

Friday, 16th March, 1962

> Five minutes to one by my watch, I wonder what time it is everywhere else in the world. It was sweet of you all to come to see me off... Papaji, Uzra, Salima, Chunmun, and my beloved Kinnoo! I saw you right up till the end,

> waving me up and off; the last glimpse was through the window as the plane turned and took off. Now up here, all sensations are changing, the ears, the slight heaviness in the head. How neat the world must look to whoever is responsible for its creation, when and if he looks down! The squalor and filth are all hidden and nothing looks unartistic. Thought of Pavan as we rose higher. He must be thinking of me today. The plane arrived at 11.05 p.m., Moscow time, two charming young ladies met me with a bunch of tulips and daffodils. They are representatives of the two societies that have invited me, Soviet Friendship Societies' Union and Indo-Soviet Cultural Society. One of them speaks surprisingly fluent Hindi. Long drive through the snow. Bhisham Sahni was with us till my hotel, Budapest, Room no: 410, 4th Floor. Goodnight![1]

All her life, Zohra had kept a list of all the cities and towns she had toured and performed in, in alphabetical order, from A to Z. This trip was no different, and now she could add Moscow, Baku, Berlin, Dresden, Prague… She loved being on the road again, revelled in the adventure and attention lavished on her, thoroughly enjoyed being treated like a VIP! This was communist Russia and Europe, there was austerity all around her, but the arts and artistes were treated with special respect, and she experienced their particular hospitality at first hand.

Particular, because it was kept firmly within prescribed limits. Zohra was accompanied throughout by her interpreter, Svetlana, a young and beautiful, and supremely accomplished, woman, fluent in Russian, Uzbek, English, Urdu and Hindi. Despite her attempts to sneak out on her own and discover places for herself, Zohra found her days were so tightly scheduled that she hardly had any time to herself. No deviation from the approved programme was allowed, so much so that

Zohra's requests to be allowed to see some plays and visit their theatre institutes fell on deaf ears—they had been told that she was a dancer, and so it was ballet, ballet, ballet all the way! It was only after she confided to Svetlana that she had not danced on stage since 1945 and was now primarily an actress, that she finally saw several plays in Moscow after her return from Baku.

Moscow in the 1960s had quite a few Indians in the city, all of them connected in one way or another with the Indian Left or with IPTA, working as translators or writing for *Soviet Land*. At the time, the USSR had cultural centres in major Indian cities, actively supported the Peoples Publishing House, and maintained close ties with the Indian intellectual community. Among the writers in Moscow then was Bhisham Sahni who translated from Russian into Hindi on a regular basis, and whom Zohra met while there. But she wasn't really meeting other Indians, not even Benoy Roy, whom she had known from her IPTA days; her interest was in meeting local artistes, and she was pleasantly surprised when introduced to the great puppeteer, Obratsor, Peoples Artist of the USSR; to actors of the Moscow Art Theatre; Bolshoi dancers; puppeteers of the State Central Puppet Theatre, and several others. She was struck by their simplicity and complete absence of pretentiousness, no matter how eminent they were in their fields. Unlike India, where, often, mediocrity strutted about as celebrity. She observed the same seriousness of purpose among students and teachers, many of whom questioned her closely and in an informed way after her lectures. As for their productions, they were generally superb—the puppet shows in particular, were witty and ironical and executed with great skill.

Baku in Azerbaijan was unexpectedly bleak and bitterly

cold, but the language was an interesting mixture of Arabic and Persian, with many familiar words: Salaam Alaikum, kebab, naan, pilav, and so on. She lectured, as scheduled, but the memorable occasion was her trip to a town 45 kms away from Baku, from where the Sputnik had been launched in 1957. The town, only ten years old, nevertheless had its own law court and ten drama societies! Back in Moscow, she accompanied the dancer Maya Rao to the Theatre Art Institute where Maya was a student, and where Stanislavsky and Nimerovich Debchenko had studied. Indeed, Zohra learnt that most of Russia's greatest singers and musicians had trained at the Institute.

On April 1, Zohra arrived in East Berlin, and got the shock of her life. A glorious city in shambles, and a courageous nation crushed. Her room in the Sofia Hotel was on the fourth floor, minus a lift and an attached bathroom. Her first impression was of desolation. 'Berlin is unrecognisable from the imposing, neat, smart and grand city I knew thirty years ago. Heartbreaking! Deserted, bleak, ruined, bleeding.'[2] She spent three rather sombre days there, watching productions of the Berliner Ensemble—*The Resistible Rise of Arturo Ui*—and the Gorky Theatre, then left for Dresden which was a relief after the heavy atmosphere of Berlin. On her return to the city, however, she was elated at the prospect of seeing two Brecht plays: *Threepenny Opera* and *Mother Courage*, the latter a filmed version of the stage production. 'What an experience! Helene Weigel is a really great actress; great economy of emotion, mobile, relaxed movement and expression… If film can have such an impact, what must the actual show be like!' Still, she was not sorry to leave Berlin for Czechoslovakia—except Prague, she felt, was even more repressed than the other cities, and the Czechs 'subdued and in certain cases, even frightened'. People were wary of meeting, of speaking freely, and avoided casual conversation.

On the whole, the trip, though unusual and educative, was not the thrilling adventure she had anticipated; too controlled and formal, and the obligation to praise all things Soviet and Russian somewhat inhibiting. Even Dresden, which she had so looked forward to for old time's sake, had been a little depressing. One morning she took time off to visit Wiener Strasse, where she had lived with the Count and Countess Zedtwitz in 1933, but found 'Not a house in sight! Only levelled ground with grass growing in patches.' It was with difficulty that she controlled her tears. She learnt later that that part of town had experienced the heaviest strafing during the war. The Zedtwitzes, in the meantime, had moved to Vienna.

Her tour of the Communist bloc over, Zohra left for London, eager now to get started on her course.

Act 3, Scene 1: Rehearsing

April 18, 1962, Heathrow, London. It was cold, not bitterly, overcoat-hugging cold as it had been in Russia, but at 9°C it wasn't yet spring. And there was no sun! Well, it was England, after all, but Zohra had forgotten how sun-less it could be. She was met at the airport by an old family friend, Sharafat Athar Ali, as well as by a Mrs Rafferty on behalf of the British Council. She spent a couple of days in one of the Council's boarding houses, but then moved to the Indian Students Hostel at 41, Fitzroy Square, whose foundation stone had been laid by Krishna Menon in 1950. It was just a short walk down the road from the British Drama League, at nos. 9-10, to which Zohra would proceed every morning. This is where she would be for the next ten weeks with other producers, actors, teachers and adjudicators, absorbing and acquiring the techniques and training in acting and production that England was renowned for.

Zohra wasn't new to England, of course, having lived in and visited it since the 1930s, but this was different. England in the 1960s was not the same as what she had experienced as a young woman, touring with Uday Shankar, under the wing of Dartington Hall, or simply holidaying with friends. She was fifty years old now, a single parent who had left her two young children in India, in uncertain circumstances. Moreover, this wasn't just another tour for a few weeks, something that Kiran and Pavan were used to from her Prithvi days. Now, even though she hadn't quite planned it, she had taken the first step towards another new beginning.

The British Drama League had been set up in 1919 as an association of individuals in amateur theatre and affiliated amateur dramatic groups, with a focus on education. It believed that theatre was 'everyone's business', and actively encouraged new writing. Its regular features were competitive festivals and its summer schools, attended by aspiring actors and producers from all over. Among Zohra's colleagues at the League that year were an Egyptian, a South African, a Hong Kong Chinese, a Spanish judge, an Israeli singer… as well as an old friend from Delhi, Kunwar Sinha, who had been with her in Begum Zaidi's Natya Academy.

Every afternoon, she and the other students would gather at the park in front of the building to have their sandwiches and tea or coffee, or, if they were feeling extravagant, a light meal at one of the Greek restaurants around the corner. The neighbourhood was home to many Cypriots, immigrants who ran Mom and Pop shops on the ground floor, and lived above. The square itself was rather shabby, although the buildings around it were handsome, even if a bit run down.

For Zohra, the course offered an opportunity to acquire formal training in a profession she had entered without its benefit. As she said to Kunwar when he asked her why she wanted to learn a skill she had been practising for over a decade, 'In India, there is no acting school. To act professionally, I must learn how to.' Now, after years of teaching, she was finding exactly how exhilarating it was to be taught again: 'I don't think I have enjoyed anything quite as much as this course, from the point of view of shedding the arthritic core inside which encases one's being as the years go by.'[1] Although it was intended primarily for producers and was rather technical in many respects, the course did require students to produce scenes from plays themselves. Zohra's interest was in acting, and here the requirement that all students analyse what they knew of acting was most instructive. Zohra reviewed her previous experience of performing intuitively, 'seeking from within for inspiration'; at the League she learnt how to hone those instinctive probes, learnt what it was to really 'act'.

The Associate of the Drama Board exam at the end of the course was not compulsory, but Zohra decided to do it anyway, and got the highest marks in her group. She was thrilled, as she had fully expected to fail! She also received a Star Certificate from the Drama League—the only Indian to be given it, apart from Ebrahim Alkazi and Habib Tanvir before her.

Now that she was in London, theatre capital of the world, she watched the greats of English theatre perform: Laurence Olivier and Maggie Smith in *Othello*, *The Master Builder* and *The Recruiting Officer*; Peter O'Toole in *Hamlet* and *Ride a Cock Horse*; Dame Peggy Ashcroft and Vanessa Redgrave in *The Seagull*; Albert Finney in *Miss Julie*; Saeed Jaffrey and Zia Mohyeddin in *Kindly Monkeys* and *Volpone*, respectively; and scores of other plays that the League insisted they see as part of their tuition. She thought Peter Ustinov in *Photo Finish* and Robert Stephen in *The Royal Hunt of the Sun* were superb, particularly the former, who reminded her of Prithviraj Kapoor in *Paisa*. In between, she took in mime by Marcel Marceau, Kathakali from Kerala, Spanish and Yugoslav dance by visiting troupes—even a trip to Stratford to meet Michael St. Denis, who worked closely with the Royal

Court Theatre. It was all very exciting and heady, and though she missed the children terribly she was in her element.

After the course, she moved out of the Indian Hostel where she had been staying, to Rashid Anwar's flat in Drayton Gardens. Rashid was a friend from her Bombay days, an entrepreneur who had made good, and had financed Chetan Anand's *Neecha Nagar*. Zohra stayed with him for a short while, then moved to Hampstead to stay with her former sister-in-law, Khadija, who was visiting from Karachi. She now made another important decision—she would stay on in England for a little longer, gain some experience, act in a few plays and build a portfolio before returning to India.

At the time, there was another kind of theatre that was throwing up tentative shoots in England, the product of immigrant communities who were beginning to experiment with both form and content. Among the South Asians, the writer Dilip Hiro staged *To Anchor a Cloud*, about the Emperor Shah Jahan, with Saeed Jaffrey as Shah Jahan, and Jamila Massey in it; and Harbhajan Virdi, an aspiring director, was working with the Southall Youth Movement, encouraging them to venture into acting, albeit in the face of stiff resistance from their families. However, what really galvanised these fledgling attempts was the arrival of East African Indians in the UK, following Idi Amin's purges. 'It gave an enormous kick up the backside of Asian culture, Indian culture, in Britain in general,' said Naseem Khan, then theatre critic for the *New Statesman* and *Time Out*, 'because you found people who had a great history and background of being involved in amateur theatre, and the taboos that someone like Virdi encountered with getting actors, basically didn't exist.'[2] The East Africa Indians were middle class, already active in the performing arts, with a number of women who were practising singers, musicians, and even actors, who carried over their involvement in the performing arts into Britain, connecting organically with the Asian community there. Their semi-amateur, semi-professional theatre, more open, less angst-ridden, made an enormous difference to the efforts of people like Virdi and Hiro.

English theatre, too, was beginning to edge out of the West End. Joan Littlewood and Gerald Raffles' Theatre Workshop had injected a touch of whimsy and the irreverent into their productions in Stratford East, then a rather derelict part of the East End. Theatre Workshop was avowedly local and political, and grew out of Joan Littlewood's vision of theatre being based in an area that was working class, and was open to all. As such, it was part of another movement taking place at the time, the community arts movement, which tried to extend the limits of where culture should be located: in smaller, non-traditional unconventional spaces, in which the role of theatre would also undergo change—that it could, and should, reflect social ills, challenge convention, pull down the fort walls. 'The role of Stratford East in giving a kick-start to political theatre was very important,' said Naseem, 'it was pioneering.' So, Theatre Workshop offered the staples, naturally—Shakespeare and Johnson and Marlowe—but then broke new ground with their productions of Brendan Behan's *The Quare Fellow*, Shelagh Delaney's *A Taste of Honey* and, in 1963, *Oh, What A Lovely War*, which won them the Grand Prix.

Zohra may or may not have seen or heard of any of these productions, and in any case, her first priority was to look for some work after the conclusion of her successful stint at the Drama League. But where were the openings? Did mainstream theatre have any roles for Asians? For an Asian woman, moreover, well past her prime, newly-arrived, and far from being a beauty? A handful of South Asian actors—Saeed Jaffrey, Gerson da Cunha, Zia Mohyeddin, Attia Hosain, Renu Setna—appeared on and off in occasional productions, but as the actress Jamila Massey noted, 'those days there was hardly any work for brown actors'.[3]

Often, black and Asian actors dropped out of drama school, or were encouraged to do so before their final year, because they knew that agents were not interested in representing them. Some that seemed to be, like the Oriental Casting Agency, were more or less nondescript, but in the absence of anything else they at least kept Asian actors' CVs on file. Renu Setna, later a well-known television actor and close friend of Zohra's, said he had a really tough time getting work, getting accepted, and that too, only after writing dozens of letters to casting directors or to people who he thought could help.[4] 'If there was a play set somewhere in the East,' said Jamila Massey, 'in India or Malaysia...the job you got was saying, Yes, sir, No, sir, three bags full, sir... Whisky, sir, pani, sir. In other words, as a serving maid. That was it...'[5]

White actors, however, were routinely cast as brown characters, just one more example of the general lack of authenticity in productions dealing with stories or features on the colonies. Waris Hussein, one of the earliest Indian television directors in England, directed the first few episodes of *The Indian Tales of Rudyard Kipling* for BBC in 1964, and said,

> Zohra was one of the few Asian actors around. The young girl (in the feature *Without Benefit of Clergy*) was played by Yolande, who was Sri Lankan, and all the Indian parts were played by Europeans!... Warren Mitchell ended up playing an Indian in a dhoti! We were absolutely circumscribed those days.[6]

But all this was somewhat in the future; right now Zohra needed to find a job that would take care of basics. At Kunwar Sinha's suggestion, she registered herself with the National Association of Theatre and Kinematic Employees (NATKE), who offered her a job as dresser at the Old Vic. Would she be interested? Indeed she would! How could she pass up an opportunity to see the plays and players, work with the great marquee names, at such close quarters? She quickly suppressed a little twinge of doubt—Zohra Mumtaz, daughter of nobles and member of the Rampur royal family, working as a glorified ayah? What would her father have said? But she was nothing if not an intrepid Pathan, and so, on September 28, 1962, she reported to the wardrobe mistress at the Old Vic, who informed her that her wage as a part-time dresser would be £5/10 a week, plus tips. 'Oh, no,' said Zohra, aghast, 'I don't want any tips.' Well, she was advised, she'd better not refuse, or she would upset the 'Ladies', the three actresses she would be dressing: 'Phil', 'Dil' and 'Nil', or Phillada Sewell, Dilys Hamlett and (possibly) Rosalind Knight.

> I was enjoying the work of dressing and undressing them until Saturday night arrived and I was handed £6/7 by each of them. Accepting this... was a humiliating experience. With difficulty I put on a smiling face but let myself go in a flood of tears as soon as I reached home. All the Nawabs of Rampur and Najibabad must have turned in their graves that night.[7]

The 1962-63 season at the Old Vic featured Ibsen's *Peer Gynt*; Shakespeare's *Merchant of Venice*, *Othello* and *Measure for Measure*; and Ben Johnson's *The Alchemist*. Zohra saw them all, of course, but what she remembered most was Ibsen's *Peer Gynt*, a dramatist she was unfamiliar with. The size of the

Company was also a revelation: forty-four actors; plus stage and set designers; music and lighting directors; sound coach; sound effects; and sundry managers. It may not have been as huge as Prithvi Theatres at its peak with 219 members, but its complement of actors alone was far higher. As she watched the season's offerings she began to recognise and appreciate the difference between professional theatre, and what they had done at Prithvi, intense and exhilarating though it had been. Realised, too, perhaps, that a ten-week course might not be sufficient but that it would have to do for the time being.

Old Vic apart, Dartington Hall, her old institution, invited her to lecture on Indian dance at the Hall, as well as at various schools in and around London, and this allowed Zohra to keep her hand in as well as make new contacts. The chance to once again teach dance came her way unexpectedly when, one day, she heard that Ram Gopal, the well-known Indian dancer, was now in London. (In fact, Ram Gopal had been in England since the 1940s; Minette de Silva recounted how he used her flat in London as a temporary dance space in 1946-47.) Ram Gopal's School for Indian Dance was located on The Kings Road, Chelsea, but students were taught in the Harlequin Ballet's headquarters, St. Andrews Hall. Classes were held several times a week, and it was a rare treat to observe Ram Gopal when he occasionally took a class. His *adavus* were a thing of sheer beauty—it was not for nothing that he was considered the equivalent of Nureyev. On an impulse Zohra phoned him, and was invited to join him as principal of his newly opened dance school. She was delighted to accept, especially as she would be paid a salary of £20 per week, for just two hours of work every morning! As she needed to be at the Old Vic only in the evenings, this was a most welcome addition to her finances.

With a modest but steady income in hand, Zohra decided to move from her nephew Kamil Mumtaz's flat to a place of her own, so that she could bring Kiran and Pavan over to join her. The immediate reason for wanting to do so was the attack on India by China in October 1962. Pavan was then a student at Sherwood College in Nainital, and Zohra was terrified that, should the situation escalate, he would be in harm's way. Kiran was safe enough at her aunt Hajrah's house, but Zohra wanted her children with her anyway. In the kind of unintended way that such decisions get made—or simply come about—it was clear that she had no immediate plans to return to India. At the back of her mind, however, would have been a more practical consideration: in England the children's education, especially Pavan's, would be free, and all medical expenses covered by the National Health Service. So she set about looking for a suitable place and was lucky enough to find a small flat, two bedrooms, with a small hall, kitchen and bathroom in the attic, in a house on 85 Abingdon Road, in the Royal Borough of Kensington and Chelsea. It was the corner house on a quiet, leafy street, and the landlady was an Anglo-Pakistani Christian, a Mrs Roach, whose daughter, it turned out, had worked as a secretary for Zohra's younger brother, Ikram, during one of his naval refresher courses in London!

Kiran and Pavan arrived in London on January 13, 1963. It was a bitterly cold day, grey, with the infamous London pea soup fog. Pavan, just ten years old, had been sick throughout the journey, and Kiran, who had never wanted to leave Delhi, was sulking and miserable. She hated London. The flat was tiny, the bathroom in the attic was freezing, and the relative austerity of London in the early 1960s was in sharp contrast to her carefree college life at Lady Sri Ram and her aunt's comfortable home on North Avenue. She was mutinous.

Zohra reassured her that they would return to India as soon as things improved and she had saved a little money, but that didn't happen soon enough for Kiran.

It was a difficult time for all. Money was tight, there were no acting assignments in the offing, Pavan had to be admitted to school, and a suitable course found for Kiran. Zohra herself was then working three jobs: at Ram Gopal's in the morning, the Old Vic in the evening, and at Pettit's, a clothing store around the corner from their flat, in their mail order department. Pavan managed to get admission into Fox's, a local primary school, and Kiran joined evening classes at St Martin's School of Art, where she studied drawing. As she had already been learning dancing in India, she accompanied her mother to Ram Gopal's classes, occasionally taking part in the dances that Zohra composed for him. Pavan, who was discovering the novelty and joy of watching television for hours on end with Mrs Roach, had no complaints, but Kiran was chafing at the bit. Didn't like the flat, didn't like being out of place, felt, rather than directly experienced, an incipient racism in the air.

Mid-Sixties Britain was restive. The immigrant community, primarily West Indian, was waking up to a realisation of its rights and its second-class status. Protest was simmering. Graffiti on city walls declared 'The Tygers of Wrath are Wiser than the Horses of Destruction!' Another scrawled 'Burn It All Down!' The ripple effect of the 1958 Notting Hill riots was still being felt in sporadic violence in inner city locations, one of them in North Kensington, not far from where the Segals lived on Abingdon Road. If blacks were becoming assertive, the reaction to their assertiveness was not long in coming. In the Midlands, especially, inhabited primarily by immigrants from the Indian subcontinent, local resentment was finding expression via local politicians. The Labour party was stoutly challenged by the Conservatives, and the racist talk of the ultra right National Front was gaining ground. The slogan, 'If you want a nigger for a neighbour, vote Labour,' coined by Conservative MP Peter Griffiths, would win him the election in Smethwick, a town north-west of Birmingham, in 1964; he claimed the slogan was only 'a manifestation of popular feeling'. Colour bars were common, according to Harbhajan Dardi of the Indian Workers Association in Sandwell. 'Barbers would make Asian customers wait three, four, five hours while they cut white people's hair,' he said.[8] Nor was it unheard of for a brown immigrant to be told, 'Why don't you go back to where you came from?'[9] Even Zohra, who tended not to take these comments to heart, confessed that she was aware now of the kind of racism that she had never encountered in England of the 1930s.

Nineteen-sixty-three was a hard year, financially, for Zohra, as well as being professionally arid. Her stint at Ram Gopal's school was shortlived—there weren't enough students, the demand for Indian dance was disappointingly low, and one fine day, students arrived at the school to find the doors closed. Ram Gopal had left England for Venice! In front of the statue of Shiva, however, the incense was still burning. But it was at Ram Gopal's school that Zohra met Jamila Massey, also a student, whose husband, Reginald, would later introduce Zohra to the director Ken Annikin for a role in his film *The Long Duel*. Work would come her way when it did, in the meantime she had her jobs, she was glad to have the children with her again and she had a growing circle of friends. Jamila and her husband, Reginald Massey, obviously, and Kunwar Sinha, but also the young Roshan Seth (in London, studying acting at Lambda), Saeed Jaffrey, the filmmaker Waris

Hussein, whose family were old friends, the actresses Soni Razdan and Rani Dube, Gerson da Cunha… Their flat might have been small, but Zohra was large-hearted and entertained with enthusiasm. Kiran remembered her throwing big parties, cooking one day in advance, then freezing the food, and on the day of the party, producing a wonderful dawat.[10]

In July that year, Zohra applied for and got a job at the India Tea Board on Oxford Street, initially as catering manageress, and later, as floor supervisor in charge of the waitresses. The little extra money came in handy, and the hours allowed her to accept the occasional radio work that came her way. Post Indian independence, BBC Radio bifurcated its service into Hindi and Urdu, with Rani Dube and Aley Hasan in charge of the former. Zohra, Jamila and Dolly Rawson took part in radio plays for the Hindi service, and although the plays—among them *Riders to the Sea* and *Dickens' Scrooge*—offered little opportunity to display her acting sills, Zohra did get to exercise her voice and to stay in practice.

Apna Hi Ghar Samajhiye (Make Yourself at Home) and *Look, Listen, Speak*, in both of which she spoke, were a radio broadcast series intended for the Asian immigrant community in Britain; both programmes were commissioned by the BBC's Continuing Education Unit, which produced community-oriented series that came out of Peppermill, its Birmingham unit. Within the BBC at the time there was quite a strong strand that felt its programming should be more embedded in the community, and believed firmly that 'everybody has a story to tell'. *Apna Hi Ghar Samajhiye* was presented in Hindustani, and was made at the initiative of Hugh Carlton-Greene, then director-general of BBC, who felt that the BBC was 'neither talking to the newest British citizens, nor doing a great deal to combat rising racial prejudice'.[11] Mahendra

Kaul, who anchored the programme from 1966 with Saleem Shahed recalled, 'We had to get our people to adapt to this new life so that they would be accepted… I felt this quite strongly, because racial tensions were very high at the time.' Then BBC director David Stride, who knew Zohra from her Uday Shankar days, recommended her as they were looking for a very special kind of voice, for which she was paid the very generous sum of sixteen guineas per programme, and as the series continued for two years it was a very lucrative assignment.

Bush House, the BBC's headquarters, became a hub for all the expat Indians associated with theatre in London at the time—Zohra, Rani Dube, Kusum Bahl, Dolly Rawson, Devi Shah, Jamila Massey—who set up something called KADA, the Kala Arts Dramatic Association, which would meet in Zohra's flat. Zohra often returned from her day at the Tea Centre to find the group draped along the stairs, waiting for her to open the door! They would pick a play, any play, and do a reading or rehearsal, even though they knew it would probably never be staged. But they were all enthusiastic, passionate about theatre, and of them, Zohra, Roshan Seth, Gerson da Gunha, Kusum Bahl (later Haider) and Jamila would later go on to perform on both stage and screen. 'We were all struggling,' recalled Dolly, 'but we were together, and there was this tremendous bonhomie among us'.[12]

In 1964 Zohra got her first break in television with the BBC commissioned television series *The Indian Tales of Rudyard Kipling*, an adaption of Kipling's stories, directed initially by Waris Hussein, who worked on two: *Without Benefit of Clergy* and *On the City Walls*. The idea was to adapt the Kipling stories, but in Waris Hussein's opinion, done without any reference to authenticity and no real research into what that involved visually. When he came on board as director, he said,

> ...they showed me the existing set for the English part of the show, and there was this set dressed like a Victorian sitting room! With wallpaper—as though we were shooting in London! I said, there's no way that anyone would put wallpaper on walls in India...so I was responsible for reversing the entire art department's idea of how to create Indian interiors.[13]

Without Benefit of Clergy, one of Kipling's less known stories, is about an Englishman in the ICS who is constrained to lead a double life; the story, Waris thought, said some very interesting things about the cross-fertilisation of relationships between the British and the Indians during the Raj. Zohra was cast as an old woman who 'sells' her young daughter to the Englishman in order to survive. Waris' decision to cast Zohra in the role was quite bold, as he was a very new and young director himself, but

> Zohra brought to the role the authenticity of a woman who had no option but to sell her child, and she brought to it a dignity, even though she was poverty-stricken. She gave it gravitas... and when I saw the finished product... it said something about colonialism, about poverty, about a man conflicted... at a time when it was thought that never the twain shall meet.[14]

Zohra appeared in four Kipling episodes, not all directed by Waris Hussein, but *Without Benefit of Clergy* remained her favourite. The series itself was reasonably popular, not because there was a large Asian audience for it but because, said Waris, 'We were looking to a colonial middle-class audience, and so we had nostalgia in buckets!' It was during the shooting of the Kipling tales that Zohra met Renu Setna, a fellow actor from India settled in England, who became one of her closest friends in the country. 'There was a rehearsal somewhere in Westbourne Grove,' Setna said, 'and I was ten minutes early, and there was this lady sitting there, looking very elegant in her sari… And I just went up and said, Hello, my name is Renu, and she said, Hello, my name is Zohra, and we got talking… It was friendship at first sight.'

Although they had roles in different episodes they would meet during rehearsals, go to lunch together when they could, and in time became family for each other. Setna had been a little tense that first day they met—what sort of impression he'd make, whether he'd get on with the director, with the rest of the cast—but Zohra was totally relaxed. Serene. And she put him at ease.[15]

After Kipling, Waris went on to direct what would become an iconic series for the BBC, *Doctor Who* and, again, he cast Zohra as the attendant to Ping-Cho, in four episodes. *Doctor Who*, a science fiction story, was created by the BBC to fill the gap between children's and young adult programming, and over its several episodes was set in periods ranging from the Stone Age to twelfth-century Palestine and contemporary Britain. The first series had the distinction of being produced by Verity Lambert, the BBC's first female producer, and being directed by Waris Hussein, then in his mid-twenties.

Zohra had small parts in both the first and second series (directed by Douglas Camfield), in the episodes *The Roof of the World*; *Marco Polo*; *The Singing Sands*; *Five Hundred Eyes* (in all of which she was uncredited), and in *The Crusade* and *The Knight of Jaffa*, both set in Palestine. Kiran, who accompanied her on shoots for *Doctor Who*, later commented, 'What I didn't like was seeing her in all these *chota-mota* roles. I didn't like it, but *she* was very happy doing them, waiting for a big break.'[16] Without realising it, Kiran had identified that singular trait of Zohra's—her 'fortitude, grit and determination', as noted by Waris—that saw her through her first couple of years in London, dealing with disappointment, with prejudice, and with the challenge of being a single woman and single parent, hoping to make it in entertainment media that were notoriously exclusionary in their casting. Zohra was the only non-white in *Doctor Who*, with all the other non-white characters being played by whites. But she loved being part of it, said Waris, this was a new medium for her and she 'got a great sense of being involved in performing'. The series was hugely successful, and now, finally, Zohra was beginning to put her years of training in theatre to use in England.

If there was one thing Zohra never did, it was to look back with regret. So, with salary from her various jobs and the additional income from her radio and television work, she decided to move out of Kensington. At Kiran's urging, they moved to Hampstead—14 Lyndhurst Gardens in Belsize Park, a two-storey, red brick house in a genteel part of the city, commonly referred to as a garden suburb. Zohra occupied flat no. 3 on the second floor. It was spacious, with enormous rooms and high ceilings and windows that looked out on a tree-lined street. Kiran finally had a room of her own ('a perpetual mess'), and because there was room to spare, Kunwar Sinha came to stay with them. Pavan was away at boarding school, Wolverstone Hall in Ipswich, but Kiran was still at St Martin's.

News from home was always welcome, and from Bombay, doubly so. It came in the form of letters from Prithviraj Kapoor who wrote and told Zohra about what mutual friends were doing: Shaukat Azmi was acting in IPTA plays; he himself was working on twelve films at the same time; but when at Juhu, he would practice his sitar and tabla. 'When I linger alone near these instruments,' he wrote, 'I find all of you here with me.' So far from home, his words brought tears to Zohra's eyes.

But visits from friends and family brought a whiff of India to Zohra in London, with both her sisters, Uzra and Hajrah, coming to stay. A temporary lull in television work meant she could spend all her free time with them, a time of warmth and affectionate reminiscing. Who also visited was her beloved guru, Prithviraj Kapoor, on his way back from Karlovy Vary, where he had received an award for his role in K.A. Abbas' film *Aasman Mahal*. She was sad to see how much he had aged, and how painful his varicose veins were—she looked away as he hobbled slowly, leaning on Pavan's shoulder for support. It was harder still to see his obvious sadness at Uzra's departure from India, and from his life. The pity of it was that Uzra, too, missed Bombay and her life there terribly, and found living in Pakistan difficult. In London, she confided in her sisters about what the loss of acting and a vibrant cultural life meant to her; and although unstated, her separation from Prithviraj was a continuing source of sorrow.

Rafiq Anwar, an acquaintance of Zohra's from India, was the Indian consultant for a film to be directed by Ken Annikin (of *Those Magnificent Men in Their Flying Machines* fame), starring Yul Brynner and Trevor Howard. *The Long Duel*, set in 1930s India, was the story of Sultan, a tribal bandit, in the remote areas of the north-west and his capture by, and subsequent escape from, the British. Zohra was offered the role of Devi, an old tribal herbalist, in what would be her first film appearance in the West; along with her were Vivien Leigh, Merle Oberon (then known as Queenie Thompson) and Imogen Hassel, all three Anglo-Indians from Calcutta! Shooting was to begin in December 1966. By now, Zohra had signed up with an agent, Lloyd Williams Associates, with whom she would continue for all the years that she remained active—Eileen and Jill Williams represented her and handled her engagements and appearances in England till well into the 2000s.

The Long Duel, shot in the Sierra Nevada hills in Grenada, is an Orientalist potboiler, complete with bandits, dancing girls (recruited from Ram Gopal's school) obsequious Indians and imperious Englishmen. Except for the women, it had an all-white cast made up to look brown in an effect that was at once hilarious and insulting. It would be unthinkable for a film like that to be made today, and yet, its storyline is oddly—and perhaps, inadvertently—subversive. The bandits foil the Brits at every step, the Empire bows to the inevitable, Britannia does not really rule the waves. For Zohra, working at such close quarters with actors she admired and with a director who was open to suggestions from his actors, was valuable experience—and she thoroughly enjoyed living in luxury in Alhambra! An odd coincidence made this film memorable for her; Sultan Dakoo's headquarters in Rohilkhand was none other than the derelict fort of Najibabad, once owned by Zohra's mother's family. The film was shot in Spain, but the terrain there immediately put her in mind of Najibabad. Family lore had it that its erstwhile owner joined the 1857 war of independence, so the British stormed the fort and executed his brothers—Zohra's direct forebears—as guilty by association. The rest of the family fled the scene.[17] Of all the coincidences, this was probably the most unexpected!

Back in London, she was happy to be in quiet Hampstead, going for walks on the Heath with Kiran, cooking for friends and family, lunching occasionally with Renu Setna and his mother, gradually returning to theatre whenever she received an offer. By the end of 1966, however, Kiran had completed her course at St Martins, found a job, and was sharing a flat with a friend in St. Johns' Wood. With Pavan away at boarding school the Hampstead flat felt rather large and empty, and so Zohra decided to move to something smaller, which she found in Highgate. The flat was indeed smaller than 14 Lyndhurst Gardens, but she continued to entertain as before—Babar Mumtaz, her elder brother Zakkan's son (and Kamil's brother), remembered all sorts of people turning up at her place, including people from the film world in India if they were visiting. He met James Ivory and Ismail Merchant there, with the cast. Zohra would cook, people would bring stuff, 'but she held all of us together'.[18] By now, Zohra had also decided to make her professional life in England, having, in one sense, burnt her bridges in India. With Kameshwar's death, Bombay was not an option, and Delhi hadn't really worked. 'I can't remember her ever saying, should I go back?' reminisced Babar, 'because it was a kind of one-way street: I've got to make a life here, and that's it.'

On March 5, 1967, the English Stage Society staged Partap Sharma's *A Touch of Brightness* at the Royal Court Theatre, with an all-brown cast for the first time ever, in London: Zohra Segal, Saeed Jaffrey, Roshan Seth, Gerson da Cunha, Dino Shafeek, Manisha Bose, Prem Bakshi, and others. The play had an interesting history. It was about life on Fortune Road in the red-light district of Bombay, and had been selected for presentation at the first Commonwealth Arts Festival in London, in the autumn of 1965. Rehearsals were conducted in India, but as the troupe prepared to leave for London their passports were impounded—it was thought that the content of the play was an embarrassment for India, so could not represent the country at the Festival. A second attempt to perform it within India in 1966 met with the same fate. The state of Maharashtra required all plays to receive censor clearance; *A Touch of Brightness* was banned as 'the play is set in one of the most infamous localities of Bombay city... and deals with matters which it is highly undesirable to show on the stage'.

The Royal Court performance, therefore, was its first public staging anywhere; it was a single performance, for which Partap Sharma was paid the royal sum of five guineas. Zohra was cast as Bhabi Rani, owner of Cage 77, whose inhabitants were Basanti, Vatsala and Suraksha. The play started with the 'advantage of a martyred work', noted the *Times*' theatre critic, who also noted that the playwright had drawn his characters—a beggar, a pavement dweller, a constable, the women—with 'a real feeling for what happens to human nature in jungle conditions'; despite this 'they still possess a harsh dignity that comes over strongly in the performances of Saeed Jaffrey and Zohra Segal'.[19] *The Jewish Chronicle* similarly complimented Zohra Segal and Dino Shafeek, who played a lovestruck young man, but Peter Ansorge of *Plays & Players* was scathing in his review of both the play and the players, saying, 'Only Saeed Jaffrey as a wily crook and master chess player managed to outwit the play's aspirations to eternity and present a credible human being.' For Zohra's first stage appearance in England, it was a case of mixed reception. Still, a first all-Indian production in London was a landmark, for the Royal Court had seen several eminent playwrights begin their careers on its stage—Samuel Beckett, John Osborne, Arnold Wesker, David Hare, Ann Jellicoe, among others. Its reputation was due in no small measure to its being known as a writers' theatre, and to its energy in discovering and cultivating new and emerging writers.

It was now five years that Zohra had been in England, and with both Kiran and Pavan away, she was missing a family. Fortunately, her cousin, the ophthalmologist Hamida Saiduzzafar, was in London for her PhD, so Zohra asked her to move in with her. Hamida's very welcome company apart, she was glad that her friendly overtures to Pavan were met without rebuff. Indeed, he warmed to her in a way that he had not been able to with his mother, and Hamida, in turn, became the not-authoritarian 'parent' whom he could relate to. She took him to the Orkney Islands on a vacation, sympathised with his adolescent escapades and withheld judgement. Zohra was grateful for this temporary truce with her rebellious son. Hamida stayed with her for three years, but Zohra, who had not returned to India since 1962, still missed the sense of home she had there.

Then, out of the blue, in December 1967, she was offered a role in the Merchant-Ivory production *The Guru*, with Madhur Jaffrey, Michael York and Rita Tushingham, and the chance to go home. She was thrilled, not a little because she was flying first-class to Bombay! The entire cast and crew were staying at the Taj, but Prithviraj Kapoor would have none of that and insisted that Zohra stay with him at Janki Kutir, in Juhu. She couldn't refuse.

The Guru was a post-Mia Farrow/George Harrison/ Maharishi Mahesh Yogi film, steeped in the counter-culture of the 1960s, and the hippie search for mysticism and the 'wisdom' of the Orient. Michael York comes out to India to learn the sitar from his guru (Utpal Dutt), Rita Tushingham is (you guessed it) the hippie, smitten by the guru, and Madhur Jaffrey is his long-suffering wife. Zohra, unsurprisingly, is a *mastani* who offers Jaffrey an amulet that will help her conceive and give birth to a son. It was a tiny role, two scenes only, in both of which Zohra had no written dialogue; but being Zohra, she ad libbed her way through and had the time of her life jabbering away in Bambaiyya Hindi.

The film had been a pleasant diversion, but her homecoming was tinged with sadness; before her departure for India, Zohra received the news that Uzra's husband, Hamid, had passed away. He had gone to the hospital for a check-up, but collapsed suddenly and couldn't be revived. After her film shoot Zohra left for Delhi to receive Uzra, who was visiting India, relieved that she could be with her and offer her the solace that she herself had received from her after Kameshwar died. When they returned to Bombay, Uzra, true to a vow she had made, neither visited nor spoke to Prithviraj in Juhu, painful though this resolve must have been. Prithviraj, able to talk about his feelings more openly to Zohra, wrote to say that after Uzra's husband's sudden death she had asked him not to write to her again, not even on her birthday. He told Zohra that Uzra said, 'I want to sacrifice everything for my duty, and I can only do so if you help me and don't even write a single word.' So that is what he did, though it broke his heart. 'I want to be very close to her, but I cannot be. When she wants someone, she calls on her own people to be near her. I am far away…Pain is ruthless, it pierces the heart like a dagger.'[20]

Later, unable to reconcile himself to Uzra's ultimatum, he wrote to Zohra to say,

> I thought I would write to Uzra complaining about her silence. I will tell her, if you get married that is your right but that doesn't mean that you stop writing, stop giving us your news. You made him your business partner, but even if you make him your life partner, you still have no right.[21]

The sisters visited family in Rampur and their father in Dehradun, a poignant reunion for Uzra. Her sorrow was palpable and her unhappiness at her distance from them very real; yet she said she would remain in Pindi or Lahore rather than return to India. Zohra, sad to see Uzra so dejected and downcast, accompanied her to Pakistan and stayed with her in Lahore, before leaving for Karachi to meet Ikram and Zakkan, Amina and Sabra. It was ages since the siblings had all been together, and Zohra was struck by how prosperous they all were. Sabra's husband was in the army, and Amina, after her break-up with Nurul Hasan, had relocated to Karachi and opened a school for girls, of which she was the principal. Zohra was pleased to find them well-settled, but a little surprised by the glimmer of conservatism that she noticed had crept into their lives and responses, an unexpected trait in the otherwise liberal Mumtazullahs.

To her dismay, she found a hint of it in Uzra, too. 'Come back with me to London,' she urged her, but Uzra refused. Then go to Karachi, suggested Zohra, but no, 'Why should I go there?' replied Uzra, 'I earn Rs. 6,000 here, I can't go.' Besides, she said, she now had a little radio and television work in Lahore which she didn't want to give up. Prithviraj, when he heard later about Uzra's reasons for staying back, wrote to Zohra to say,

> I cannot believe that Sukhiya (his name for her, the character she played in *Kisaan*) attaches such importance to money. She has never desired luxury, then why couldn't she come here, to this humble jhonpra?... There is no scarcity of work here, the theatre is gasping for breath... I can't understand why she did not even consider this alternative.[22]

Zohra was sorry that she hadn't been able to persuade Uzra, but as she had now been away for over two months, she made plans to return to London.

In 1969, fifty-seven years old and with a little time on her hands, Zohra began writing her memoirs. She bought ruled foolscap paper on which she wrote by hand, then ever frugal, had her friend, Firdous Aly, type her text on the backs of used playscripts. In much the same way as she had maintained a scrapbook, she thought she would put down her life as she recalled it, while she could. 'My main reason for writing,' she said, 'is to create an absorbing task for myself, as well as to put down whatever happened in my life before I forget it entirely. A lot of it seems to have taken place very, very long ago, as if in another life, and yet parts of it are as vivid as yesterday.' But with the kind of clarity that comes with age, she also realised that one writes about oneself 'because one is afraid to lose the link with existence after one's death'.[23]

The next couple of years were somewhat lean, work-wise, with sporadic, small assignments in film and for BBC TV. Even for Zohra, who never turned down an offer, the pickings were slender, so she took a job as a machinist at Pettits, a homestore, sewing curtains. Kiran was working as a display artist at Accurist, a watch company, and Pavan, who had completed his A Levels at Wolverstone, returned to London to stay with Zohra. It was a tension-filled time. Pavan, at home after a long stretch away and somewhat distant, was at odds with his mother, and she with him. He didn't want to go to the university, didn't want to get a job, sat around all day watching television. Money was tight, and Zohra showed her irritation with what she saw as his laziness—'*Hosh nahin hai*,' (not in his senses) she told Kiran. Pavan, in turn, retaliated, 'You call yourself a mother, is this what a mother should be?' What he meant by 'this' could be anything—a mother working as a seamstress; a mother accepting any opportunity to act, no matter what the role was; or simply, a mother in reduced circumstances. For his part, Pavan was actually unused to 'family life'—he had never known it. Except for the first six years of his life in Bombay—an idyllic time in his memory—he had spent his entire childhood away from home. At Welham, when he was seven, followed by Sherwood, and then England and boarding school again.

By his own admission he was direction-less, and in the way of teenagers in the 1960s, had begun experimenting with hallucinogens.[24] Tripping on LSD. Of course, he did not tell his mother but she, no stranger to substance abuse with Kameshwar, would have recognised the symptoms. She was worried sick—was Pavan going the way of his father? How would she ever be able to deal with that? She wished there was a male member of the family around to whom she could turn for help.

Meanwhile, Kiran was marching on the streets, supporting leftists and other radicals shouting slogans in praise of Mao tseTung and *The Red Book*. Prithviraj Kapoor, in whom Zohra confided her unease, wrote back to say, 'Now what has happened to Kiran? Where has she got this madness from?... You don't have to shout and march... No, I don't like this at all, not at all.' Sloganeering, he said, was for people who had nothing better to do—Kiran had her dance, she was a good dancer, so tell her, he said, 'You are the falcon/To soar is your destiny/ The skies above are within your reach.'[25]

They needn't have worried, for Kiran was in the grip of

a happier madness that overshadowed everything else: love! Walter Bötschi was a young Swiss designer-jeweller working at Accurist, where he was an apprentice. They met at a friend's party. Walter would have been around twenty years old, and Kiran, a couple of years older. He knew no English, and she no French, but it was love at first sight—or rather, love via sign language. 'He was so lovely to look at!' Kiran smiled, reminiscing about their first meeting, 'really, really yummy.' They became very close, and after Walter completed his compulsory military service in Switzerland, decided to get married. A civil ceremony was performed at the registry in Highgate in June 1970. Zohra was delighted, for she had taken to Walter immediately. He was gentle, amiable, fun-loving, respectful towards her and, in her view, the ideal son-in-law.

But the couple decided to move to Switzerland, to spend time with Walter's parents. The Bötschis owned a hotel in the little town of Bielle in Switzerland, where he and Kiran returned after their wedding, and began working with them. 'My god, what HARD WORK!' recalled Kiran. 'On my feet all day, not really speaking the language, serving in the café, but also in the restaurant—and no salary! Only tips.'[26]

Two years after moving to Switzerland, Kiran found she was pregnant and she and Walter returned to London for her delivery. Babar, Zohra's nephew, sublet his flat on Oxford Street to Kiran, and in June 1972, their daughter, Sujata, was born at St Mary's Hospital in Highgate. Zohra was thrilled with the baby and happy to have Kiran and Walter back in England. Walter had never wanted to live in Switzerland; he disliked the regimentation of everyday life in the country, and hated the police. His experience with conscription only hardened his feelings, so Kiran's pregnancy and the return to England were fortuitous.

Slowly, things settled down with Pavan, too. He did a year's course in art at the North London Polytechnic in Walthamstow, and moved out to a tiny flat of his own near the school. After applying for all sorts of jobs, including training as a pilot for BOAC, he managed to get a job at the State Bank of India in London, as a junior clerk. Sujata was now one year old, Kiran had resumed her dancing, performing in London and elsewhere, and so in September the following year, 1973, Zohra took six-weeks' leave from Pettits and left for a short break in India.

She hadn't had much work the last couple of years, but hoped that when she returned her luck would turn. 'Zohra was always a supporting actor, never a lead in those early days,' said Jill Williams, 'and she never made much money—just had a steady income.' Inevitably, she was typecast because of her age, but she was a 'rare character actress'.

{SECOND INTERMISSION}

Somehow, the unexpected managed to follow Zohra to India. One day, the dancer Maya Rao, whom she had met in Moscow in 1962, invited her to a reception she was holding at the Institute of Choreography in Delhi, at which her students would show Zohra their work. With Zohra were her friends Usha Bhagat, then Indira Gandhi's social secretary, and Shanta Gandhi, Director of Bal Bhawan. Maya persuaded Zohra to reminisce about her days with Uday Shankar and Prithviraj Kapoor for the benefit of her students, and Zohra gladly obliged. Recalling those years with the two men she thought of as her gurus was filled with nostalgia and a curious feeling of loss, so that when Usha Bhagat and Shanta Gandhi told her it was time she returned to India she responded with, 'I would like nothing better!' But where was the opportunity of worthwhile work for her, at her age?

Well, work was found. Mrs Gandhi had been toying with the idea of setting up a National Folk Dance Ensemble, and applications for the post of director had been solicited. No appointment had yet been made, however, so Usha Bhagat suggested to the Prime Minister that she consider Zohra Segal for the post. Mrs Gandhi agreed immediately, and before she knew it, Zohra not only had a job, but an offer that accepted her terms, including accommodation for herself—a rented flat in Curzon Road Apartments built as transit housing for officers of the Indian Foreign Service—a small one-bedroom place, and a convenient ten-minute walk from the Sangeet Natak Akademi on Copernicus Marg, where she would have her office.

The offer had come at an opportune time. There was a hiatus in her acting career in London, with no real work in the offing; Pavan was now employed in the city; and Kiran, to Zohra's chagrin, had separated from Walter in order to devote herself to dance. Kiran's break with Walter upset Zohra greatly, but there was little she could do to change the situation. She understood Kiran's dissatisfaction with life in London and her passionate pursuit of her vocation, for hadn't she, Zohra, done the same? Had she not left home and hearth, both her children and her family, to relocate to London and take her chances when even fewer real options were available?

So she returned to London to dismantle the house, distribute her belongings in various trunks two of which she left with Walter, and the rest with her friends Renu Setna and Prayag Raj. It was far more difficult to deal with Pavan, however, who was visibly unhappy with his mother's decision. She managed to find him a flat in Finchley before she left, but he was not to be appeased. Some amount of guilt mixed with an aching love for him had always been a part of her relationship with Pavan—Kameshwar's death when Pavan was little more than a boy; boarding schools, both in India and London, which meant depriving him of home and the remaining parent; and her own itinerant life and frequent absences, tore at her heartstrings. Leaving him again now when he had just begun to settle down and was living with her again, was agonising—but what else was she to do? She could hardly spend the rest of her life sewing curtains…

January 1, 1974, Zohra arrived in Delhi, eager to begin work, but a little uncertain about how to do so. She hadn't been actively involved with dance for a long time and knew little or nothing about folk forms. Her earlier experience with the Delhi Natya Academy had ended unhappily, and the National Dance Ensemble was, if anything, even more high profile—failure here would be that much more galling. But nothing ventured, nothing gained, and so she set about planning the development of the Ensemble, meeting Usha Bhagat and Shanta Gandhi on several occasions to discuss what she had in mind with them.

Zohra set about recruiting prospective students by sending the Ensemble's prospectus to various dance schools and academies and university colleges, which effort netted her sixteen students, eight boys and eight girls. She then contacted former colleagues and students from the Almora Centre, including the dancer Narendra Sharma, but he was unable to spare much time. Others, too, were unavailable for one reason or another, but somehow, a few teachers were found, including the gifted poet-singer Mohan Upreti from Kumaon.

Unsurprisingly, the Sangeet Natak Akademi (SNA), which administered the Ensemble, was obstructive and unhelpful—dance and music were its turf, why was the Ensemble encroaching on it? And so, red tape apart, it was unwilling even to spare some space for the teaching and training of dancers. The Prime Minister's secretariat was not forthcoming either, so Zohra prevailed upon her personal network to obtain the use of the basement at Lalit Kala Akademi (the National Academy of Arts, right next door) in the evening and afternoon, and a large hall in the Bharatiya Kala Kendra (also nearby) in the morning. It was only after eight months that the

Ensemble was able to occupy a wing of Bahawalpur House, down the road from the SNA.

Yet, against the odds and despite her best efforts, the Ensemble could not take off. In the face of total indifference from the SNA and lack of intervention by the Prime Minister's secretariat, Mrs Gandhi decided to close the Ensemble even before it could present its first programme in public. It had barely been functioning for nine months. Zohra was in despair. She turned to Usha Bhagat, with the plea that she be given at least three months to wind up the Ensemble and perform once, in public. It was an uphill task, but she was able to continue till March 31, 1975, and managed to present a programme at Mavalankar Hall, to an invited audience. It was a huge success—but the die had been cast.

The problems with the Ensemble couldn't have come at a worse time, for Mrs Gandhi was having problems of her own, with the Allahabad High Court trial proceeding against her. News of the Ensemble's imminent closure created a furore in the media as well as among artistes, with letters of protest and public meetings condemning the SNA's decision. But the situation on the ground and the political climate in the country made any reasonable discussion on the matter difficult; moreover, it was clear that for the powers that be, the fate of the Ensemble was the least of its preoccupations. On June 16, 1975, the vice-chairman of the SNA put out a notice withdrawing administrative support to the Ensemble; and one week later on June 25, 1975, Mrs Gandhi declared an Emergency, which effectively and irrevocably sealed its fate.

Mrs Gandhi, Zohra had been told, was finding it embarrassing to meet her, and so Zohra did the next best thing—she wrote to her:

June 1975

Dear Indira ji,

I am sending you the final report of the National Folk Dance Ensemble, which sums up briefly the activities of this project for the past year and a half.

I am grateful to you for giving me this opportunity of working in my own country and in a field which has been close to my heart for many years. I have gained a tremendous amount of experience in this short time, which however, compared to what still awaits exploration, is a mere drop in the ocean.

My only regret is that the hard work of my staff and students, together with my own enthusiasm, was nipped in the bud. Perhaps, in the years to come, a way out will be found to continue this worthwhile task.

With best wishes,

Yours sincerely,
(Mrs Zohra Segal)
Director
National Folk Dance Ensemble

On June 29, 1975, Zohra returned to London, sixty-three years old and with no work in hand, having been out of circulation for a while. Thanks to some radio interviews she had done with Sir Ralph Richardson and Dame Flora Robson earlier, she now had an EQUITY card—which gave her membership of the actors' union—but no offers. She put in her application for old-age pension, which at least meant that she didn't have to go back to Pettits! Her sewing days might well be over, but she did wonder whether her acting days might not also have come to an end. At her age, and as an Asian woman in England, not much would have been forthcoming, anyway.

But then, not much had come her way in India, either. What would she have done there? In London, she had a community of friends, actors and others, Indian and British, and she had grown accustomed to—in fact, liked—the work culture and its professionalism. It was what she had missed in India on the few occasions she had acted there. And, really, apart from Joy Michael, a few other colleagues and, of course, Hajrah and her brother-in-law, who else was there in Delhi?

Among those in England whom she thought of as close friends, were the writer/artist Kit Williams and his first wife, Helen, who lived and worked in the Cotswolds. Helen had been to a dance performance by Kiran at the Commonwealth Institute some time in the early 1970s, and been much struck by her dancing. They became friendly, and meanwhile, Walter, on a visit to a gallery in London, discovered Kit Williams' art and struck up a friendship with him! The Segals were frequent visitors at the Williamses' home in the country, and Kit, Helen, Zohra, Kiran and Walter developed a close bond.

'Our minds met on whimsicality,' recalled Kit Williams, speaking of his particular relationship with Zohra. She responded to the quirkiness of much of his art—a clock sculpture he did in Cheltenham, with little creatures popping out of it; his phenomenally successful book-cum-treasure-hunt, *Masquerade*, which she enjoyed reading, and to his poetic sensibility. 'I think she relaxed when she came to the country,' he remarked, felt at ease with the rhythm of their lives.[1]

But London was where she had decided to return, and where she needed to stay if she wanted to act. Kiran, meanwhile, had been dancing and performing all across Europe and England, receiving a very good response, and had decided to return permanently to India to study with Guru Sada Shivam Pillai and Guru Nana Kasar. Come back with me, she urged Zohra, just for a change, till you find something. Zohra wasn't in the least inclined to accompany her. She might have, had it seemed likely that her efforts to find a place in the National School of Drama repertory company would succeed. But she had accepted now that this was unlikely. It was discouraging, for after all, Ebrahim Alkazi as Director of NSD and a long-time associate, could have put in a word for her; but, as she lamented, 'lots of charming promises were made but no concrete offer'.

Zohra decided, instead, to go to Pakistan, having obtained a visa to visit, and took little Sujata, Kiran's daughter, with her. It was only the second time after Partition that she had been able to meet her brothers there, so she spent several weeks with them in Karachi, and with her beloved Uzra in Rawalpindi. She didn't have the slightest inkling, then, that this time when she returned to England, her luck would indeed turn.

Act 3, Scene 2: Breakthrough

In 1975, the British Actors' Equity Association produced a report entitled 'Employment of Afro-Asian Artists in the Theatre', prepared by its Afro-Asian Artists' Committee, which presented the results of a survey on the employment of 'coloured' artists in theatre and television. (Coloured included West Indian, Black African, African-American, Asian and Oriental.) The background for the report is worth noting.[1]

In early 1974, Equity sent out a letter to its members, and also to every provincial theatre in the country, reminding artistic directors of Equity's 1968 policy regarding 'integrated casting'. In the normal course, when actors graduated from drama school they became members of local repertory companies, generally regarded as 'post-graduate' training; work in television and films, as well as in the West End, usually followed a stint in provincial theatre.

This opportunity was more or less absent for Afro-Asian actors, and was reflected in Equity's survey findings. In the 147 provincial theatres surveyed, of the 1306 actors employed by them, only nineteen were Afro-Asian. In the West End, of the thirty-three theatres that employed 850 actors, eighteen were Afro-Asian; of the three national companies—National,

Royal Shakespeare Stratford, and RSC Aldwych—with 210 actors, only four were of Afro-Asian origin.

At the time, Equity's membership was in the region of 20,000, of whom 500 were Afro-Asian—roughly 2.5%; the report concluded that based on survey findings, of the total number of roles covered—3,398—fifty-six or 1.5% were played by Afro-Asian artists; the lowest figures pertained to provincial and repertory theatre. Yet, the report noted that cities like Birmingham, Bristol, Manchester, Liverpool, Wolverhampton, Leeds, Bradford and Glasgow had a high concentration of immigrants and a substantial number of theatres—'it would be socially justifiable,' it said, 'for employment opportunities to be offered to Afro-Asian artists' and thereby, to engage a largely untapped audience.

It could be argued, as artistic directors did, that theatre and television programming had few roles for Afro-Asian actors, and that most repertory companies operated on shoestring budgets—they couldn't afford to 'carry' an actor who would be used in, at most, only one play or two, for the whole season. To which, the report responded that the problem of casting Afro-Asians could be addressed when choosing the plays for the season for 'there are many plays with characters who could be played by blacks or whites'. In modern plays, moreover, a character's skin colour may have no relevance. More importantly, however, the report noted that

> Black people appear to be alienated from the theatre as it is known today, since they see nothing on stage which relates to their daily lives. It is the view of the Committee that many of today's social problems could have been averted and their escalation could still be prevented, if they felt some measure of identification with the native population in this country through the media and the Arts. It would

> appear, in certain parts of the country, that the education system has failed to achieve this sense of identification.[2]

Not all Afro-Asian actors were in agreement with the report's conclusions. Renu Setna 'didn't like the idea of a separate committee' because it meant that Afro-Asians were being thought of differently. 'Madhav Sharma and I ran the charge at the Equity meeting against this...because people love being on committees. I don't think they did anything but serve themselves.'[3] Actors like Setna objected to being typecast; to a kind of tokenism that took the place of real opportunity. Very early in his acting career, he had addressed a meeting of the Council of Repertory Theatres (CORT) where he said, 'It's all very well to be asked to speak at your meeting but I'd rather be speaking in one of your plays. When will you cast us as people, not just as Asian, Chinese, Indians, Africans?' He remembered going to see directors, writers, producers... and saying to them,

> Look, you know, there's a considerable number of us in this country and we're never seen, we're practically invisible. We don't have two heads, we don't have horns, we're just normal members of society, but we're only ever cast as ethnics... Think of the number of Asian doctors, of other professions... but we're never seen in any of those things, we're only ever seen as servants or minor characters.[4]

Madhav Sharma, though agreeing with Setna, did say that the big problem was

> ...this very polite way the British have of finding why they can't use your talent for anything... whilst in America they start by saying, 'How can we make this happen?'... That's the kind of discrimination that exists in this country.[5]

As it happened, the Afro-Asian community in England wasn't sitting around and wringing its hands, waiting to be noticed by the mainstream. Already in 1975, there were two major West Indian street carnivals; runs for fourteen West Indian and African plays; three Bengali plays and dance dramas; about a dozen mass-attended Urdu mehfils; three Gujarati plays; two Hindi plays; and several performances of Bengali, Cypriot, Ukrainian, Serbian and Polish folk songs and dances. This sub-culture of ethnic arts was not only energetic, it was jostling for space to express its version of the performing arts, that reflected its reality and experiences in its adopted country. But it was a struggle, and their problems were those of every endeavour that sought to break the mould, to break out: lack of rehearsal space, lack of acceptance within the arts structure, and lack of exposure.[6]

These 'ethnic arts', as they came to be known, received little attention to begin with, being seen generally as colourful local custom. At a more considered level, it was thought that encouraging minority arts could be divisive, leading to a perpetuation of difference; in fact, of course, the opposite is true—rejection or ghettoisation reinforces stereotypes and may well lead to a reactionary response by the very communities that should be integrated.

In 1976, the year Zohra returned to England, the Arts Council of Great Britain put out a report entitled *The Arts Britain Ignores* by Naseem Khan. She had been commissioned by the Arts Council, the Calouste Gulbenkian Foundation and the Community Relations Commission to identify the existence, range and status of minority arts in Britain, 'with a view to making recommendations regarding financial support; infrastructure support; programming; employment; and policy changes; in order to reflect the heterogeneity of British society in the arts, and to foster an active multiculturalism'.

The report was wide-ranging and comprehensive, detailing all the arts in practice among the several ethnicities in Britain at the time—Afro-Asian; Caribbean; Cypriot; Chinese; Ukrainian; East and Central European—from song and dance to folk and classical, encompassing fledgling theatre and literary activity, as well. It was an exemplary report, in that it sent its recommendations to the various councils and institutions keeping their specific mandate in mind; and so the suggestions for the Home Office or the British Council were obviously not quite the same as those for the Race Relations Committee, the Arts Council, Regional Arts Associations—or the BBC, and the Independent Broadcasters Association.

The latter two dominated public and private broadcasting and provided the most extensive programming in the country; it was important that their response to the recommendations be positive—although both emphasised the fact that their criteria for *all* programming was 'excellence', not equal representation. Both opted to include immigrant content in general programmes, rather than create specialist ones for ethnic minorities. Nevertheless, the BBC acknowledged that a 'middle course' needed to be steered between 'being plausible and being patronising'; to be conscious at all times 'never to leave behind in any programme a sediment that could be construed as likely to exacerbate racial tension'.[7] Independent television, it seemed, was more proactive, having produced what they called 'Access' programmes—notably by London Weekend HTV and Tyne Tees—to provide an opportunity to minorities to express their point of view. Documentaries like *A Passage to England*, about a Pakistani girl in England; or *The Bradford Godfather*, about a Muslim community in Bradford; or *Love Thy Neighbour*, about community relations, were examples of efforts at reflecting the realities of immigrant life.

Community-specific programming was the brief at BBC's Asian Unit at Pebble Mill in Birmingham, which produced magazine programmes, news, and community oriented features, in a way encouraging Asian performers but in another sense, compartmentalising them. It stirred the old debate between mainstreaming and separatism, ironically falling into the 'plausible but not patronising' pitfall that the BBC consciously wanted to avoid.

Serendipitously, Zohra arrived on the scene just as the BBC was grappling with multicultural programming, at a time when there was a very strong community arts movement that was also very political and very vocal. 'Everybody has a story to tell' became a slogan of sorts, and there was a strand within the BBC that wanted to get embedded in the community in order to create content. The community arts movement was also very much a part of the theatre in education, or TIE, initiatives of the 1970s, and quite a bit of early 'multicultural' programming had an educational impulse.

In 1977, the BBC's Further Education Unit produced one of its most successful series called *Parosi* (Neighbours) directed by Paul Kriwaczek, with early episodes written by Naseem Khan and Dilip Hiro. The aim of the series was to encourage immigrants to learn English so that they could better deal with the problems they might encounter in a new country. Language as empowerment, in other words. Zohra was the connecting thread, the *sutradhar*, if you like, who popped up in every episode. 'She was like everybody's aunt,' recalled Naseem, 'she would look at the audience and say, "Tsk, oh that poor man! Now if only he had done so and so… now, don't fall into his trap, you know, this is what you should be doing.' And of course, she was wonderful.'[8] Zohra was Mrs Chowdhry, 'the social worker, teacher, busybody, loudmouth', whose diary recorded the weekly happenings in the neighbourhood. The episodes were shot and recorded over six months, from January to May 1977, it was aired in October that year, and repeated in 1978.

Parosi was immensely popular, a show with a friendly, chatty tone which connected directly with its audience. It might, in retrospect, have teetered on the edge of the stereotypical but it seemed to click, and as Naseem Khan noted, 'it certainly got a place in history'. It just as surely got Zohra the kind of recognition she loved—and deserved. 'Only another actress can appreciate the joy I felt when children ran up to me in the street to make sure I was 'Mrs Chowdhry',' she recalled, 'and I lapped it up to my heart's content!'[9]

One place where large crowds would gather was at cinema halls in Southall, where Zohra occasionally conducted workshops for young women. One of her most endearing qualities was her spontaneous professional generosity, her encouragement of talent whenever she spotted it. She realised, too, that although some of the young hopefuls were politically and socially conscious, they were untrained and not terribly knowledgeable about India. She urged them to travel to the country, to learn at first hand, watch films and videos, recognise the difference between popular and elite culture. If they were going to perform in plays with an Indian setting, they should do their homework. Don't just shake your head from side to side and do a caricature, acting is hard work, she said.

Southall, then, was seething after the murder of a seventeen-year-old Indian boy, a tragedy that ignited the community and saw the birth of the Asian civil liberties movement. It also saw the birth of Tara Arts, co-founded by Jatinder Verma, an East African Indian, part of the Asian exodus from Kenya in

1968. It was among the earliest wholly British Asian theatre companies, whose first production in 1977 was an adaptation of Tagore's *Sacrifice*, which attacked religious bigotry. In a shabby local authority centre in Tooting, Tara Arts put up a gritty no-holds barred play about the downside of Asian-ness. A young girl is trapped by a boy into sleeping with him and gets pregnant; unable to face the consequences she commits suicide. The play was based on a true event that shook all three founders of Tara Arts, made them think. 'Watching it,' wrote Naseem Khan, 'felt slightly risky, like reading a forbidden book, but it's exhilarating, it's fresh, and I sit up straight.'[10]

Still, at the time, this was fringe theatre, very cheap, touch and go, not something that Zohra would have looked to for herself—fringe was young, it was sporadic; she was already in her mid-sixties, and community theatre was not really an option.

The Tricycle and Joan Littlewood's Stratford East, the two places that were pushing Black and Asian theatre, were a possibility, but they, too, were battling what came to be called 'the lack of fit'. Where exactly was this kind of theatre or music or film to be slotted? The mainstream wasn't really interested in opening out, widening its perspective, creating roles for actresses like Zohra—or even someone like Madhur Jaffrey. Asian performers complained that they were always being interviewed but never offered opportunities. And as one academic insightfully put it, even if an opportunity came knocking, 'Don't look at the entry points, don't look at the doors, look at the position of the walls.' Meaning, look at the structures that have been constructed to keep people out.

Theatre, then, where Zohra's versatility could have had full play, was more or less out. Television, on the other hand, was opening up and after *Parosi*, Zohra became 'bankable'. But she had promised Pavan that she would take him to India after she finished shooting *Parosi*, and so in October 1977, she left for India with him. Just a short trip, but they managed to take in Aligarh, Agra and Banaras.

Brief appearances in a London Weekend Television series called *Mind Your Language*, apart, Zohra had few offers of work, and in late 1978 she left for Karachi, with Kiran and Sujata, to celebrate her father's 100th birthday, on March 11, 1979, with the family. It was a historic occasion, the first time that all seven siblings were present since their mother's death, sixty years earlier. All the children and grandchildren—except Pavan, whose visa hadn't come through—were there, and Kiran presented her beloved Nana with a most precious gift—she danced for him. Zohra's eyes brimmed over to see her daughter surpass her own performances as a dancer. When one of her sisters remarked that Kiran had excelled her mother, she remembered a maxim from the *Atharva Veda*: 'The father is the string, the mother the bow, and the child is the arrow. Could I wish for anything more from life than an arrow of such true aim?'

Six months later, Zohra's father passed away in Karachi on September 4. She was alone in London when she got the news. Distraught, she just about managed to go to the post office to send a condolence cable to her brothers and sisters in Pakistan, then called Pavan—and broke down. Abbajan had been her rock-solid reference point, her emotional safety-net when she faced reversals in her personal life, and an unfailing moral support in all the unconventional choices she made in her life. She knew he was irreplaceable—he had been one of the four pillars of her life, along with Memphis, Uday Shankar and Prithviraj Kapoor; the four people to whom she owed everything in her life and her work.

Early in 1980, Zohra received an unexpected offer to act on stage in a play called *The Primary English Class* by the American playwright Israel Horovitz. It used the familiar trope of language, with seven characters—Polish, Italian, French, German, Chinese, Japanese and American—thrown together in an English-teaching class. In his notes to the play Horovitz wrote:

> Language is *not* the clarifier: neither a friend to thought nor a twin to meaning. Language is the first mask. The fence between neighbours' emotions, between their ideas, their needs. Wars are fought over a word. Marriages begin or end with a simple 'I do' or 'I don't'. *The Primary English Class* exists to express my love and my wonder.

To Zohra the script and the play seemed to be a lot like *Mind Your Language*, but she liked her role, Mrs Pong, the Chinese woman, and it was a chance to act on stage again. The play, directed by Sam Walters, was performed in March 1980, an off-season discount production at Wyndham's in the West End, and again at the Orangetree Theatre in Richmond. Its reception was tepid. *The Sunday Times*, while acknowledging that the play had 'all the possibilities of a quick-paced farce, based on that trusty stand-by, the English phrase-book', regretted that it descended into hysteria. Only the Japanese and Chinese characters, it said, shared the honours, the others collapsing into caricature.

For Zohra, the stage was the ultimate venue, and so she put all her energy into Mrs Pong, developing, and indeed, *becoming* the character. The scene she played 'was the only scene that was spot on,' recalled Renu Setna, 'absolutely marvellous, the way she attacked it. She attacked it like a Palestinian attacks an Israeli or an Israeli attacks a Palestinian... she gave it her all.'[11]

That window of opportunity that was just a crack opened wide in a most surprising way over the next couple of years; Zohra appeared in *The Good Person of Szechwan* as Mrs Shin, produced by the Kick Theatre Company in 1981; in *Our Own People*, also in 1981, by Actors Unlimited; and in *Hedda in India* by the Upstream Theatre Company in 1983; the last two directed by Madhav Sharma. Sharma, along with Harbhajan Virdi of Southall Youth Movement and Jatinder Verma of Tara Arts, was one of the few Indians who had a theatre company in London, performing and intervening, via theatre, against terrific odds. One of their biggest challenges was to resist the stereotyping of Asians in the UK that was common not only in the arts, but on television as well. Unlike Virdi and Verma, Madhav Sharma had not been born and brought up in England, so his quest as a producer and director was to address the issue of Asians in British theatre as an outsider looking in. Why, he asked, should he only work with Indian plays, playwrights and actors? Stage only Tagore or Kalidasa? Why shouldn't he deal with the question of race in general terms? As he said, 'Here, you think everybody dances the bhangra or owns a restaurant, that's all they know about us, and that's all that's publicised. It's political, because you're not allowed to go beyond that.'[12] He decided he was not going to fall in line.

Sharma didn't believe in the separatism that was gaining ground in Brit-Asian theatre, because he worried that the liberals were keeping them separate as a way of keeping them down—they didn't want them to cross over. And so he directed plays by the English playwright David Edgar (*Our Own People*), and in 1983 he staged *Hedda in India*, an adaptation of Ibsen's classic *Hedda Gabler*. The play was set in India, soon after Partition; Sharma cast Zohra as Aunt

Julie/Jabeen; Jamila Massey was the wife (now ex-wife); Jenny Seagrove, Sharma's wife, played Hedda; Tariq Younus was the lover, called Sarkar. Said Sharma, 'I cast actors who I thought were actors, who had talent, I didn't want them to come and do *Oh, My Goodness, Me* acting.'

Zohra was happy and relieved that she wasn't expected to play a caricature, glad that Sharma's decision would breach the establishment's idea of Indian-ness. She also appreciated the rehearsal regimen—in at 9:30 in the morning till 6:00 in the evening, every day, for three weeks. A stickler for punctuality herself, she was never late—indeed, on the day of the performance she would reach the theatre two hours before curtain up, go on stage to familiarise herself with the space, with the exits and entries, check her props and costumes, and then do her exercises for half an hour before washing up and applying her make-up. 'Not having to rush before a performance makes the all-important concentration possible, so that when the curtain goes up, the audience is all yours.'[13] This was her Uday Shankar discipline, and she kept to it, throughout.

Zohra was brilliant as Aunt Julie/Jabeen. They got rave reviews, 'the critics were wonderful about it, but could we get a producer to do it commercially in the West End?' asked Sharma. Not a chance. 'People came from the National Theatre, Royal Shakespeare, to see it, but in those days they weren't interested in employing us unless there was an 'Indian' role,'[14] and so *Hedda in India* never had a commercial release in the UK.

Pavan got married in 1982, an arranged marriage, as he wanted to marry an Indian girl. He was twenty-nine, had a good job as a data processing manager in the Bank of Baroda in London, where he had been working since 1978. A match was arranged for him by his aunt—Kameshwar's elder brother's wife—with Seema Rai, also from a Hindu-Muslim family in Allahabad. Kiran was the go-between! Instructed by Zohra to check out the family and meet the young woman as Pavan and she herself were in London, Kiran attended Seema's younger sister Sara's wedding in Delhi. With no idea about what she was supposed to check out or whom she should speak to, Kiran exchanged pleasantries with Seema's mother, after which she was besieged by phone calls from Pavan. Did you meet her? What is she like?? What could Kiran say? She advised him to come and see for himself. Which he did. Seema and he liked each other, a date was decided, and they were married in Delhi, at the Jagannath Mandir in Hauz Khas. A Hindu wedding. 'We were never religious,' Zohra has said,

> Kiran and Pavan were not brought up as Hindus, but certainly not as Muslims, either... My in-laws wanted me to bring up my children as Muslims, but I didn't do so because I myself was not a Muslim after I returned from Germany—I had gradually shifted to atheism. Kameshwar was also absolutely non-religious... I told my children, my background is Muslim and your father's background is Hindu; all religions lead to the same thing. They are hooks on which you can hang your trust... This is what I taught them, which is why neither is a Hindu or a Muslim.[15]

Pavan, like Kiran, was secular, and not being an observing Hindu or Muslim it probably didn't matter that his wedding took place in a temple—for him it had as much meaning as any other venue. The couple returned to London, to the small, two-bedroom flat Pavan had bought in Windsor, but Seema found life in England difficult. Pavan was away at work, Windsor was not London, and she was lonely, without family or friends in a country far from home. They left England within a year and were back in India, where Pavan now had a job with the World Health Organisation. He would not return to England again, and after a longish stint in India for fourteen years, Pavan moved to Denmark, then to Zimbabwe, the Congo, Burkina Faso, and finally, Malaysia. A major part of his life was spent away from his immediate family, and Zohra, as Kiran remarked, 'was always pining for him'.[16]

Unlike Pavan, Kiran remained firmly rooted in India, developing and gaining recognition as a dancer, but this meant that Zohra saw relatively little of her, as well. Kiran seldom had occasion to visit England so that it was only when, or if, Zohra travelled to India that they met. Fortunately, in 1986 the BBC commissioned the making of *The Maneaters of Kumaon*, a docu-drama based on the life and work of Jim Corbett, to be directed by Alex Kirby. Zohra was cast as Corbett's grandmother, and the shooting took her to Kaladhungi—Corbett's home base—followed by a wonderful break in Delhi and Bombay.

In Delhi, Aruna Asaf Ali invited Zohra to speak at a special screening of Chetan Anand's first film, *Neecha Nagar*—a film that had become a classic but, as Zohra recalled, 'was an absolute flop in the beginning—people threw chairs at the screen when it was released in Bombay'. Unbeknownst to her audience, Zohra said, her brother-in-law, Hamid Butt, also in *Neecha Nagar*, is Salman Rushdie's nephew (his sister's son) and figures in *Midnight's Children* as Hanif, the protagonist's uncle, a film director. Rushdie, she told her audience, was often a guest at her flat in Hampstead while he was a student at Cambridge.

For the rest, she spent some lovely time with Kiran and Sujata, and because she had so enjoyed shooting in the foothills of the Himalayas, she discussed with Kiran the possibility of buying a small house for herself in Mussoorie or Nainital for when she finally returned to India. It remained an unrealised plan, but this visit more or less decided Zohra—it was time to wrap up her affairs in London and come home.

One occurrence, about which she had no say at all but which had caused her some considerable unhappiness, was Kiran's marriage to the artist Jatin Das. Zohra neither liked nor trusted him. She said as much to Kiran, told her that he would not be welcome in her house, but Kiran paid her no heed. She had met Jatin at Habib and Monica Tanvir's house in Delhi, where she used to practise her dance. They met again later, at an event organised by the India Tourism office in London, and Kiran was swept off her feet by his pursuit of her. She responded to Jatin's overtures but resisted his pleas to get married, till one day the photographer Raghu Rai said, '*Kar le, yaar, kyon nahin karti? Dekh,* Sujata *ke liye bhi ghar ban jayega.*' (Do it, why don't you? Look, Sujata will find a home too.) That did it. She married Jatin in Khajuraho in 1984, and lived to regret her decision. Called it 'the biggest mistake' of her life. Jatin, she soon realised, would take advantage of her contacts and invitations to dance abroad to further his own career and promote his art. He was selfish and cavalier, undermined her dancing and her performances, and far from providing a home for Sujata, encouraged Kiran to send her to the hostel at Mother's International School.

Their marriage lasted three unsatisfactory years—one evening in 1987, when Jatin was away in Manipur, Kiran packed her bags, left a note for him, and walked out.[17] Zohra was glad that Kiran had finally seen him for what he was, relieved that she wouldn't need to either be impolite or tolerate him for her daughter's sake. But she regretted deeply Kiran and Walter's divorce.

In 1983 Sir Denis Forman, then chairman of Granada Productions, decided to produce an adaptation of Paul Scott's *The Raj Quartet* as a mini-series called *The Jewel in the Crown*, in which Zohra had a role in the initial episodes. She called it her lucky break: 'After slogging away from 1962 to 1982 it was the first real break in my career, not counting *Parosi*, because, in spite of the fact that I appeared in twenty-six episodes, it was only viewed by Asians.' Her character in *Jewel*, Lady Lili Chatterjee, suited her to a T, a high-class Indian woman used to ordering the servants around. The filming was done in Mysore for a few weeks, and then in Manchester; but before the shoot, the director, Christopher Morahan, went through the whole script once with the cast in London, and once more before the actual shooting. Zohra, being a perfectionist herself, totally approved of what she called 'this extra-professional approach'.

It was India, of course, that was the jewel in the British crown, but it had become clear to the English that it was also the riddle they couldn't crack. It had been subjugated, but not conquered. By the mid-1940s the sun had begun to set on the Empire—in 1942, when the series opens, England was in the middle of fighting—and losing to—the Japanese in Burma and Malaya, Gandhi had launched his Quit India campaign, and desertions from the Indian Army to Bose's INA were a cause of some concern. Things were beginning to fall apart. The ugly face of imperialism—embodied in Ronald Merrick, the Superintendent of Police in the fictional town of Mayapuri—had been exposed and was being questioned by some of its own. The intrinsically conflicted relationship between ruler and ruled, the forbidden love between black and white, are brought to crisis in the rape of Daphne Manners, a young English woman newly arrived in India. Rape, as metaphor, had already made its appearance in E.M. Forster's *A Passage to India*; it reappeared here as representing the violence of the relationship between ruler and ruled. In this, *Jewel* was ironically more subversive than nostalgic about the Raj.

Zohra loved being Lady Lili. Loved showing off her aristocratic manners, educating the directors on the niceties of her status, and of crucial details like: servants never stepped inside with shoes on, or without a head covering, either turban or cap. As she walked along the corridors of the luxury hotel they stayed in and stole a glance at herself in the mirrors, she felt rather gratified by what she saw: a wealthy matron, grey hair parted at the side, lipstick, rings on her fingers, wearing a delicate white sari and living in a grand bungalow called McGreggor House. She knew all about such people, having grown up in a palace and been to school with an assortment of princesses. And she greatly enjoyed working with brilliant actors, among them Susan Wooldridge, who played Daphne Manners, Tim Piggot-Smith, the young Art Malik and another Indian, Shreela Ghosh, who looked to Zohra for advice and support.

When the series premièred on January 9, 1984, Zohra was alone in her flat in Hornsey. She put together an evening meal for herself, placed it on a tray, and sat in front of the television, waiting with bated breath for the show to begin. But, 'as one scene changed to the next, I felt deeper and deeper shock and disappointment at my acting. At the end of the first episode I undressed and got into bed. With tears in my eyes I told myself, "If this is all you're capable of, Zohra Segal, it would be better if you gave up acting".'[18]

Zohra hated herself as Lady Lili. She thought her dialogues were artificial and brittle and her appearance, far from aristocratic, was 'like a trumped-up ayah'. Her sister Uzra and the talented actress Indira Joshi, then in London, agreed with her (as did Pavan), but TV audiences in Britain didn't seem to mind. Indeed, the *Herald* complimented her on a 'pucca performance', and the *Daily Express* declared that the principal actors were 'acted off the set by Zohra Segal… given to bright utterances'. For the first time, ordinary people on the street, in buses and on the Underground, came up to her and congratulated her on her performance. With the success of the series in the US came more offers from producers and directors, and of course, much to her great delight, her fees went up considerably.

Why did Zohra, who (as she acknowledged) was to the manner born, not bring to her role the nuance that she was capable of? Was it a matter of direction? 'I felt there were certain things that needed to be done with the character (Lili Chatterjee),' said Waris Hussein, 'things that weren't done because Christopher Morahan wasn't to know how. He got the British side right, but he didn't get the Indian side right.'[19] But Zohra knew how upper-class Indians were likely to conduct themselves, so was she, in effect, playing Zohra, rather than Lady Lili Chatterjee? Looking at herself playing a role? For when she 'forgot' herself and inhabited Lady Lili's skin, she confirmed that she was indeed a fine actress. One must conclude that it is those moments that the critic Gerard Dempsey was thinking of when he wrote that Art Malik, Tim Piggott-Smith and Susan Wooldridge. 'are outstandingly good, but they are acted off the stage by Zohra Segal'.[20]

Two Raj films, both based on novels—M.M. Kaye's *The Far Pavilions* and Paul Scott's *The Raj Quartet*—opened within six days of each other in 1984. Both were made with budgets of £5 million each and both were filmed on location in India. Both dealt with a native-born Indian, unsettled in his own country, and both were very successful in their own way. It seemed there was a large enough audience in the country that lapped up Raj glory and Empire exotica, but was there something else at work there, as well? Could it be that Raj nostalgia had *its* takers, while the unsettled Indian experience found an echo among second-generation Indians in the UK?

Jewel had a generous sprinkling of Indian actors in it, another plus, for in addition to Zohra and Art Malik, it had Saeed Jaffrey, Zia Mohyeuddin, Kamini Kaushal, a young Om Puri, Jamila Massey, Kunal Kapoor (Shashi Kapoor's son) and Shreela Ghosh. Identification with the Indian cast apart, could it also be that the film's subtext—and, as it unfolded, its representation of the 'inevitable corruption of imperialism'—struck a chord with post Indian Independence viewers who had never experienced the Raj? Difficult to say, but following close on the heels of *Far Pavilions*, BBCs Channel 4 (which produced *Pavilions*) commissioned an unusual programme on Hindi cinema called *Movie Mahal*, conceived and directed by the film buff, filmmaker and writer Nasreen Munni Kabir. It was a mix of film clips, interviews, song sequences and commentary, cleverly spliced and expertly edited to offer a fascinating—and hugely enjoyable—glimpse into what makes Hindi films the unique genre that they are. It debuted in 1986-87, was seen by between 250,000 and 450,000 viewers in the UK and overseas, and became the yardstick by which programmes in this format would be produced. Kabir herself went on to make others like it on song-writers, marquee actors, and legendary directors like Guru Dutt.

The South Asian diaspora was making its presence felt

in other arts, as well. Tara Arts had become a fixture on the theatre scene by the early 1980s, and in 1983 was established enough to acquire its own premises. Madhav Sharma's Actors Unlimited and Upstream Theatre were experimenting with adaptations of western classics, writers like Salman Rushdie, the British Pakistanis Aamer Hussein and Hanif Kureshi were being noticed, and Kureshi's *My Beautiful Laundrette* was heading towards cult status. Attenborough's *Gandhi* (1982) and David Lean's A *Passage to India* (1984) had already opened to very favourable response, so India had, in the words of the *New York Times* critic, John O'Connor, been receiving 'unusual attention in major entertainment productions'.

After *Jewel*, Zohra appeared in two films in quick succession: *The Honorary Consul*, based on the novel by Graham Greene, starring Michael Caine, a young and very good-looking, Richard Gere, and Zohra as the Consul's maid, Maria. Theme music by Paul McCartney. Zohra's was the tiniest role possible but she looked every bit the part—iron gray hair pulled into a tight bun, severe black uniform, patrician demeanour. The second was an unusual film, a docu-drama called *The Courtesans of Bombay*, directed by Ismail Merchant, in 1983. It was Zohra's second film with them after *The Guru*, and here, too, the screenplay was by Ruth Jhabvala. The story is set in a chawl, Pavan Pul, and focuses on a group of courtesans who dance for patrons during the day and—it is suggested—ply their trade by night, in the hope of making it as movie stars. Saeed Jaffrey plays an actor enamoured of one of the dancers, Zohra is a sometime courtesan, now a maker of pickles.

Courtesans is a curious film, doesn't quite succeed either as documentary or as feature, but Zohra had a substantial role, and for once, was not cast as an older woman. Her role is carefully calibrated, allowing her to display her particular skill as both a dancer—her facial expressions emoting nostalgia, tenderness, mischief, are a sheer joy to watch—and as a character actress. She holds the screen, appearing mostly solo, reminiscing easily as she chops and slices and seasons her pickles. Where occasionally—and certainly earlier in *The Guru*—she could be a bit over the top, in *Courtesans* she is subtle and understated, confirming Madhav Sharma's assessment of her: 'Anybody who's ever seen Zohra act properly in a good part goes away saying, "That's a fantastic performer there".' *Courtesans* was broadcast by Channel 4 and had a limited release in the US in 1986, with the *New York Times* calling it 'a fascinating 73 minutes of sociology, human interest and exotic entertainment'.

Films were fun, Zohra travelled to exotic locations, met and acted with many of the big names in the business and, of course, it was work, which she enjoyed. But her heart was in theatre, its daily physical contact with an audience, and the charge that accompanied each performance. An unusual opportunity came her way in 1983-84 when the Joint Stock Company staged a play called *The Great Celestial Cow* at the Royal Court Theatre. Unusual, because it was Zohra's first experience with community and ensemble theatre, and because she played four roles in it.

The play was a tenth anniversary production for Joint Stock, which had toured in Leicester before concluding its season in London. It grew out of extended workshops and rehearsals and was finally scripted by Sue Townsend, famous author of the superb *The Secret Life of Adrian Mole*. Zohra observed the way Joint Stock worked with great interest—a theme was picked, the company's director, Carole Hayman, did the research, visiting Indian families in Leicester, going to temples and the cinema, and after three weeks returned with the information she had collected for the workshops, where the story was developed through constant interaction among participants. Sue Townsend then 'wrote' the play. *Cow* was a fantastical extravaganza, tracing the life of a young woman, Sita, from the time she leaves her beloved cow in her village in India and sets out, with her two sons, to meet Ram and her relatives in Leicester. The story unfolds through music (which included *Sgt. Pepper's Lonely Hearts Club*, 'Kabhie, Kabhie', Bob Marley and the Wailers and Gloria Gaynor), dance, laughter and tears, and follows Sita as she tries to adjust to her new surroundings.

Zohra was the Spirit of Kali, the Mother-in-Law, the Muslim Girl, and the second Official, and had the time of her life playing all four! Others in the cast included Lou Wakefield (the only white actor, with whom Zohra would work again later) and old friends Shreela Ghosh and Jamila Massey. The Royal Court guaranteed Joint Stock takings of £8000, and a 70-30 split (70 to JS, 30 to RCT) should box office net receipts exceed £16,000. Seats were a modest £6, 4 & 2. Royalties would be shared by all.

In a refreshing and welcome change the women were neither 'wallpaper' (Jamila Massey's word) nor 'victims' (Shreela Ghosh), 'weak' (Zohra) or 'quiet' (Souad Faress, who played Sita). In fact, the story is about women's strength, about warmth, humour 'and sheer bloody-mindedness' that keeps Sita going. About Zohra, *The Times* said she displayed 'ageless grace and a sense of mischief, whether as a precocious little horror in a school nativity play, or an old dear, shocked after telling her grandson to shut up'.

The play was well received in London and Leicester but when it was performed in Bradford, everybody in the

Company got a letter from the Asian community in Bradford, saying, 'How dare you take our culture and make fun of it.' It was 'nasty, horrible stuff' recalled Lou Wakefield, and the community's strong reaction came as something of a shock to them all.[21]

In the summer of 1986, Zohra had an unusual visitor, neither family nor friend, but a potential co-author: the American anthropologist Joan Erdman, who had met Zohra in 1983 while she was researching her study on Uday Shankar. Zohra gave Joan her unfinished memoirs—which she had called *The Name-Dropper*—saying Joan could read about her years with Dada in it. Erdman, intrigued by what she read about Zohra and her life, suggested that she interview her, bring her story up to date, and present her life to the public in a co-authored work. She spent three weeks with Zohra in London in 1986, stayed in her flat, and talked to her about the circumstances in which she had worked and lived, and about her career as an actress.

Meanwhile, Zohra was back in business with a role in the celebrated avant-garde director Derek Jarman's shockingly original interpretation of the life of the Italian painter Caravaggio, in a film of the same name (rated R, and described as 'a kinky ode to… the dark side of the Renaissance'![22]). Zohra appeared in a single scene, right at the beginning, but her performance was pitch perfect. It would appear unusual, perhaps incredible, that someone of Zohra's background was finding work with directors as boldly experimental and provocative as Jarman. Yes, it was a bit part, and she almost never refused a role; but then again, even starting with her decision to learn modern dance back in the early 1930s, and working with pioneers like Uday Shankar, she had always found herself in artistic projects that pushed the boundaries and broke new ground.

It seemed to Zohra, now in her mid-seventies, that she was having the time of her life! She was in demand, the work was fun and varied, she was acting alongside the best in the business, actors and directors, and was comfortably off financially. With Kiran and Pavan both independent of her, she had no pressing responsibilities on either front. And England held its senior citizens in uncommon regard in its provision of services—she was living in a lovely (attic) council flat in Hornsey, her travel on buses and the Underground was free, and she had a pension from Equity, in addition to the fees she earned. She missed Kiran and Pavan, naturally, but Babar, her nephew, lived in the city, and Uzra and Hamida visited often—visits she enjoyed very much because there was nothing like family to recharge one's emotional resources. Much as she appreciated what England had to offer, she still wasn't used to the formality that governed social relations.

In 1985, BBC's Channel 4 produced a six-part series called *Tandoori Nights*, scripted by Farrukh Dhondy, featuring Indians and Indian restaurants (called, quaintly, 'curry houses') in London. The two competing restaurants here are The Jewel in the Crown (run by Jimmy, Saeed Jaffrey's character) and The Far Pavilions, an upstart across the road set up by a former waiter of Jimmy's. Zohra plays Jimmy's mother, grandmother to one of his daughters, Bubbly, whose marriage prospects are of great concern to her.

The six episodes were hilarious, pure comedy, and an indication of how far the diasporic community had come if it could laugh at itself *and* at its host society. Saeed Jaffrey and Zohra stole the show with splendid performances, with Zohra resisting the temptation to outdo herself as herself! Her grandmother is irascible when she needs to be, sulking when she feels neglected—declaring, 'I'm going back to Jalandhar *now*!'—bossy when looking for a suitable boy for her granddaughter, and utterly believable every minute that she's on the screen. 'This gran is a tough old biddy,' wrote Tony Pratt in his review, 'and I love her... Nobody should be an extra in a family, but grans should always be the stars!'[23]

Channel 4, concerned that this all-Asian series would lose a British audience, was delighted with the result—*Tandoori Nights* was a resounding success and went on to a second series. When the second series went on air in 1987, however, fans were more than disappointed, for though the original lively cast was still in it, the scriptwriter, director and editor were all new—and, sadly, not up to the game. Meera Syal's script was lacklustre, the situations stilted and poorly directed. Repeats often ran the risk of slipping into cliché or predictability, and it seemed that *Tandoori Nights* had succumbed to both.

Still, Zohra enjoyed playing opposite Saeed, an old friend and co-actor, with whom she had worked in several productions, including, most recently, *Partition*—and, of course, *Masala*. She greatly admired his acting ability but wished he would cut down on his drinking, it worried her considerably.

The unusual attention that India had been receiving by the entertainment industry in Britain in the 1980s continued unabated over the decade, propelled now by the 40th anniversary of Indian independence in 1988. It is tempting to think of this interest in terms of Raj nostalgia or catering to second-generation Brit-Asians, but this can only be a partial explanation. Had Independence not been accompanied by Partition and the bloodbath that followed, the tone and tenor of the films made would have been of another order. Filmmakers, writers and producers understood that any representation of the transfer of power would have to acknowledge, in any rendering, the close to irresponsible role of the departing power at the time, and include the perspective of those left to deal with the consequences. Some vestiges of guilt, a prickling of conscience, perhaps, underlay both the choice of subject and its treatment.

Jewel in the Crown presaged this dis-ease by counterpointing the policeman Ronald Merrick's racism-masquerading-as-duty with the disquiet of the women missionaries and two young Englishwomen, who can see the writing on the wall. A third young Englishwoman, daughter of a military family widowed by the war, internalises the dis-ease and simply loses her mind: hers is the psychotic response to the tragic anomalies of her situation. Hari Kumar—the not-Indian-but-not-English-either central character—represents, literally, the violated body, brutally beaten and imprisoned on a trumped-up charge. His is the body of India, metaphorically speaking, hovering between humiliating subjugation and resolute non-cooperation.

Partition, Ken McMullen and Tariq Ali's 1987 film (commissioned by Channel 4's Farrukh Dhondy), brings body and mind together in its adaptation of *Toba Tek Singh*, Saadat Hasan Manto's tragic take on the sheer insanity of drawing lines of division across the subcontinent. The story is set in a lunatic asylum, and the problem before the administrators is how to divide its inmates: Hindu lunatics to India and Muslim lunatics to Pakistan? This makes no sense to the lunatics, and one of them, Bishan Singh (aka Toba Tek Singh), refuses to acknowledge this new geography. His mind is frozen in incomprehension, his body immobilised by a profound confusion.

Ali and McMullen's version of the story and the film they made, was a radical departure not only from the original tale but from all the earlier films made on Britain's 250 years in India. It was radical both politically and aesthetically, as noted by Ian Johnston in his 2007 review, because it was avowedly political cinema, reflecting the socialist politics of its makers who inflected Manto's sparingly simple story with Brechtian and Tarkovskian accents and symbolic devices.[24] Part of the film's unusual rendering was also a result of McMullen's own family history; his father had been conscripted into the Army and served in India during the war. He developed what McMullen called 'a great affection for the country and felt that the Empire was not wholly honourable' in its practice. McMullen was influenced by his father's memories and wanted to incorporate their essence into the film. The character played by John Shrapnel in it—wily Raj administrator/Anglo-Indian engine-driver—is a direct result of this intention.[25]

Zohra Segal, cast as Everywoman, opens and closes the film. She sweeps the courtyard of the asylum—indeed, the sound of the broom sweeping rhythmically is the first sound we hear in the film, following an image, in close-up, of a silent Zohra wiping a mirror in which her face is reflected. She never speaks in the film, but her inner voice is heard as voice-over commentary on the deliberations taking place between Indians and Englishmen on the transfer of power. In a brilliant—and stunningly subversive—intervention, all the lunatics play double roles; they are simultaneously inmates and administrators, begging the question—who is insane in this absurd and diabolical enactment? Saeed Jaffrey, Roshan Seth, Zia Mohyeddin, John Shrapnel are disoriented, babbling madmen in one scene, and suave, dissimulating civil servants in another; the film suggests that there is little difference between the two.

There is no Everywoman in Manto's story. In *Partition* she does the womanly job of cleaning up the debris, sweeping out the rubbish, picking up the pieces. As one who plays no role in the affairs of state, is only an observer carrying out her menial tasks, Everywoman/Zohra nevertheless knows what it's all about. 'Money, money, money,' she mutters to herself in the anteroom to the negotiating table, 'how much for India? And how much for poor orphaned Pakistan?' As she wipes the mirrors, mirrors that reflect reality but also distort it, we see her own face in them, all-knowing, all-seeing. 'Zohra was India,' Roshan Seth said to me when I discussed the film with him, 'her character represented India. The power struggle was between Jinnah and Nehru, and if you put it in a wider frame, between Hindu and Muslim... But Zohra was India. She carried on sweeping, no matter what happened, just swept the dust from one place to another.'[26]

But how did her character emerge on screen in the first place? McMullen says that Zohra chose her role herself. He wanted a double role for her, just like Roshan Seth, Saeed Jaffrey, and John Shrapnel but Zohra declined. 'I want to play the lowest, humblest character,' she told him, no Lili Chatterjee for her this time. So she became the sweeper, but, said McMullen, 'she incorporated dance in the role... see how she sweeps, her movements, the movements of a dancer. We discussed her moves, but the movement was all hers. She was perfect.' There was another insight she provided, one that was crucial to the visual impact of the film. 'We were having dinner,' said McMullen, 'and she said, "The British have never understood the Indian sense of time... so many dynasties, the Mughals, then the British, all dust in the wind." It was an extraordinary statement!' And so her character developed—Everywoman, sweeping the dust from one place to another, and in the end, over Roshan's body.[27]

Zohra's Everywoman India is superb. No improvisations this time, every move was scripted. There was not a whiff of overacting or caricaturing. Every twist of her wrist as she plies the broom, every glance from her unblinking eye, every wrinkle on her face, tells the untold story, the words unspoken. She depicts the lives of the lunatics she lives among, of why they have lost their minds. Their worlds. And when the film ends it is her face that is etched on the screen, her gaze unflinching. Everywoman as witness. Seth concluded, 'Zohra never realised that just to look at her face... is to look at her life, at the story of India, its happiness, its tragedies, everything is there in her face...'

Partition was shot over ten days with long stretches without any action, waiting for the light to change or the scene to take shape. The pace is slow, the colour palette an unrelieved black and white. And grey. The mood and tone are sombre. But 'there was great rapport between the actors, young and old,' recalled McMullen, 'and it was a great privilege to work with people like Zohra and Roshan and Saeed.' The film was panned when it was shown on Channel 4. Perhaps because its message was unpalatable, perhaps because it demanded too much from its audience—or perhaps, as Seth suggested, because of McMullen himself. 'Nobody saw Ken's films, they never went anywhere... he was the mad genius, no proven track record, but he had a reputation.' McMullen himself thought it was unlikely that a film like it could be made in the same way again. 'In some ways,' he told film historian James Leahy, 'I think this film is a kind of guided, concrete meditation on the events of 1947… indeed on all imperial history.'[28]

Partition was shown at the Edinburgh Festival in August 1987, and Zohra accompanied McMullen to the première and press conference that followed. About the film, Zohra herself felt, 'In spite of brilliant acting by top artistes like Zia Mohyeddin, Saeed Jaffrey, Roshan Seth and John Shrapnel, to my mind this detracted from the touching and simple statement of the original.'[29] In 2007, Second Run reissued *Partition* in a DVD format and this time it received a decidedly warmer reception, especially in the US. By 2007, the events of 1947 were already in the last century, and too much water had flowed under the bridge for the film to find wide viewership, but it remains an exceptional representation.

In 1987, at the age of seventy-five, Zohra decided to pack up in England and return to India for good. Another of her impulsive decisions? She was busy, she had enough work, her social life was active; yet she had made up her mind to leave. Being Zohra, once she had decided she lost no time on second thoughts or doubt—she simply booked her ticket to Delhi for September 26, on Thai Airways. How hectic this leave-taking would be, even she had no idea. Contacting shippers to transport her belongings; informing her landlords, the Hornsey Housing Trust, that she was vacating the flat; disconnecting gas, electricity and telephone connections; calling the municipal authorities to clear the rubbish; the plumber to disconnect her washing machine. The bank, the post office, her pension and income tax accounts, informing everyone that all correspondence needed to be forwarded—except, she had no address in India!

But there was no time to worry about any of that because there were so many going-away parties to attend! The one thrown by her old friend Firdous Ali—who had helped to have the manuscript of her memoirs typed in 1969—was special, as he had invited several eminent theatre personalities, as well as almost everyone who had worked with Zohra in England, as colleagues and friends. But the friend she found it most difficult to say goodbye to was Renu Setna. Renu was her family in London—in whose house she had often left Kiran, and Pavan when he was very young. Later, when Kiran's daughter Sujata was born, it was Renu's mother who looked after her when Kiran was away performing. With Renu, Zohra was completely at ease, could talk about almost anything because she knew she would not be misunderstood or misjudged. So it was Renu who met her at the airport on Saturday, September 26, to help her with her luggage and checking-in, after which she bade him an affectionate farewell, promising to write.

Why did Zohra choose to leave at that particular point in her life and career?

> Call it whim or sixth sense or some guidance from an unknown source, but I felt that this was the moment for me to end my self-imposed exile. Both my children, Kiran and Pavan, were settled in Delhi and yet I, nucleus of this little family, was living miles away in a foreign land. True, I had at least achieved a measure of recognition, I was extremely comfortable in my pretty and elegant attic flat, I had dear friends and relatives a phone call away. I had saved up just about enough to feel secure financially, the

> London climate suited me and kept me fitter than most of my younger colleagues, and the social security system of the UK enabled me to live very economically.[30]

And yet. England wasn't home for her, never could be. No matter how many years you lived there, you were always an outsider, a foreigner. Coloured. On your best behaviour, never wanting to give the wrong impression, always setting an example to younger South Asians to follow. Time now to unwind, to feel at home, and at ease, in India. She was nearing the end of a journey, she felt, and she wanted it to terminate in her own country. And then, there were Kiran, and Pavan and his children, Rohan and Tamra, who were almost like strangers to her as they had never lived in the same country. The emotional tug was irresistible now.

Zohra in the 1930s.

All photos and images courtesy of Kiran Segal, unless otherwise mentioned.

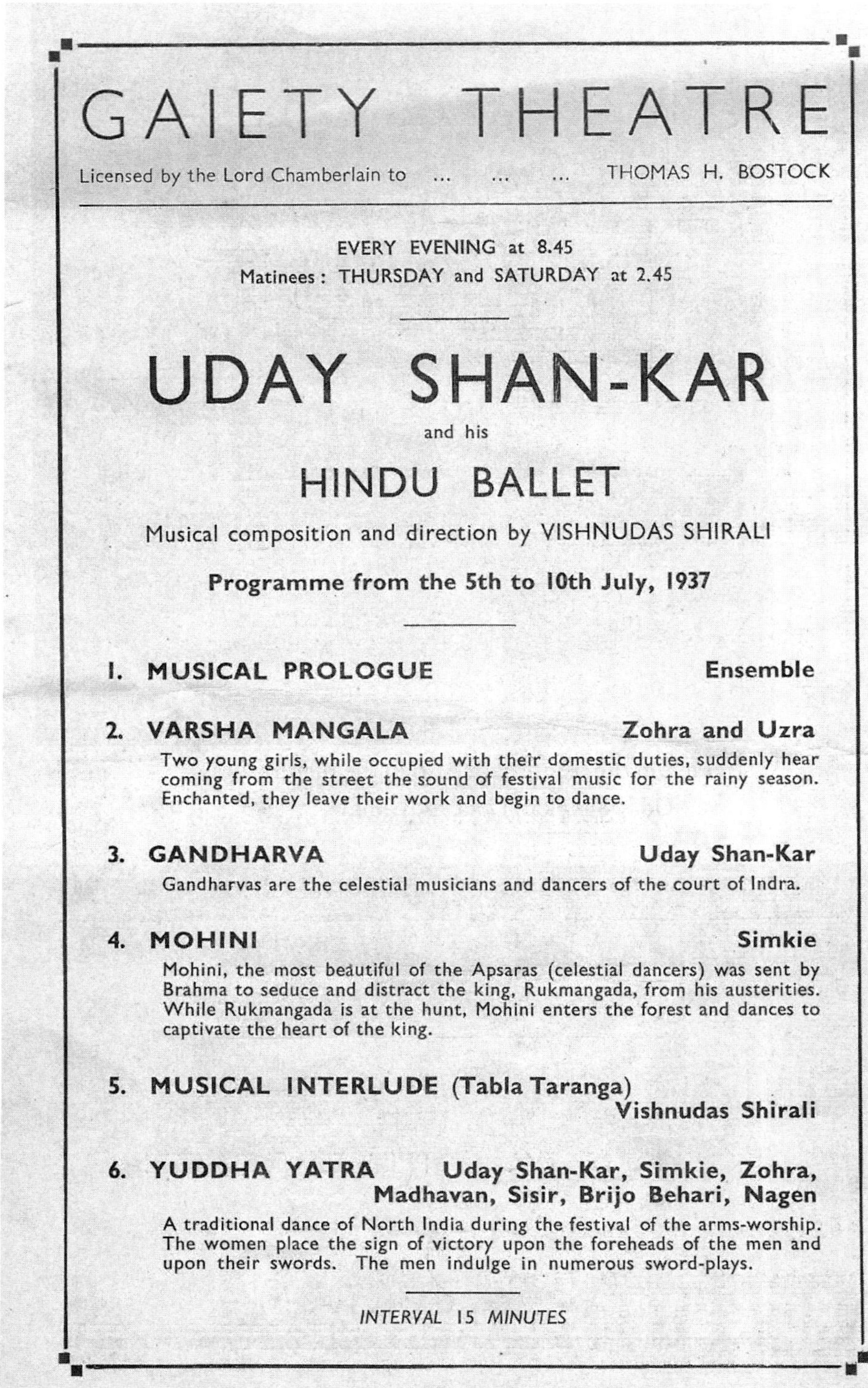

GAIETY THEATRE

Licensed by the Lord Chamberlain to ... ... THOMAS H. BOSTOCK

EVERY EVENING at 8.45
Matinees: THURSDAY and SATURDAY at 2.45

UDAY SHAN-KAR

and his

HINDU BALLET

Musical composition and direction by VISHNUDAS SHIRALI

Programme from the 5th to 10th July, 1937

1. **MUSICAL PROLOGUE** — **Ensemble**

2. **VARSHA MANGALA** — **Zohra and Uzra**
   Two young girls, while occupied with their domestic duties, suddenly hear coming from the street the sound of festival music for the rainy season. Enchanted, they leave their work and begin to dance.

3. **GANDHARVA** — **Uday Shan-Kar**
   Gandharvas are the celestial musicians and dancers of the court of Indra.

4. **MOHINI** — **Simkie**
   Mohini, the most beautiful of the Apsaras (celestial dancers) was sent by Brahma to seduce and distract the king, Rukmangada, from his austerities. While Rukmangada is at the hunt, Mohini enters the forest and dances to captivate the heart of the king.

5. **MUSICAL INTERLUDE (Tabla Taranga)** — **Vishnudas Shirali**

6. **YUDDHA YATRA** — **Uday Shan-Kar, Simkie, Zohra, Madhavan, Sisir, Brijo Behari, Nagen**
   A traditional dance of North India during the festival of the arms-worship. The women place the sign of victory upon the foreheads of the men and upon their swords. The men indulge in numerous sword-plays.

INTERVAL 15 MINUTES

Programme card of a performance by 'Uday Shan-Kar and His Hindu Ballet' in London, 1937.

At the Uday Shankar Dance Academy, Almora, around 1940.

Simkie, Uzra and Zohra in Almora.

Four generations: Zohra with (L to R) great-granddaughter Madhyama, daughter Kiran and granddaughter Sujata.

Act 4, Scene 1: In Character Again

September 27, 1987 dawned bright and clear—and hot. The humidity slammed Zohra as soon as she stepped out of the terminal building in Delhi, but for her, just experiencing sunshine again was marvellous. Every day, without fail, a blue sky, a more or less guaranteed absence of rain, and splendid September sunsets. No wonder people were cheerful and sunny-tempered!

Kiran met her at the airport and they drove to her spacious three-bedroom flat in Alaknanda; Zohra moved in with them, an arrangement that would continue, with just one break, till the end of her days. The flat was a duplex, with Zohra and Sujata on the top floor and Kiran below, from where she conducted her dance classes. Not far from them was Pavan with his family; for the first time, Zohra, her children and grandchildren were together in the same city. She couldn't have been happier.

For the next few months it was travel with and to family; her beloved Hamida and she went to Kaladhungi (where she had shot *Maneaters of Kumaon*) and Bhimtal, visiting friends who were planning to build a tourist camp in the valley. December was hardly the right time of year to be in the hills or the jungle, but at Camp Corbett they sat around a campfire at night, in the bitter cold, eating roasted fish caught in the stream that flowed below them. Jim Corbett's bungalow in Kaladhungi would soon be made into a museum, but Zohra remembered it from her shoot, much the same as it had been then.

Rampur, to which they repaired after Bhimtal and Camp Corbett, was sheer luxury after the makeshift conditions of their earlier stay. They were put up in Zohra's uncle's spacious house, Lalazar, which had been designed by her older brother, Zakkan. Acres of green lawn, verdant gardens, an army of servants, excellent food, the warm embrace of her family after a very long time away from them. Zohra relaxed into a sense of well-being such that she had not known in all her years in England: being indulged and looked after, as she knew only an Indian family could.

But life as a lady of leisure was not something she could slip into easily, it was not a habit she had ever cultivated. Besides, she liked to work. Where and how, though? Theatre was still not an easy option, and all or most film work was in Bombay. Plus, she was now seventy-seven years old. Still, you never knew what might turn up, so she contacted her old friend, Dolly Rawson (now Thakore) in Bombay, asking her to let her know if she heard of anything interesting for Zohra. Dolly, active in theatre and in with the film crowd, had been casting director in India for Attenborough's *Gandhi*—for which Zohra, in London, had turned down a part because she refused to appear as a starving village woman during the Bengal famine. Fortunately, however, television in India was opening up, and in the early days Doordarshan was fairly adventurous in its programming. Late in the year, and into January and February, 1988, Zohra appeared in an Urdu adaptation of Chekov's *Anniversary*, in which she played a crafty old woman who elbows her way into a series of offices, demanding her husband's pension. It was a tiny opening and might never develop into anything more, but Zohra enjoyed her role and the fact that she now had an audience, via a new medium, in India.

An experience with 'street' theatre came her way in July that year, with a production of *Moteram ka Satyagraha*, written and produced jointly by Habib Tanvir and Safdar Hashmi for Jana Natya Manch (Janam), the theatre group of the Communist Party (Marxist). It was directed by Tanvir, Zohra played the crochety Panditayani, and the play was performed on July 30 & 31 at Pyarelal Bhavan. Sudhanva Deshpande, an actor with Janam, writes:

> 'Zohra is back in India and looking for work', said Habib sa'ab. 'She wants to work with me. Do you think we can cast her in this play?' Habib sa'ab, Moneekadi and I were chatting at the end of rehearsal one day, when Habib sa'ab sprang this on us. I had no idea who he was talking about. But Safdar jumped with joy. 'Zohra Segal? *The* Zohra Segal? Of Prithvi Theatres? She needs work? Of course! It would be a privilege for us to work with her.'[1]

The play was enormously successful, with repeat shows at the All India Fine Arts & Crafts Society (AIFACS) auditorium in September 1988, but Zohra was not part of this staging—she knew Janam couldn't afford to pay her, and she couldn't afford to perform without being paid.

Deshpande recalls Zohra's performance as being extraordinary. Older than the actor who played Moteram by thirty years, she 'matched him step for step… her agility and lightfootedness were to be seen to be believed'. And her voice, clear as a bell, projected perfectly 'down to the last syllable of a long line right to the back of the auditorium'.

Zohra's brief encounter with Safdar Hashmi would end in a terrible tragedy barely six months later—in January 1989, Hashmi was brutally done to death while on his way to Sahibabad, on the outskirts of Delhi, where Janam was scheduled to perform *Halla Bol*! Zohra was shocked and deeply saddened by this murderous act (done, she was told, at the behest of the Congress party), at the death of a kind and gentle soul, a talented actor, and committed playwright. Later, when friends and comrades of Safdar set up SAHMAT, a trust in his memory, Zohra readily agreed (as she felt she must) to recite at the very first memorial event held publicly to commemorate his death. She would do so again, over the years, whenever she was asked to.

Word had spread that Zohra Segal was back in India, but despite her Doordarshan appearance and Tanvir's and Hashmi's play, the pickings were slender. 'I will go on acting as long as I have the strength and somebody casts me in something,' declared Zohra, but there seemed to be no roles.

Some months would pass before she was approached again, this time by Theatre Royal Stratford East of London for a role specially written for her—an old immigrant woman in a building in the East End of London slated for demolition. *Down Every Street* featured four old women—a Cockney, a Jamaican, an Austrian Jew and an Indian—interviewed by a researcher about their lives and the impending change in their circumstances. The play was a hopeless flop. The combination of documentary and narrative became monotonous, with no interaction between or among the women. The interviewer was stilted, unable to hold viewers' attention. Panned by reviewers, one of whom said it was like flogging a dead horse, the play nevertheless got some genuine appreciation for Zohra's performance; she herself thought it had no tension or conflict—how could it possibly succeed as theatre? No wonder Arnold Wesker, the famous dramatist, who came to see it on opening night, May 18, 1989, left after the interval saying he couldn't take the monotony and 'non-drama' character of the play.

Down Every Street may not have been much but it was wonderful to be onstage in London again, and Zohra was also happy renewing her contacts and meeting friends, all the while living comfortably with Babar and Emma in Hampstead. After the play's run was over on June 17, she moved to her good friend Meenakshi Cherian's (Minnie's) bed-sit near St. James Court Hotel in Westminster. Minnie was Zohra's old dance-mate Simkie's daughter, who had gone to school with Kiran in Bombay. The very next month, July, Zohra was offered a role in a Thames TV series, *The Bill*, in between which she travelled to Coventry to do a TV film for the Royal Society for Prevention of Accidents, about an old-age pensioner whose legs are badly affected by arthritis and by a recent stroke which leaves her with little feeling in her limbs. An accident is inevitable.

This surprise four-month sojourn in England proved to be a great pick-me-up for Zohra. It was a tremendous morale booster, she was in demand by the profession, by family and friends—and she was back in the limelight! Or, if not exactly the limelight, at least in the footlights.

Back in India, towards the end of 1989, her old friend and colleague Ebrahim Alkazi's daughter, Amal Allana, approached Zohra to act in a television serial, *Mullah Nasruddin*, that she was directing for Times Television. Nasruddin is a Sufi mendicant who travels from place to place, hoodwinking corrupt officials and rich businessmen in order to benefit the poor. Nasruddin's escapades are the stuff of folk tales from

China to Mesopotamia, which Allana was to encapsulate in thirteen episodes, set in Turkey and rendered in Urdu. The cast included Raghubir Yadav and the National School of Drama actor Manohar Singh, and was shot in Haryana and Rajasthan over several weeks.

It turned out to be one of the most arduous shoots Zohra had been on, more exhausting than the one-month-long stage appearances she had managed easily with *Down Every Street*. Long drives to Haryana and equally long shoots, often extending till late in the evening without a break or a meal, were more than she had signed up for. Often, there were no chairs for them to sit on or loos for the women to use, and the living arrangements, when necessary, were rudimentary. The production and direction left much to be desired, Zohra felt, but Manohar Singh and Yadav were a pleasure to work with. 'Professionalism, at last!' she said. Of her performance Amal Allana said, 'The impact she made in that small role as a storyteller was tremendous. People wanted to know who she was and from where she'd surfaced...'

It was theatre where Zohra felt she could probably give her best; but theatre in India then was not professional enough, in her opinion, and though she seldom turned down an offer she couldn't reconcile herself to the casual approach that most productions adopted in their work. For her part, she never let up on her daily routine of exercise, yoga and voice projection, for 'The body, as well as the mind, have to be kept polished and ready, alert and alive at all times.'

Her day began with a big mugful of milk with Nescafé ('I hate tea') which was her breakfast. Then one hour of Uday Shankar's movement exercises, followed by Mary Wigman's eurhythmics, and then recitation—34 poems in all, 17 that she recited on the front balcony of her flat, and 17 on the rear balcony. Faiz, Jafri, Iqbal, and two English poems—'Generations' by a Pakistani woman, and 'I Could Have Been' by Brian Langley, which ended with 'If I had lived instead of dreaming/ Who knows what I could have done.' Then the day's crossword puzzle, because 'it enlarges the mind and broadens the vision, apart from enriching one's vocabulary'. In the evening, *The Bold and the Beautiful* or *Santa Barbara*, if they were showing, or cricket! Zohra was a cricketaholic.

Working was important not only because keeping active was basic ('that's why I take up all the assignments I am offered') but because she was supporting a three-generations-of-women household. Kiran's dance school, Pallavi, did bring in a regular income and Zohra herself had her pension from Equity, but there was Sujata, her granddaughter, and her teenage expenses to cover. Zohra couldn't really afford to be without work, nor could she afford to work for free.

Besides, there was some tension now with Kiran, as Zohra strongly disapproved of her relationship with one of her musicians who had become her live-in partner. She worried that Kiran was making the same mistake with him as she had with Jatin, but this time around, the man in question was in the same house as them. Best to move out, she thought. Her repeated requests to the central government for an allotment in the artists' quota at Asiad Village, off August Kranti Marg, had yielded no results. But—serendipity!—she managed to find a flat in Ganga Apartments, down the road from Kiran. Once again, she was happily on her own—she hadn't realised quite how much she missed being mistress of her own time and space. Living alone, cooking and doing everything herself, active and independent. 'Life is lovely!' she declared.

Out of the blue, in 1990, Jill Williams, her agent in London, called to say that there could be a role for her in a Canadian film directed by a young twenty-five-year-old Canadian-Indian, Srinivas Krishna. 'Take it, take it!' cried Zohra, without asking too many questions about the script. The film was a comedy (right up her street) called *Masala*. She was cast as Grandmother Tikkoo (a role that fit her like a glove) and Lord Krishna, the object of her fantasies, was played by none other than Saeed Jaffrey, with whom she had enjoyed acting in the past, most memorably in *Tandoori Nights*.

The film was audacious and quirky, a jumble of stories, and a combination of what the *New York Times* called 'Indian phantasmagoria and Bombay-style movie kitsch', full of improbable subplots. Zohra, as the grandmother, is an avid television junkie, and one of the subplots has her summoning Lord Krishna on the set so that she can engage in a running argument with him. The sheer wackiness of her character who has a hotline to God, allowed Zohra to improvise to her heart's content and to do so at her shocking best. The NRI community in Canada was furious with the film for portraying the Lord in a 'crazy fashion'; and it was withdrawn from the film festival in Bangalore in 1991 for the same reason. Said Zohra, '[Srinivas] Krishna was not too bothered about the outcome of the film—he knew it would raise a controversy.'[2] The young director himself said, '*Masala* is a conscious subversion of genre. The moment we recognise that the plots and subplots are all different stories, and they are all subjective and power-grabs of one kind or another, what is the legitimate story? And what makes sense?'[3] In Toronto, the film grossed more than Steven Spielberg's *Hook*, and went on to win the Samuelson Award in Birmingham for the 'most innovative and original portrayal of contemporary urban life'.

Funnily enough, *Masala* cracked open the possibility of more roles in diaspora films made by the first generation of BritAsian directors in the UK, the most successful of them being Gurinder Chadha, a Kenyan Indian woman in Southall. Before this, however, Zohra teamed up with Madhur Jaffrey (Saeed Jaffrey's ex-wife) in 1991 for a television series, *Firm Friends*, made for Tyne Tees TV (UK), scripted by Lou Wakefield and directed by her partner and lover, Carole Hayman, and first broadcast on ITV on June 16, 1992.

Set in Newcastle, *Firm Friends* is about two women—a middle-class white woman (Rose Gutteridge/Billie Whitelaw) and her cleaning lady (Jayshree Kapoor/Madhur Jaffrey) who start a restaurant because *a*) they like cooking together, and *b*) the white woman's husband has walked out on her, after cleaning out their bank account. Wakefield had worked with Zohra on *The Great Celestial Cow* and knew she wanted her in *Firm Friends*, so wrote a role specifically for her—Suvira Bhatia, the cleaning lady's mother. Lou Wakefield told the producer that Madhur and Zohra were crucial, otherwise they couldn't pull the series off. 'We managed to get Madhur sorted,' Lou said, 'provided she could stay at the Ritz, all expenses paid, and she would choose where I would take her to dinner!' (Zohra, on the other hand, would invite the whole cast home and 'cook up a *storm*'.) But why a mother for the cleaning lady, when the story was really about Whitelaw's and Jaffrey's characters? 'Oh, but it was Zohra!' exclaimed Lou. 'You would wait for her, you were looking for her all the time, and she went down really well.'[4]

Firm Friends was a completely woman-centric series—'although,' said Lou, 'I can't imagine any sane person trying to pitch anything like that, only women, then'—and utterly delightful because it had all the right ingredients. Family, a bit of drama, Indian food (Britain's favourite food at the time), an award-winning actress (Whitelaw) and a world-famous cook (Jaffrey)—and then, the 'secret ingredient', a feisty eighty-year-old who thinks nothing of spicing up the fare. The series had a peak viewership of ten million!

Zohra loved every minute of it. It was a plum role because, as she said, 'Suvira has all the pay-off lines. In a typical scene, Billie and Madhur will have been going on for hours, doing wonderful emotional acting, and then here I come with one line and clinch the scene!'[5] Which, of course, was exactly what Lou Wakefield had in mind: 'Zohra would put in a bit of mischief any time she got a chance, which is why I was writing specifically for her.' By now Zohra had perfected the art of infusing the tiniest of roles or the blandest of lines with energy and her irrepressible in-your-face delivery. It may not always have worked, but in *Firm Friends*, with Carole Hayman's skilful direction and Lou Wakefield's clever scripting, she simply sailed through.

All of a sudden, Zohra found that she was flooded with work, in Delhi as well as in London, and she was rushing to and fro between the two cities for the next couple of years, appearing in plays, television serials and films. Balwant Gargi's *Bua Fatima* for Doordarshan; *Bhaji on the Beach* with Gurinder Chadha; shooting for the second series of *Firm Friends*; 'So much work coming my way at this late age, I tell you, it's marvellous!'[6]

Bua Fatima, a six-episode serial, was commissioned by Doordarshan (at a cost of Rs. 2.5 lakhs per episode), and was set in pre-Partition India. Fatima is a village midwife, loved by Hindus and Muslims alike, and her faith in the goodness of human nature remains undimmed even amid the burning fires of communalism. By refusing to surrender her humanity she becomes the moral force in her community. The series was shot in Mewat, in late 1992, including 6 December, the day the Babri Masjid was torn down in Ayodhya, and the following days, as riots erupted across Uttar Pradesh. After months and years of showing religious epics which, noted Khushwant Singh in his column in the *Hindustan Times*, 'whipped up feelings of communal exclusiveness, Doordarshan realised its folly and tried to make up by commissioning films stressing inter-religious unity'.[7] The story is melodramatic, almost farfetched, but, said Gargi, Zohra 'not only caught onto and absorbed her role immediately, she lent a new dimension to it. She is the only choice I would have made'.[8]

In 1961, when she was one year old, Gurinder Chadha moved from Kenya to Britain with her parents, just before Kenya's independence. She grew up in Southall, where her father first got a job in a post office and later opened a series of shops in the London suburbs of Ealing, Croydon and Walthamstow. Gurinder had the conventional upbringing of a young Sikh girl, which included not being overly ambitious. She decided to confound everyone's expectations and enter the media, rather than join a secretarial course.

In 1990 she set up Umbi Films, her own production company; after training as a news reporter and radio journalist she made her first documentary, *I'm British, But*...which set the tone for what would become her trademark: addressing the mainstream from the vantage point of the margins. Or, as she has said, 'making films about England, but seen through black eyes'. 'I think the reason I have the drive I do,' she continued, 'is ultimately about racism. It's about finding ways to diminish the impact of difference.'[9]

In 1993, Gurinder Chadha burst upon the scene with her first feature film, *Bhaji on the Beach*, a comedy about three generations of British Asian women on a day out in Blackpool. The organiser of the trip, a young BritAsian woman, stands at the front of the bus and says: 'It's not often we women get away from the patriarchal demands made on us in our daily lives, struggling between the double yoke of racism and sexism that we bear. This is your day—have a female-fun time!' *Bhaji* introduced a strikingly attractive newcomer, Sarita Khajuria, in the cast and included the rather better known Kim Vithane (also seen in *Firm Friends*), Tanveer Ghani—and Zohra, as Pushpa, the older woman in the group, racist in ways that only Indians can be.

The film (scripted by Meera Syal) and made in association with Channel 4 at a rumoured budget of £1 million was a huge hit, catapulting it into the kind of commercial success and critical attention that few first films manage to attain. Reviewing it for the *Evening Standard*, Alexander Walker remarked, 'To turn this tale of a seaside outing into such a complex excursion into multi-ethnic manners and make it funny and comprehensive, too, is an uncommon achievement. To make it racially truthful, is a brave one.'[10]

Nikesh Shukla, writing on the 25th anniversary of the film's screening, said, 'In those days, if there was a brown person on television you'd go and call everyone in the house to come and watch… Then *Bhaji on the Beach* arrived and put our community on screen. I remember watching the film curled up on the sofa, with my Mum's feet in my lap. I understood that, at that moment, she was those women on the screen.'[11]

Gurinder Chadha had seen Zohra in *Parosi* as she was growing up, and was reminded of her when she was casting

Pushpa. She contacted Jill Williams to enquire whether Zohra was available and in England; she wasn't, but Chadha decided that she wanted her for the role, regardless.

Gurinder Chadha has said that *Bhaji* 'was a very unorthodox take on Indian womanhood… we don't think of Indian women beyond a certain age as being capable of or eligible for fun. But here was Zohra and her friends doing forbidden fun… I don't think the film would've worked without her feisty personality. She liked to challenge people's perception of Indian women and how they should behave, so she was subversive in her portrayal…' In the scene with the male strippers, for example, when they lift her up and carry her onto the dance floor, Chadha worried that Zohra would take offence. Not at all. 'It was the coolest thing,' exclaimed Zohra, 'we never get to do scenes like this!'

She loved the comedic value of behaving and dressing younger than her age, said Chadha, but 'she was also sensitive to what I was trying to do, to present our lives as we live them. She was very appreciative of the politics of what I was doing.'[12]

And yet, *Bhaji* is one film in which Zohra's over-the-top acting and risqué improvisations begin to jar. Although she had told Chadha to stop her if she thought she was overdoing it ('I want to act, not over-act'), it's evident that Chadha didn't think she was doing so. Indeed, she believed Zohra's improvisations 'worked wonderfully well… she played a racist in the film and she went the whole hog'. Less than that, in this case, might have been better, but in any case, her future appearances in Chadha's films were almost foretold.

A brief return to television with *Little Napoleans*, a drama serial for Channel 4, again with Saeed Jaffrey, and Zohra was ready to go back to Delhi. But only to pack her bags for a four-month sojourn in Pakistan. This trip was special, not only because she would be meeting her siblings again, but because she and Uzra would be onstage together, in an Ajoka Theatre production called *Ek Thi Nani*. She had no idea what to expect. Her emotions swung between intense excitement and a little trepidation—acting with Uzra again, in a play written specifically for them, was an extraordinary development, but acting as an Indian in post-Zia ul Haq Pakistan where plays were performed surreptitiously, gave her some pause. And then, this was not just any old group staging a play, it was Ajoka—statedly political, always pressing against the boundaries, literally, metaphorically and theatrically.

Shahid Nadeem and Madeeha Gauhar's Ajoka Theatre, established in 1984, at the height of Zia ul Haq's thrust towards Islamisation, boldly announced its aim: theatre for social change, in the full knowledge that its path would be strewn with all manner of potentially treacherous obstacles. Public performances in auditoriums were out of the question; private venues were few, afraid of risking their premises and incurring the wrath of the powers-that-be. Government institutions or universities were obviously ruled out. That left the street. Ajoka swiftly made the street its very own space, enacting plays that held up a mirror to the times, performed by an amateur cast that had more than enough conviction to compensate for lack of experience. They swept up the public and curious passers-by into their subversive intent, for their theatre was in full view, and open to all.

Zohra was an old IPTA hand and knew what the pull of the street could do for a performer. But this was Pakistan, unfamiliar territory, she was in the hands of people she didn't know—and she didn't want Uzra to face the music should anything go amiss. Fortunately for her, her 'tour' began in Karachi at the Goethe Institute, with solo performances by her, reciting from the work of well-known poets—Hafiz Jalandhari, Faiz, Iqbal, Kaifi Azmi, Majaz. Her audience sat spellbound as her voice resonated with the lyrical power of the poems she had selected for this visit: Jalandhari's *Abhi to Main Jawan Hoon*; Iqbal's *Naya Shiwala*; Majaz's *Nanhi si Pujaran*; Kaifi Azmi's *Andeshey*; Faiz's *Intesab*. And then, as a kind of signing off, she did an enactment of excerpts from *Bua Fatima* and *Din ke Andhere*. As the shadows descended on the lawns of the Goethe Institute, Zohra gathered her accompanists—her speaking hands and fluently expressive face—into herself and walked off the stage, to thunderous applause. By herself for just a split second before the crowd surged, she heaved a sigh of relief. She had won her audience over.

Of course, the real test would be the reception they got with *Ek Thi Nani*—not only would the sisters be playing opposite each other and enacting a largely true-to-life story, the object of their concern was none other than their real-life grandniece, Samia Mumtaz, their brother Zakkan's granddaughter. A family drama; albeit with a feminist twist.

On April 12, 1993, *Ek Thi Nani* opened at Kinnaird College, Lahore, with the following synopsis:

> There was once a country where people were forced to renounce their history, their culture, their heritage. There was once a society where people had to denounce art, humanity, free-thinking; disallowed to be what they were and forced to be what they were not. There was once a grandmother who was living a double life, suppressing her past and preventing her granddaughter's future. And there was once a 'Nani' who had fought to lead her life, her way, and had paid the price. The house where status quo reigned supreme was thrown into turmoil. No one could resist the irresistible 'Nani' and a 'culture revolution' unfolded.

Uzra was the fastidious and convention-bound Dadi, Zohra the Nani who took the road less travelled and charted her own destiny. Sabeen, Dadi's granddaughter, rebels against the conformity required of her and finds a champion in her Nani, visiting from India. Dadi naturally protests her wayward sister's influence on Sabeen, but the script cleverly introduces an underlying tension within her; like the real-life Uzra, Dadi is haunted by her subconscious, craving a life of creativity, freedom and, yes, abandon—the kind she sees in her sister.

In one stroke *Ek Thi Nani* exposed the hypocrisy of a culture that endorses one set of norms for men and another for women, and struck a blow for freedom of choice and from social mores that militate against spontaneity and individualism. But its barely-concealed subtext was even more subversive: by importing this Nani from India it held a mirror up to Pakistan's own authoritarian control over society and culture; its message rang out, loudly and clearly, to audiences across the country.

The play travelled to Karachi, at the invitation of the activist group Women's Action Forum, where it was performed at the Goethe Institute on April 19 and 20. It was sold out weeks in advance and performed to a rapturous reception, but at least one reviewer slammed its egregious comparison with India. Fatema Kizilbash, writing in the magazine *You*, said:

> The play would have been excellent entertainment if the writer hadn't decided to give expression to his low national esteem… ridiculing and mocking the contempt with which society regards dance, the eminent writer forgets that dance was never a part of Muslim culture in the subcontinent… to an average person it remained strictly associated with the '*Kotha*'.

Like every other reviewer, however, Kizilbash commended Zohra's performance, and in particular the infectious energy she displayed onstage.

Later that evening at her brother Ikram's house, with Amina and Sabra present as well, Zohra relaxed in the warm glow of satisfaction and the affectionate presence of her family. They reminisced in the way siblings do when they meet after a long time, but she realised that the performing arts in Pakistan were up against tremendous odds, and that for someone like her it would be a virtual dead end. She knew what the move had meant for Uzra, and in conversations with the dancer Sheema Kirmani, and with Shahid and Madeeha, she heard first-hand accounts of their experiences with the custodians of culture. And yet, it was Shahid and Madeeha's Ajoka that had taken the initiative to invite her to Pakistan and to write for her and Uzra their play, *Ek Thi Nani*.

It had been an emotionally intense, yet poignant experience for both sisters. Acting together again after forty-five years, but in circumstances so altered and a context so ambivalent, evoked memories and nostalgia not unmixed with a certain sense of loss. Zohra recalled Uzra's real unhappiness during her early years in Pakistan and the absolute restriction on her performing in public; enacting Dadi was like enacting her own experience, and the sharp contrast with Nani only reflected the freedom that Zohra's choices had allowed her. Uzra's later retreat into religiosity and customary observances had always saddened Zohra, so that there was a fair degree of personal conviction in her support of Sabeen in the play. In the end, it was only after Uzra's husband passed away and her children were independent of her, that she could return to acting. Zohra was grateful to Shahid and Madeeha not only for *Ek Thi Nani*, their tribute to the two grande dames of theatre, but for persuading Uzra to join Ajoka—she had been part of the company ever since its inception. Of her own experience with them, and in Pakistan, Zohra said, 'I have never received such adulation, such respect... such standing ovations, ever before. And to think I was a nationalist-minded [Indian] actress in Pakistan.'

Nineteen ninety-three was Zohra's year of travel within India, too, with a production of Aamir Raza Husain's adaptation of *My Fair Lady*. It was sponsored by ITC's Welcome Group Theatre and played in Bangalore, Chennai and Delhi, with Victor Bannerjee as Prof Higgins. Zohra would work with Husain the following year as well, in his mega production *Legend of Ram*, in which she played Manthara. The play was dogged by controversy from the word go. Unlike Gargi who shot *Bua Fatima* in the immediate aftermath of the demolition of the Babri Masjid as a clear statement against communalism, Husain showed the script to L.K. Advani for his clearance, a shocking concession to the man who had personally orchestrated the Rath Yatra to Ayodhya and the destruction of the mosque. Then there was the over-the-top budget, close to one crore rupees; an outdoor location—a barren and rocky stretch of land leased from the Ministry of Urban Development at Rs. 20,000 per day—with nineteen elaborate sets spread over three acres; a 100-member crew, thirty-five character roles, and trolleys that moved on railway tracks to transport the audience from one location to the next. Said Husain, 'We staged the play for 700 people per evening, for months, and performed for about 70,000.'

Unfortunately for him, the production was panned on

every single count—script ('a bald, unilinear concatenation of incidents'—*Times of India*); performance ('uniformly unremarkable' except for 'the amazing energy of Zohra Segal'); costumes ('drab, outlandish outfits'); sets ('the whole thing unfolds mechanically as a series of static tableaux'); and budget ('the sponsors would have done better to have pitched in with this Rs. 70 lakhs for ten good plays'—*Hindustan Times*).

Zohra knew of Husain's tendency to flamboyance, both by reputation and her own experience with *My Fair Lady*, but she was appalled by the sheer unprofessionalism of this production. The row over roles, with Victor Bannerjee wanting Ravana, but getting Ram; the unseemly spat between art critic Kavita Nagpal and Husain, when he tried to get her evicted from the site and was forced to apologise by the Delhi Union of Journalists; the endless rehearsals because actors arrived unprepared or lines were changed at the last minute; and what was inexcusable in her view, the tackiness of the sets. Long before Husain—and with no funds to speak of—Prithviraj Kapoor had devised sets that were not only spectacular but added immeasurably to the theatricality of his productions. Here, in *The Legend of Ram*, they were extravagant but not necessarily appropriate to the story. Perhaps Husain had been overly influenced by the excesses of the television *Ramayana* and *Mahabharata*.

It was with relief and a feeling of happy anticipation then, that Zohra accepted a second tour of *Ek Thi Nani* in Pakistan in 1995, visiting Lahore, Karachi and Islamabad. The next eighteen months were taken up by small roles in a couple of plays by Sohaila Kapur in Delhi, and Pooja Bhatt in Mumbai—*Skirmishes* and *Tamanna*—and then, in 1996, a larger role in the Doordarshan serial *Amma and Family*, with thirty-two episodes. By now she was back with Kiran in Alaknanda, having given her flat in Ganga Apartments to Pavan for him and his family. In the meantime, Sujata had married a young Syrian Christian, Roy Daniels, in 1992; before long both Zohra and Kiran realised that the young man—an ad filmmaker—was physically abusive and well on the way to becoming an alcoholic. Sujata now had a baby daughter, and mother and grandmother, both, were worried about what the future held for her and little Madhyama. In the event, Sujata left her husband in 1993-94, and returned to live with Kiran and Zohra; they were relieved, naturally, but it meant that theirs was now a household of four generations of single women, with Zohra as the primary income earner. Though she loved the theatre and enjoyed the exposure she got from the occasional television serial, there was little money in either.

In 1994, Zohra experienced the kind of setback to her health that she could never have imagined—she was diagnosed with cancer. A large tumour on her leg, the size of a ball, was found to be malignant. The news shattered her. She locked herself in her room and wept bitterly. 'Then,' she told an interviewer ten years later, 'I realised that if I could handle Kameshwar's death, I could handle cancer, too. After all these years I was ready for anything.'[13] She was operated upon and the tumour removed. The minute she regained consciousness she opened one eye and asked the doctor, 'So will I be able to walk again?!' Only half-jokingly. 'Why only walk?' he responded, 'You can dance again!' Years of disciplining her body with exercise and a controlled diet paid off, for she was soon back to normal, and before long, back to work.

In 1997, the feminist press Kali for Women in Delhi published Zohra's autobiography, *Stages: The Art and*

Adventures of Zohra Segal, co-authored by Joan Erdman. Ten years after she had been interviewed by Erdman and had written letters to various members of her family regarding family history, her original manuscript, *The Name-Dropper*, was now out, expanded and reworked, and with a new title. The book was widely reviewed and Zohra herself was interviewed and featured across the media, but she was not well-pleased. As she said to her publisher,

> I spent several years in painstaking research collecting material for *The Name-Dropper*... all that Joan did was to juxtapose the sequence of the chapters when we finally started working on the book in 1989. The additional material is based on interviews, 27 hours of interviews, with me, plus eight new drafts... it is *my* voice and *my* writing...

Zohra minded that Erdman claimed copyright on the material in the book, as well as royalties, which she said should, in all fairness, have been equally shared; she regretted having been persuaded by Erdman to relinquish her rights on both.

Act 4, Scene 2: The Third Bell

To her complete surprise, in October 1996, Zohra received an offer from a company called Mona Lisa Films to appear in their film *Hum Panchhi Ek Daal Ke*, with Aishwarya Rai and Suniel Shetty, for a fee of Rs. 15,000 per day. Well, it wasn't much, but it was a toehold in Bollywood, so Zohra accepted. Although the projected schedule was a ten- or twelve-day shoot, she shot only four days so was paid Rs. 60,000.

Within six months of *Hum Panhchi*..., Zohra was hired for a joint production between Vijayta Films in Bombay and Gurinder Chadha's Umbi Films to play the role of Dadiji in a feature film, *London*, co-directed by Chadha and Raheel Rawail, starring Sunny Deol, Bobby Deol and Karishma Kapoor, and her old friend Saeed Jaffrey. Lyrics by Gulzar, music by Vishal Bhardwaj, costumes by the then young designer Manish Malhotra. This time, Zohra's fee was Rs. 3 lakhs.

London was shot in London from July through September 1997, during which time Zohra filmed for approximately twenty days. Working with two directors on a film was a new experience for her, but Gurinder and Saeed were old friends and Sunny Deol (who, it appeared, was the man behind Vijayta Films) had indicated that *London* would have a Hindi adaptation called *Dillagi* to be directed by him! All in a day's work, thought Zohra.

While in London, she received a script from the producer-director Sanjay Leela Bhansali for his film-without-a-title, which later became *Hum Dil De Chuke Sanam*, but before that released she would appear in Mani Ratnam's *Dil Se*, and sign a contract with Vijay Productions for *Chalo Ishq Ladayen*. Zohra was going to be rushed off her feet trying to juggle shooting schedules, but she wrote to Dolly Thakore anyway, asking her to co-ordinate with Jill Williams in London as she was fielding possible offers for Zohra there!

In all these films Zohra was the grandmother (the universal Dadi, she used to say), a role she could probably perform with her eyes closed, but each story and each director had a different take on her character, and then of course, she introduced her own improvisations. Of her growing presence on the silver screen in India she would always say, 'Eight years with Dada, fourteen years with Papaji, but no one knew my name till I slapped Govinda!' (in *Chalo Ishq Ladayen*). She respected Mani Ratnam and, in *Dil Se*, the cast, too—Shah Rukh Khan, Manisha Koirala, Preity Zinta, Raghuvir Yadav—was competent. But filmmaking in India, or at any rate, in Bombay, was far removed from what she had known in England, with last-minute changes, shooting days reduced, actors arriving unprepared, fudging their lines because the dialogues would be dubbed later—she said later, of an actor she worked with, that she had studied the script for his role, memorised her lines but '*Woh ladka, woh bolta hi nahin! Aake mere kaan mein phus-phus kar jaye. Toh maine usko daant diya, ki kuch toh emote karo, kuch bolo* (That boy, he wouldn't speak! He'd come and he'd just whisper in my ear. So I gave him a scolding—emote a little, speak your lines)—after all,

I have to react to you!'[1] The professional in Zohra disliked this anything-goes attitude, but even she could not complain when the box office takings were so high—*Dil Se*, made on a budget of Rs. 11 crores, netted Rs. 28.5 crores; *Hum Dil De Chuke Sanam* (with Salman Khan, Aishwarya Rai and Ajay Devgun) with a budget of Rs. 16 crores, made a whopping Rs. 51.4 crores, and went on to win the Best Film, Best Director and Best Actress awards at the 45th Filmfare Awards.

Meanwhile, *Ek Thi Nani* had clearly won the hearts of Pakistanis for she was in Karachi and Lahore yet again, with Ajoka, for two weeks in March 1999. Its India tour, however, was cancelled, much to Zohra's disappointment, largely because of trouble on the border; but Kiran had taken her whole troupe up to Kargil that August and danced at a height of 11,000 ft., with shells falling all around the open-air stage! Zohra's heart swelled with pride at Kiran's courageous and admirable decision. A month with Pavan and his family who were now in Zimbabwe was delightful and just the break she needed, after a very satisfying run in July with *Ek Thi Nani* at the Bloomsbury Theatre in London.

In October 2000, when she was eighty-eight years old, Zohra wrote to Jill Williams to say that she had been offered a role in a new Ivory-Merchant production, a film of V.S. Naipaul's *The Mystic Masseur*, to be shot in Trinidad in January–February 2001. She would accept, she wrote, but

> This is the third time I am working with Ismail Merchant and each time I have found him to be close-fisted… This Trinidad contract adds up to only $4000 including the 10 days' per diem [compared to the US$5000 per week she had been paid for *Masala*]… However, I am content with the arrangements as I shall visit a new country and meet my actress friend, Barbara Assoon, in Port of Spain.[2]

Assoon had acted with Zohra in *Down Every Street*, and she would again in *Masseur*. Zohra would be working together with Om Puri, too, who had been with her in *Jewel in the Crown*, and with young Ayesha Dharker, who had acted with her in *Manika, Manika*. Zohra had already read Naipaul's novel and was now waiting for the script. She would be playing the Auntie in the film.

Merchant's reputation for pulling tight the purse-strings was apparently on full display during the filming; Om Puri (who played the storekeeper, Ram Logan) said there were only six chairs available to sit on for sixty people, and that lunch on the sets was rice and chicken curry, a few local vegetables, and a slice of currant cake. The producers had hoped to make the film on a budget of $3 million, assuming that Trinidad would be like Bombay. As it turned out, the locals would demand to be paid not just to come on as extras, but be paid to leave the set![3]

By mid-January 2001, Zohra was in Port of Spain sharing a lovely bungalow-flat with Ayesha, but as she had four weeks between her shoots—four days in the first week of January, and a final shoot in the first week of February—she was hoping to spend the intervening time in London, provided Merchant–Ivory paid for her stay. They had already drastically truncated her role, cut out all the amusing bits, so she had no idea what the end result would be. Well, the end result had a tepid reception, with one reviewer calling the film 'a limp though not dislikeable affair'.[4] Zohra herself certainly felt that better use could have been made of her comic potential.

In June, she was back in London, this time for *An Evening with Zohra Segal* with Jon Harris, Director of Stratford Circus, East London's centre for all performing arts. Club class travel, five nights in London, a one-on-one conversation, and a fee of £1000! While she was at it, she also appeared in *This Is Your Life: a tribute to Saeed Jaffrey*, something she was more than happy to do for her friend. And then, when she was least expecting another offer of a film role, she was hired to play Naanima in *Anita and Me*, based on Meera Syal's highly successful novel of the same name.

The film is a 1970s nostalgia trip, based on Syal's own upbringing in Staffordshire, about a young Punjabi girl's coming of age in the West Midlands. It received the kind of indulgent reviews reserved for voices from the margins, but did surprisingly well at the box office. Within one month of opening in cinemas across the UK it had earned £1,753,880; and on October 15, 2001, Jill Williams sent Zohra a cheque for £4,492, being the final amount due to her for *Anita and Me* and the programme for Stratford Circus.

In London that August, Zohra had met David Abel, a Canadian, and executive producer of the Canadian theatre company CanStage, Canada's largest contemporary theatre. She now received a script from him, *Rice Boy*, written by a young Canadian-Indian, Sunil Kuruvilla, which interested her immensely; the play, she said, was 'very profound in its message, using crisp, concise dialogue, in a novel presentation'. She was keen to accept, she told Jill Williams, even though the fee offered was minimal, but admitted that she hadn't written to Abel directly because she didn't know whether she would 'still be around in March 2003!'[5] The projected dates for the show were March 3 to April 10, 2003.

Well, she was very much around in 2003 and spent a most enjoyable month in Toronto, cracking jokes with the rest of the mostly Asian cast and making them laugh at her 'atrocious remarks'. In Micheline Chévrier, the director, she found the kind of fine sensibility that in her experience made for the best theatre.[6]

In India, between films or the stage, Zohra also made several ad films for, among others, Cadbury's chocolates, Titan watches, Gobain glass, Widex Hearing Aids, Mirinda Cold Drinks and Pepsi Leher, for fees ranging from one to ten lakh rupees, depending on her role. But much more fun than the ad films was her guest appearance at the launch of a book, *Bollywood—the Popular Indian Cinema*, in Bombay, in September 2002, that showed a clip from a yet-to-be-released-film in which she appears. At her cue, Zohra zoomed onto the stage, clinging onto a young man on a motorbike who wove through the tables seating 700 assembled guests, before depositing her on the stage. She pocketed a cool Rs. 10,000 for this caper!

Back in Delhi, she participated in workshops conducted by theatre director Royston Abel, who had been commissioned by the Embassy of the Netherlands to produce a play based on *The Diary of Anne Frank*. He declined, as he said he didn't adapt, only worked on an original script; and so he devised a play based on the post-Godhra communal violence in Gujarat in February 2002 and called it *The Spirit of Anne Frank*. Zohra was afraid it would be censored because of its content, but in fact Abel produced a powerful, and powerfully acted, play with Zohra, Shabana Azmi and Nandita Das as an ensemble cast. Five women in a train compartment, threatened with imminent violence, and their individual responses to the threat. It opened to a very good response in December 2002 in Delhi, and was a success elsewhere too, with full houses and standing ovations in Ahmedabad, Kolkata and Bangalore.

The decade of the 2000s coincided with Zohra in her nineties, which were probably her busiest and most lucrative years.

Theatre, films, television serials, commercials, one-woman shows, poetry recitations—she was whizzing around the country at top speed, frantically adjusting shooting schedules, personal appearances, and travel abroad. The only concession she made to her age was to ask for a wheelchair at airports—not because she couldn't walk, but because it saved her standing around in queues!

In 2001-2002, she worked with Gurinder Chadha once again in what would be Chadha's most successful film, *Bend It Like Beckham*, about a young Sikh girl's passion for football and her determination to pursue her love of it. Her parents (Anupam Kher and Shaheen Khan) forbid her, but unbeknownst to them, she joins an all-women team and makes it to the top. The film hit all the right spots: sport, a Gen-Next BritAsian woman overcoming stereotypes, and good rollicking fun. Good film-making, too. It became the highest grossing sports film ever, raking in $76.6 million at the box office; and Jamie Russell at BBC said, 'Mr Beckham ought to be proud to have his name on such a great film.'

Zohra's role in *Beckham* was tiny, but her association with Chadha and the film's phenomenal success were a bonus. Still, a year later when Gurinder Chadha asked her for a one-day shoot in her film *Bride and Prejudice*, she declined—the company did not agree to her fee of £1500 per day. 'Gurinder got all high and mighty', wrote Zohra to Jill Williams, 'saying "Zohra shouldn't forget it was I who raised her film career", to which Zohra retorted, 'She forgets that it was *Jewel in the Crown* which gave me my first break in 1982, and the first film I acted in in 1946 (Chetan Anand's *Neecha Nagar*) went to the Cannes Film Festival and won the Grand Prix—Gurinder wasn't even born then!'[7]

In any case, 2003 was so busy that she hardly had time

to catch her breath. Two shows of *Ek Thi Nani* with Uzra in Delhi, in August, before which she had participated in The Other Festival in Chennai, where she recited eleven poems from Urdu, all of which had to be translated into English in order to obtain police permission! And then, a spate of film shoots. *Saya*, directed by Anurag Basu and produced by Mahesh Bhatt, for which she was paid Rs. 4 lakhs; followed by *Veer Zara* from Yashraj Films (Rs. 3 lakhs); and then Karan Johar's *Kal Ho Naa Ho* directed by Nikhil Advani, with a star-studded cast: Shahrukh Khan, Preity Zinta, Saif Ali Khan, Jaya Bachchan but, as Zohra acknowledged ruefully, 'I got a gob of egg on my face' because her entire role in the film was deleted. One week before the film released Johar called her to apologise, saying the film had become too long. Zohra was most upset, having shot for four full days (and been paid) and 'to rub salt on my wounds' she wrote to Jill, 'this very film has become a smashing hit!'[8] In fact, *Kal Ho Naa Ho* was the highest grossing film of 2003.

However, the sweetest recognition came Zohra's way in December 2003, when Thespo Five, a theatre outfit started by Qasar Padamsee—Dolly Thakore and Alyque Padamsee's son—gave Zohra their Lifetime Achievement Award. An award from a group of young actors and theatre-lovers was especially precious as it proceeded from an un-jaded, uncompetitive and un-cynical appreciation of her work. She loved the enthusiasm of these young thespians.

A most unusual offer came her way in early 2004—three days of shooting in a film on 1857, the first war of Indian independence, called *The Rising*. Produced by Maya Films, it was a modest production and her fee was equally modest, but she recalled what her Uncle Memphis had told her about their ancestors' role in the great uprising, and felt an odd sort of connection with them in her role.

Seven Spice Productions, an Indian production company in Preston, England, signed a contract with Zohra early in 2004 for a role in their forthcoming film, *Chicken Tikka Masala*, to be directed by Harmage Kalirai. It was an unusual script written by Roopesh Parekh, an eighteen-year-old, about a gay couple whose relationship is threatened by a conventional arranged marriage. Kalirai was a Lancashire lad, keen to set his first feature film in his hometown. As usual, Zohra would play the Punjabi Dadi, the film would be shot in Manchester over a two/three-week period in April-May 2004, and she would be paid £10,000 for her appearance. Her old friends Jamila Massey and Saeed Jaffrey were also part of the cast.

Zohra arrived in London on April 23, 2004, from where she proceeded to Manchester but, much to her surprise, was not met by anyone from Seven Spices at either destination. She was taken by a young volunteer and deposited in a barren sort of building where she was accommodated in a single room with a camp bed, a tiny shower, no toilet paper, no water, and no arrangement for meals! This was most reprehensible on the part of the producers, and she felt cross and miserable. The next day she informed Sanjay Tandon, the producer, that she had spent a most uncomfortable night alone in her room, and asked to be moved to a hotel. Fortunately for her, Jamila was arriving a week later so she could use her room, but before that Sanjay had done her proud on April 27, her 92nd birthday—'a huge bouquet given to me on location, chocolate cake at lunch, a Ganesh statue at tea, and a sumptuous dinner with a second HUGE cake!'[9] All was forgiven.

She filmed for twenty-seven days with Saeed ('pissed most of the time') and Jamila, and on May 18, left to be with her cousin Afreen in Prestwick, which was her real break. She slept till 9:30 a.m., woke up for her coffee, did an hour's mandatory exercise, wrote letters, ate a light lunch, slept again till 4:00 p.m. After a bath and short walk she waited for Afreen's return from work, followed by a delicious dinner and gossip! Two-and-a-half weeks with Afreen and another short visit to relatives in Stoke-on-Trent, after which Zohra arrived in London to spend some time with Jill Williams and her husband George in their house at Primrose Hill.

London was almost home. And Jill and George were almost family. Jill always organised a small party for her when she visited, so that she could meet her friends in one place without having to travel across town to do so. This time, too, Jill arranged a get-together in her garden and invited the writer Kit Williams and his wife Eleyne, Renu Setna, Jamila and Reginald Massey, Mini Cherian, Zohra's nephew Babar and his wife, Emma, and Walter, her former son-in-law. It was a wholly enjoyable, warm and relaxed evening.

On a subsequent evening, however, at around five-thirty or so, Zohra put her head around the door of Jill's home-office to say she was going for a walk. Wait for a bit, said Jill, and I'll come with you. No, no, she replied, I'll be fine, it's just a short walk. An hour later Jill closed her office, and half an hour after that George returned home—but no Zohra. Jill walked up to Primrose Hill, thinking Zohra would be sitting on one of the benches in the sun, but no, there was no sign of her. Three hours later and really worried now, Jill called the local hospital A & E, asking if an elderly Indian woman had been brought in. No. Jill was beside herself with worry—how could she possibly explain to Kiran what had happened? Tell the world that Zohra had gone missing on Jill's watch?

Then, three and a half hours later, the key clicked in the lock and in walked Zohra. 'Zohra, thank god you're back, where have you been? We've been so worried!' Well, Zohra had left their house, walked along the road to Belsize Park, all the way up Haverstock Hill, practically to Hampstead, to one of her favourite Indian restaurants, and asked if they had any of her favourite hottest chillies to take home to Jill's place! Of course, they all knew her at the restaurant so she sat down, they gave her tea and things to nibble, and she chatted and made them all laugh, and then she walked all the way back![10] 'You shouldn't have worried,' said the incorrigible Zohra, 'this is London and I know my way around!'

Back in Delhi after her three months in the UK, Zohra wrote to Jill in July to say,

> I am again caught up in a whirl of activity. Flying to Bombay for four days on the 4th of August to shoot a Girl Guides documentary. Then a press conference on 20th August for the hearing aid people, plus 2 photo shoots... I have already attended two book launches, and on 10th October I am launching a CD for a singer poetess in which I will have recorded 2 poems by next week. On 25th October I fly to Amritsar for *Ek Thi Nani*...back to Delhi with my sister, then on to Bombay to perform the same play with Uzra at Prithvi.[11]

As she was only ninety-two years old it wasn't such a hectic schedule, after all. Exactly one year later, in July 2005, she was back in England shooting for Gurinder Chadha's *The Mistress of Spices*, travelling to Leicester, Manchester, London, and to her relatives in Stoke-on-Trent. Chitra Divakaruni Banerjee's novel (on which the film was based), an exotic and unlikely story about the magical attributes of spices—sandalwood to dispel painful memories, black cumin to protect against the evil eye—didn't quite work as a book and worked even less as a film, despite Aishwarya Rai in the lead role as the mistress of spices. Zohra was not a granny this time but a First Mother, who warns Rai about the imperative of obeying all the rules by which mistresses of spices must abide. Rai flouts the rules with the inevitable consequences. The film received mostly negative notices with the *Guardian* asking about Rai '…is there a wishier, washier, wimpier actor anywhere in the known universe, wafting and simpering through yet another film?' Box office takings were a low $1,337,846, Zohra declared that it had 'bombed miserably', but she still got more than her guaranteed minimum payment of £2000. Plus, she and Kiran had enjoyed the shooting in Cochin, staying in idyllic surroundings near the beach.

Soon after her return to Delhi, she received an award from the President of India, the fellowship of the Sangeet Natak Akademi. Irrepressible, Zohra wrote to Dolly Thakore to say she was 'looking forward to the day (August 26) when the President will change my sex and make me a 'Fellow' of the SNA. Surely they could have changed it to 'FILLY'!'[12]

That September she was operated upon for cataracts in both eyes, and the following year, in January 2006, was admitted to Escorts Hospital for knee surgery. A long recuperation followed: she thought she should let Dolly know that she would be unavailable for work, 'as I know you have great difficulty in keeping Hollywood directors off my skin!' Come April, and she was back in harness.

In a letter to Jill Williams in 2006 Zohra wrote, 'I am loaded with money… have never seen so much in my life! My accountant tells me that I have earned nearly Rs. 75,00,000 this year, which works out to nearly £100,000!… The older and uglier and shakier I get, the more they want me in Bombay! I am thrilled to bits!'[13]

Two thousand six would be the last year that Zohra acted in Bollywood, her two main roles being with Amitabh Bachchan and Tabu in *Cheeni Kum*, and with Ranbir Kapoor, Rani Mukherjee and Sonam Kapoor in *Saanwariya*. In the former, Amitabh is a master chef in a restaurant in London, famous for its biryani and other Hyderabadi delicacies. Tabu is a pretty good cook herself, and tells the cooks at Amitabh's restaurant that their biryani isn't up to scratch. That bothers the maestro and he challenges her to improve on his recipe; she does, and the story unfolds more or less predicably. Zohra is Amitabh's feisty mother who can't understand why he prefers bachelorhood to a companionate life. Then he falls in love with Tabu who is half his age, and sets things aflutter.

On April 27, Zohra's birthday, she was at an early morning shoot for the film at Delhi's Qutub Minar. Amitabh greeted her with roses on the set, having already sent her a bottle of champagne with a letter to say 'how wonderful it has been working with you—your unflinching energy is a great inspiration to all us youngsters'. Well, that was a lovely gesture, the champagne would be popped that evening when everyone gathered to celebrate—but the best present of all was Sujata's surprise visit from Bombay! Flowers, presents, a grand feast in a restaurant with the whole family. 'I THINK IT WAS ONE OF MY HAPPIEST BIRTHDAYS,' she gushed in a letter to Jill written in capital letters, 'My 94th!'

Guest appearances in two productions—a staging of William Dalrymple's book *City of Djinns*, and a documentary on Bhagat Singh directed by Gauhar Raza—plus a couple of ad films and her recitations of poems kept Zohra busy the next couple of years, so that by the time her 98th birthday came around she thought she could now retire. But then her dear friend Indira Joshi came to visit from London, and told her that she was going to meet the Karmapa, the young head of the Karma Kagyu, to get his blessings. Curious, Zohra began reading the book on Buddhism that Indira had brought with her, and announced that she would accompany her on her visit. They arrived at the hotel where the Karmapa was staying and found that they were an audience of two!

The Karmapa entered the room and asked what he could do for them. Zohra said, 'I'm so old, I don't know what I can ask you for,' and when one of the monks asked if she wanted to be blessed by him, she replied, 'No, no, I being old, I will bless him. He's very young.' The Karmapa graciously accepted.

On the way back in the cab, she said to Indira, 'You know, it is actually quite extraordinary because I had made up my mind, before we went to see the Karmapa, that now that I am 98, perhaps I should retire. But after I saw him, and as I was walking out, I heard a voice in my heart saying, "Not yet".'[16]

And so she carried on.

Curtain Call

In 1992, when Zohra was eighty, she told a young journalist:

> It is not easy to evaluate a lifetime's work... I feel that my only contribution is that I might have inspired some people to do what they most wanted to do...
>
> Dedication is essential... seriousness and devotion are imperative. You cannot flirt with either acting or dancing... you have got to be a professional, you cannot cheat or pretend—it shows.[1]

In 1930, when Zohra was eighteen and zoomed across the Continent in a souped-up car, nothing could have been further from her mind than dedication, devotion and seriousness. Then, it was all impulse and adventure; she wanted to see the world, to enjoy herself, to experience the unexpected and exciting, to escape from the conventional. Above all, she knew she didn't want to get married.

She knew, too, that she was a child of privilege, able to indulge her fancy because her circumstances and her liberal, cosmopolitan upbringing allowed her to defy convention. No young woman from her background would have been left alone in Europe, unchaperoned, to pursue a choice arrived at by fluke—dance! She had never danced in her life, and at eighteen was too old to begin training in a classical form. So it had to be movement and eurhythmics, which is what she studied at the Mary Wigman school. No young woman, then, would have been encouraged to develop her inclination further by joining the troupe of a dancer who, although famous for his creativity, was already notorious for his bohemian lifestyle. And few, very few, young Muslim women would have had the confidence to marry a Hindu man much younger than them, against parental approval—but by then, living an unconventional life had become Zohra's signature.

For all that one might think that hers was a life crowded with serendipitous events, look closely and you realise that at every stage she carved out her own path, making the most of the small, mixed opportunities that came her way. She might well have said, 'You cannot flirt with life.'

In Europe, Zohra met a variety of men socially: '[I] fell in love, had crushes on men, and men were interested in me—all this would have been impossible for me in India.'[2] She discovered the splendours of the world through travel, and the exhilaration, the sheer artistry of what she could do with her body through dance. She cultivated both passions assiduously, and the joy she derived from them remained with her for the rest of her life. At the Wigman school, she understood the importance of discipline, of the daily routine of exercise and repetition, and had her first lessons in what she later extolled: seriousness of purpose. Stretching the body to its limits, recognising that her body was her medium, her means of communicating, her key to increasing self-awareness and to nurturing her individuality. Dancing with Uday Shankar she realised its glorious potential, and the intoxication of the stage—footlights, applause, recognition. As part of his troupe, she could indulge both her love of travel and her love of dance.

At the Almora Dance Academy, she discovered a new love, the love of teaching, where she could finally put her pedagogic diploma to use. She excelled at it, and when she left Almora for Lahore she chose to start a school of dance rather than continue to perform. The offer to be dance choreographer at Prithvi Theatres gave her an opportunity to teach as well as to create, even though she herself did not dance on stage. By a happy coincidence she taught again, briefly, at Ram Gopal's school in London, but she admitted many years later that she had been 'too lazy to take on the entire responsibility of teaching or directing my own pupils according to my convictions and experience'.[3]

Zohra was an accidental actor. As she said repeatedly, she had neither the face nor the figure for playing a heroine, so it is no surprise that she was never cast as one. 'My face is like Ho Chi Minh's,' she once joked, 'and my profile resembles that of Alfred Hitchock.' Yet, she made her name as an actress. Hitchock and Ho Chi Minh she could deal with, but Uzra as leading lady in Prithvi Theatres was another matter. Zohra adored her younger sister, but as they were both with the company incipient rivalry could not be ruled out. 'Uzra was the beauty of the family', she told reporters in Lahore 'and I was wildly jealous of her, but I wasn't about to give up without a fight! I exercised madly and set out to cultivate my charm till everyone thought I was beautiful. Plus, I could act.'[4]

As a dancer in Uday Shankar's Company, Zohra's looks had never been a consideration. His productions usually called for ensemble performances, and on the few occasions that she danced a duet her partner was always male—Uday Shankar himself or Kameshwar. Now on stage with Prithvi Theatres, with actors like Indumati, Uzra, Shaukat Azmi, Pushpa and others, she realised she would need to focus on her strengths and hone her acting skills, and do so assiduously. Fortunately, for her, she discovered that she loved to act almost as much as, if not more than, she had loved to dance. It marked a turning point in her development as an artiste.

The fourteen years in Bombay, and with Prithviraj Kapoor and Prithvi Theatres, were possibly the happiest in Zohra's life, professionally. She was living in a community of artistes—filmmakers, actors, writers, journalists—all of whom were pressing against the boundaries of their chosen vocations, furiously experimenting and creating, intervening energetically in the social and political churning taking place in the country. In IPTA, for the first time, she was part of theatre for the common person, performed in neighbourhoods and at street corners, accessible to everyone. This was theatre with a specific purpose, communicating a progressive, political message. It was new for her. Uday Shankar had been radical in his own way, a creative powerhouse, but politically, more or less disengaged. IPTA's productions brought her face to face with social realities that, in the years preceding independence, had begun to stir the national conscience.

Prithviraj's theatre for social change, theatre with which he sought to cover the length and breadth of the country, complemented what Zohra experienced at IPTA; but here, the scope for enhancing her potential was far greater, as theatre was the primary purpose of the Company. It was at Prithvi, and through Prithviraj, that she understood what dedication to a vocation implied and entailed. That understanding was foundational. As she toured with the Company and carefully observed Prithviraj's charisma, his apparently effortless skill in drawing people out—actors, audiences, stagehands, children—

she realised that in order to communicate effectively you had to shed your ego, cultivate the common touch.

IPTA, the Progressive Writers' Movement, Prithvi Theatres were at the cusp of change in the decade just prior to Independence and the decade after. This period saw an explosion of innovation in the arts, architecture and cinema. Uday Shankar had already introduced the modern in his choreography and his compositions, and Zohra collaborated actively with him in many of his productions. She did little of that at Prithvi, but her years with the Company convinced her that acting was her life. She owed this awakening to Prithviraj Kapoor. 'I am in love with acting,' she was to say later, 'I do not think I can survive without it.'[5]

Kameshwar died in 1959, Prithvi Theatres closed down, and Zohra stopped acting. For three years she lived in a kind of suspended animation, bereft of all the resources, relationships and activities that had sustained her. Kameshwar's death, the more or less simultaneous closure of Prithvi Theatres and Uzra's final departure for Pakistan marked the kind of turning point in her life from which there would be no going back. A subtle transformation was taking place within her—she realised that the only skills she had were dancing and acting, and that, thus far, she had simply, and conveniently, attached herself first to one celebrated artiste and then another, 'basking in their glory'. She was on her own now, single, the sole breadwinner, not just for the time being but for the foreseeable future. And she was forty-eight years old, with two very young children to look after. A stock-taking was necessary.

Yes, she had been with Prithvi Theatres for fourteen years and acted in all their productions, but she was aware that she had no formal training at all. Looking and learning from Prithviraj Kapoor—who readily admitted that he was not qualified to teach anyone how to act—was sufficient for the kind of theatre they were doing; but she knew intuitively that for her to make acting her career she needed to be more professional. Hence the British Drama League.

There was nothing impulsive about her decision to seek work as an actor in England, just a practical reckoning that any experience gained on the London stage—should it come her way—could only be to her advantage. She needed to work as an actor, but also to earn a living, and so she arrived at the second critical decision in her current situation: she would take whatever she was offered with regard to both. She would suppress her ego as an actor; and as an individual, relegate her aristocratic lineage to the background. She would, in a manner of speaking, make herself over. Acquire a persona. Present another face to the world. A dresser at the Old Vic, a glorified ayah? Why not? No one knew who she was in London and, looking on the bright side, she could see as many plays as she liked at the Old Vic. A seamstress at Pettits? A new skill. Managress at the Tea Centre? The better to entertain her friends and co-workers at the BBC with. Waiting for her luck to turn, recalling, at every low point, Kameshwar's adage: 'If you don't mind, it doesn't matter.'

In the beginning all her roles were fillers, her screen presence often no longer than a few minutes. Producers would send their scripts to agents with a breakdown of the characters, and if the agents had clients who seemed to fit the roles they would send their details on and hope they were called for an interview. 'With Zohra, people came to us because they wanted Zohra,' said Jill Williams, 'and I don't remember her ever turning down a job.'

Zohra told Roshan Seth, 'I'm more than fully aware of my shortcomings.' But she persevered. 'I didn't,' said Roshan.

'I gave up, returned to India, she didn't.'[6] Madhur Jaffrey, too, gave up her acting career for want of good roles and developed as a TV personality, focussing on food. Rani Dube moved into production, Jamila Massey slowly branched out into writing, and Indira Joshi retired early. Zohra waited. Used her voice initially to good advantage on BBC's 'English by Radio', 'Look, Listen, Speak' and 'Make Yourself at Home.' She accepted bit parts whenever an offer came her way, made herself available, kept her body in trim. Her mantra:

> Eat a good diet.
> Do all things in moderation.
> Exercise every morning.
> Keep happy.

The roles she got were like that of the Ayah in the Kipling series—and that, too (as she told her cousin Muneeza Shamsie), 'because Waris Hussein stood by me'—but she didn't discriminate (unlike other Indian actors in London at the time) because, as Roshan Seth said, 'to discriminate was a luxury, and she didn't have that. She never turned anything down—she needed the money, she needed the work, she needed to be seen'.[7]

She needed to be seen, and to be seen by as many people as possible, for which television was the perfect medium. She loved theatre, believed that the best training for an actor is the stage, and always maintained that '[the] stage is like a sari, the TV screen like a rumaal. You can make a rumaal out of a sari, but not the other way around.'[8] But she also knew that television was far more likely to have an opening for her than the West End, and also likely to be much better paid.

Through the hard times that continued for several years and gave little indication that they would end soon, or for long, Zohra never looked back or retraced her steps. 'It was a kind of one-way street,' recalled her nephew Babar, 'because she had burnt her bridges. She never dwelt on her adversity.'[9] Indeed, adversity, it almost seemed, brought out the best in her. Although she herself thought she was bad-tempered, selfish and impatient, no one (other than her children, obviously) ever recalled her being so, on any occasion. The Zohra they saw, knew and worked with was never disparaging or judgemental, was always game—'creatively lovable', in Dolly Thakore's words, and 'life-enhancing', in Jill Williams' opinion. In England, in a social environment that was never completely home to her, working in a field characterised by competitiveness, rivalry and professional jealousies, a field, moreover, where a subtle racism was never far from the surface, Zohra developed the habit of stiff-upper-lip-with-a-smile. She activated her personal and professional relationships by deploying that famous charm of hers, differently with different people, but always with warmth and a genuineness that was immediately reciprocated. 'It is a fact that I had to fight my looks,' she told a young reporter. 'To overcome my ugliness, I have made myself a charming woman.'[10] Madhav Sharma recounted the following as an example of Zohra's effect on most people:

> I remember going to see one of the brothers of the dance company of the Kumar brothers—Uday? Ram?—the third one who was living with Sir John Gielgud, who was gay... I went to see Sir John about something and this brother was there, and I said to him, 'Oh, and Zohra Segal is coming,' and his face just lit up. Everybody has that reaction to Zohra, everybody. I've never met anyone who hasn't liked her.[11]

More than her charm and gregariousness, however, was her spontaneous interest in people, and her compassion.

> 'When Mum died,' said Renu Setna, 'Zohra literally dropped everything and came over to offer her condolences, to comfort the family as best she could...she sat with us, talked to us, nothing specific, you know, it was just the manner in which she spoke, made us feel good, made us comfortable, made us feel, well, it's part of life...[12]

These qualities of truth and heart that were also her qualities as an actress—'she had so much passion, so much energy, so much feeling,' said Roshan Seth—communicated wonderfully well on television, and it was here that she found her audiences, as well as, in time, recognition. She found her métier.

As she had with Uday Shankar and Prithviraj Kapoor, both of whom innovated and forged an idiom that was ahead of its time, now in England, Zohra partook of another kind of novelty—the emergence of the BritAsian in the arts, and as an audience. This audience warmed to her screen personality, felt a kinship and empathised with her as they would with their own older relatives. 'She'd make the characters 'real' with her natural joie de vivre, her love of life and people, and would always bring a sense of humour...' said Sharma, 'when Zohra bursts into laughter it's like the sun coming out after a very dark winter.'

With rare exceptions—*Jewel in the Crown*, *Firm Friends*, her early films—Zohra was cast as what Jill Williams called the 'funny granny', and it was a role she made her own. In a way, a nani's or dadi's personality and place in Indian families almost comes ready-made; what Zohra did was to give it an added twist: she improvised. Often, dialogues were bland or boring or in broken English, and roles could be skimpy. She made something of them, regardless, even if it was only to add gibberish Bambaiyya lingo to the twinkle in her eye. Rather her own nonsense than the Peter Sellers accents that directors often wanted. Not only did Zohra speak a cultured English, she defied every stereotype of the Indian woman in films by keeping a bottle of Scotch near at hand, happily tippling as she watched her favourite Hindi films on television.

'She was a great comedic actor,' said Lou Wakefield, who scripted *Firm Friends*, 'if you can do comedy, you can do straight.' Comedy, and playing—or, rather, hamming—the irascible older woman became Zohra's signature, with roles being written for her. 'She always followed the brief,' said Gurinder Chadha, 'but also kept the balance between making a character believable and infusing the role with mischief.' This may have worked to her disadvantage, because as time went on, she acted in fewer and fewer serious roles where the range of her skill and ability would have had freer play. 'She should have been in the National,' maintains Madhav Sharma, and adds:

> ...in the RSC, she could have played all the mothers, the nurse in *Romeo and Juliet*—she would have been fantastic. She could have developed into a wonderful character actress...
>
> Zohra's career didn't reach the heights it should have done here [London] because she was doing stuff which was in a very infant stage of Asian theatre... so the plays weren't always very good, but *she* was always excellent in everything... I compare her to Dame Sybil Thorndke, she should have had that kind of status in this country, and the only reason she hasn't got it is because she's dark-skinned.[13]

Professionalism was an article of faith for Zohra and it stood her in very good stead in relation to others who malingered. She learnt her lines, arrived on the dot of time, could still come up with the goods well into her late nineties. She might not have had the same stamina or energy as before but she had the discipline, and there was no compromising on that.

> When I am given a script I first read it thoroughly, then see what my role is about, the scenes I appear in—then I memorise my lines in two or three different ways. I am of the firm opinion that unless an actor's lines—apart from improvisation—are not word perfect, he or she will not be able to act the part well.[14]

This unfailing reliability endeared her to directors, and the complete absence of an ego—on the sets or stage, that is—made her an ideal colleague. Anyone, and everyone, who had worked with her remarked on her capacity to put them at ease. She would make them laugh, crack silly jokes, just have fun. Moreover, she was a team player. Other actors might be tense, worried because it was their first day, or they may not have known how the director would respond to them, whether they would get on with the rest of the cast, but Zohra, said Setna, had 'a wonderful aura about her. She just oozed this quality, she had this way of being totally charming, totally relaxed, and she influenced everybody. She was so giving, so giving in every possible way.'[15]

Young people, especially, found her both reassuring and encouraging. 'You can be anything you want,' she'd tell them, 'look at me… stop worrying about what people think of you, do what you really want to.'[16] But young or old, if she could help anyone, she did. When they acted together in *Parosi*, Indira Joshi said Zohra helped her with Urdu and Punjabi words, with her accent, and even with her lines. Scripts couldn't help you with that, nor with fleshing out a character. 'Zohra would help me, because she was full of these little things that make a character, they just add zest to it.'[17] Shelley King, who was Zohra's granddaughter Bubbly in *Tandoori Nights*, said that her conversations with Zohra over the years had helped her realise her role in many serials, including *Coronation Street*, which she was currently shooting, as a character caught in a relationship of coercive control.[18]

That Zohra had undeniable stage and screen presence was a fact, but was she actor or performer? Was she playing a role, or playing Zohra? Onstage or off, on screen or not, wasn't she always just playing a part, and hadn't she always said, 'Whatever I do is for an audience'? Did she actually ever stop acting? She loved being complimented, loved the applause, never tired of enquiring about her performance: 'Did you really like it? I was good, wasn't I?' But she could also overdo it, become a caricature of herself. 'If she had been directed properly,' commented Roshan Seth, 'her performances would probably have been very different.' So, why wasn't she? 'Because of her age, because of who she was, because she was SO sincere, SO honest, SO truthful… Nobody told her, "Try not to try.' Seth believed it was her early exposure in the Prithviraj mode of acting that was responsible for many of her over-the-top performances, that when 'you are not given the tools to do the job, you think excess energy will do it for you'. Yet it was the same Roshan Seth who also believed that 'there was something in Zohra of Mother Courage, taking the ploughshares on her shoulders, something in her of the tigress'.[19]

So, who was she—the actor or the act? The popular, lovable, gregarious, warm and generous friend and mentor, or the private Zohra whom no one really knew? The grey-haired, sari-clad grandmother-figure or the shocker who could be quite crude late in life and say things like 'My main interest in men is sex' or 'I had a host of lovers, that's what's kept me young'? The down-to-earth, sensible mother of two, who nevertheless embarked on a life of uncertainty because she had to 'get on with it', or a rebel who took her chances?

In a 1992 interview Zohra told her young interviewer,

> Have you seen these *pahari* women who carry a *kangri* under their shirts to keep themselves warm? Every few minutes they flick the ash to keep the fire going. Kameshwar's memory is like that. I laugh most of the time, but once in a while I flick the ash and cry. That's what keeps me going.[20]

Was this one of Zohra's rehearsed statements regarding Kameshwar's death, or an uncharacteristic public admission of her feelings? At various times, and with different friends, she had recounted the circumstances of his suicide, an uncannily similar telling on each occasion. Yet, she kept the details of his death from her son, Pavan, for most of his adult life despite his pleas to be told what really happened. 'Why did he kill himself? I never got a straight answer from her. To this day, I don't know why he did what he did, and I never got that from her. It's a puzzle... When she talked about it, it was always in positives, she was never negative... maybe she herself didn't understand.'[21]

Or perhaps she knew that suicide, any suicide, could never really be understood. Better to put a positive cast on memories, present a brave front. In private, with a very few close confidantes, she could share her feelings more openly, as she would have done with Uzra or her cousin Hamida; and as she did with Shelley King, to whom she spoke about the difficulty of living with a man who is insecure and a depressive, and about why and how, despite this, you remain emotionally entangled.[22]

'Inside,' said Pavan, 'I think she was a quiet person… In her psyche there was… not darkness, but there was a silence.' Zohra's public self was bright and breezy, but a core of aloneness allowed her to respond immediately to those who needed succour. 'What Zohra did, what Zohra recognised about me,' said Madhav Sharma, 'was the pain in me, and she knew that one way I had dealt with the pain in me was by completely cutting India out of my life. And she brought me back to realising that I could be both, that I could be international and still be Indian, and for that I'm very grateful to her.' It could be that in Sharma's pain, Zohra recognised something akin to her own feeling of displacement in a country where she was always an outsider. 'I think she was actually a very shy person,' continued Sharma, 'a very sensitive, very shy person, who was coping with a lot of pain and tragedy with humour… but she didn't like talking about herself.' Or, he added, looking at herself.

For all the talk in her later interviews about boyfriends and her wisecracks about lovers and sex, Zohra remained unattached, except as a friend, for the rest of her life after Kameshwar. Sharma maintained that 'she found British men difficult to deal with. She was asked out by producers once or twice, but she found it difficult.' The bawdy and the scatological became part of her performance, her delight in shocking her listeners, a diversionary tactic—the joker in the pack—but she found the explosion of so-called sexual freedom in England distasteful. 'Not because she was against it,' clarified Sharma, 'but she thought it took away all the mystery, and it took all the romance out of relationships… And Zohra was very much a romantic.'

Success came to Zohra when most actors are getting ready to retire, but for her, retirement was not an option. Not because she needed the money—of course, it was always welcome—

but because she couldn't keep away from work. 'The thing about Zohra's work was—there was always a twinkle in her eye when she worked,' said Renu Setna, 'because she loved her work.' And yet, oddly enough, she never took *herself* seriously as an actor. She was completely serious about her acting, about professionalism, about work, but she had no exalted notions of herself as an actor—she was as good or as bad as anyone else. Acting was what she knew how to do, it was bread and butter, it allowed her to do what she loved—but did she think she needed to compete? To decline an offer because it was unimportant? To make a fuss? She took her work, and her experience and skill, seriously enough to decline working for free and insisted that she be paid what she asked for, but she was never unreasonable. Before she left England for good, her friend and fellow actor Shreela Ghosh asked her if she thought she had achieved her goal. 'Truthfully speaking,' she replied, 'I could have done much more. I was given the opportunity to make my talent flourish. What did I do with these talents?'[23] In the clearest indication of what she considered were her talents she mentioned dancing, choreography and her work with Prithvi Theatres; her subsequent career in acting was not part of her reckoning, no matter that she had already achieved a degree of fame by then. She only ever said that she was 'a fairly good actress'.

Zohra lived to be 102 years old, and spanned not only the twentieth century, but a century of the arts in India. She was, and remains, the only artiste who was active in theatre, in film and television, and as a dancer, within India and abroad, at a time when there was no such thing as cross-over. It was partly an accident of the times that she happened to be at the cusp of change in all the arts that she was part of: with Uday Shankar, when he broke away from the classical tradition and developed a new dance vocabulary; with IPTA, which pioneered people's theatre; and with Prithviraj Kapoor when he seized the post-Independence moment and hitched his theatrical intervention to the nation-building wagon, also taking his theatre to the people and infusing it with social as well as dramatic meaning. The decade of the 1950s was arguably one of the most dynamically creative in the arts and cinema in India, and Zohra was at its centre.

England, too, was changing when Zohra arrived there in the mid-1960s, although it would be at least another decade before the social and political churning found an echo in the cultural environment. When it did, however, it ushered in the kind of developments that would define media—especially broadcast media—and programming for the next couple of decades or more. The immigrant—Indian, Pakistani, West Indian, Kenyan Indian, Caribbean, South Asian, Chinese—a hitherto visible but silent figure, was now seen and heard, and voices and experiences on the fringes slowly made their way into the living rooms of more mainstream society. This entry, it goes without saying, was met with resistance, and with a fair share of racist reaction. But it was only a matter of time before the next generation began scripting and choreographing and performing its own stories, and claiming its legitimate cultural space. Zohra was there, in the right place and at more or less the right time. In the mid-1970s she was already in her mid-sixties, but there were few, if any, actors with her experience on stage and screen who could play the older woman with flair. Over time, she not only made the feisty granny role her own, she made her over in her own image—irreverent, forthright, spirited. And no one has managed to replace her as the irascible old woman in family dramas. No one else had her playfulness, said Gurinder Chadha.

On April 27, 2012, Zohra's 100th birthday, her daughter Kiran organised an event for the launch of her own book of reminiscences about her mother, called *Fatty*! One hundred red roses, a birthday cake and an auditorium full of friends, family and fans awaited Zohra as she was wheeled onstage. A burst of applause greeted her, she cracked her famous crooked smile, raised her hand in a royal wave, said, 'Hello, fans!' and proceeded to steal the show.

Friends, fans and colleagues gathered at the Nehru Centre in London as well, to celebrate her century, with directors like Christopher Morahan, Ken McMullen, Malcolm Craddock, Madhav Sharma and Waris Hussein; friends Kit Williams, Shelley King and Jill Williams and her husband George; actors Indira Joshi, Jamila Massey and many others, recalling their relationships with Zohra.

At the end of the evening in Delhi, when a friend asked Zohra if she would now like to have a cup of tea, she exclaimed, 'Tea? Where's my whisky!'

Zohra Segal died of a cardiac arrest in Delhi's Max Hospital on July 10, 2014, at the age of 102, having lived more or less on her own terms for most of her long life. 'I never set out to be a pioneer, never. I did what I did not to set an example for others, but because I wanted power, I wanted fame. And I wanted to enjoy myself.'[24] She may not have acquired the kind of power she imagined, but she certainly had her fair share of fame and an extraordinary amount of love, admiration and respect. From all accounts, she also managed to enjoy herself, despite the odds. When asked once what kept her going in the face of personal tragedy and despite adversity, she replied, 'I never look back, and I have no regrets.'

A Select Listing of Performances

Dance and Theatre Companies

1935-43 One of the leading dancers of the Uday Shankar Ballet Company; main teacher at the Uday Shankar India Culture Centre, Almora. Danced in the major cities of the West and the East. Several all-India tours. Over 1000 dance performances.

1943-45 Co-director of Zoresh Dance Institute, Lahore, with husband Kameshwar Segal. All India tour with students, March-July 1945.

1945-59 Leading actress and dance director with Prithvi Theatres, Bombay. Toured in over 100 towns of India, participating in approximately 2000 performances. Vice-president, Indian Peoples' Theatre Association (IPTA), Bombay, 1946-47. Dance director for Bombay films, 1945-55.

1959-62 Principal, Natya Academy, Delhi. Lectures on Indian dance and drama in USSR, East Germany and Czechoslovakia.

1974-75 Director, National Folk Dance Ensemble, India.

Plays

Mid-1940s Clifford Odets' *Waiting for Lefty* (IPTA). As Zeenat.

1946 *Deewar* (Director: Prithviraj Kapoor; Prithvi Theatres). As the foreign woman.

1947 *Pathan* (Director: Prithviraj Kapoor; Prithvi Theatres). As Khairunissa, the Pathan's wife.

1947 *Ghaddar* (Director: Prithviraj Kapoor; Prithvi Theatres). As Bari Bi, the maidservant.

1949 *Ahooti* (Director: Prithviraj Kapoor; Prithvi Theatres). As Visheshran, the hero's mother.

1951 *Kalakar* (Director: Prithviraj Kapoor; Prithvi Theatres). In a masked dance-duet.

1953 *Paisa* (Director: Prithviraj Kapoor; Prithvi Theatres). As a social butterfly.

1956 *Kisan* (Director: Prithviraj Kapoor; Prithvi Theatres). As Gajmukhi Bua.

1967 *A Touch of Brightness* (Director: Ian Watt Smith; Royal Court Theatre). As Bhabhi Rani.

1979-80 *The Primary English Class* (Director: Sam Walters; Orange Tree Theatre and Richmond and Wyndhams Theatre). As Mrs Pong.

1980 *The Good Person of Szechwan* (Director: Deborah Warner; Kick Theatre Company). As Mrs Shin and The First God.

1981 *Our Own People* (Director: Madhav Sharma; Actors Unlimited). As Mrs Bhandari.

1983 *Hedda in India* (Director: Madhav Sharma; Actors Unlimited). As Aunt Jabeen.

1984 *The Great Celestial Cow* (Director: Carole Hayman; John Stock Theatre Group). Dadima and three other roles.

1988 *Moteram ka Satyagraha* (Director: Habib Tanvir; Naya Theatre). As Mrs Moteram.

1989 *Down Every Street* (Director: Jeff Tears; Theatre Royal, Stratford East). As Beena.

1992 *Din ke Andhere* (Director: Ebrahim Alkazi; National School of Drama Repertory, New Delhi). As the Matriarch.

1993 *Ek Thi Nani* (Director: Madeeha Gauhar; Ajoka Theatre, Lahore). As Nani.

1994 *My Fair Lady* (Director: Aamir Raza Husain; Stagedoor). As Mrs Higgins. *The Legend of Ram* (Director: Aamir Raza Husain; Showbiz). As Manthara.

1995 *The Yearning* (Director: Kristine Landon-Smith; Tamasha Theatre Company). As the old woman.

1996 *Skirmishes* (Director: Sohaila Kapoor)

1998 *Harvest* (Director: Joy Michael)

2001 *An Evening with Zohra Segal* (Director: John Harris. Opening show for Stratfor Circus.)

2002 *Spirit of Anne Frank* (Director: Royston Abel)

2003 *Rice Boy (*Director: Michelene Cheyres; Canadian Stage Company, Toronto)

2007 *City of Djinns* (Director: Rudradeep Chakraborti)

Television

1964 *The Indian Tales of Rudyard Kipling* (BBC). As Fareda/ Ameera's mother/Ayah/Mrs Hauksbee's Ayah.

1965 *Doctor Who* (BBC). As Sheyrah.

1968 *The Expert* (BBC). As Mrs. Singh.

1973 *The Regiment* (BBC). As Nani Ji.

1974 *It Ain't Half Hot Mum* (BBC). As Rangi's mother-in-law.

1977 *Parosi* (BBC). As Mrs Chowdhry. *Gideon's Way* (BBC).

1978 *Mind Your Language* (ITV). As Mrs Singh.

1984 *The Jewel in the Crown* (Granada TV/ ITV).
As Lady Lili Chatterjee.
Inspector Ghote (ITV). As the ayah.
Come to Mecca (BBC). As the grandmother.

1985-87 *Tandoori Nights* (Channel 4). As Gran.

1987 *Never Say Die* (Yorkshire Television). As Gajmukhi.

1989 *The Bill* (Thames TV/ITV). As Mrs Gunn.

1989-90 *Mullah Nasruddin* (Doordarshan). As Old Woman/ Storyteller.

1991 *Firm Friends* (Zenith/TyneTees TV). As Suvira.

1992 *Bua Fatima* (Doordarshan). As Bua Fatima.

1994 *Little Napoleons* (Channel 4). As Jayaben Shah.
Partyana (Doordarshan). As Auntie.
Tandoori Nights, 2nd Series. Channel 4. As Gran.

1995 *Amma and Family* (Home TV). As Amma.
Ek Tha Rusty (Doordarshan). As the Rani.
Mian Khoji (Doordarshan). As the Begum.
Akhri Parao (Ddoordarshan). As Maji.

1999 *Khwahish* (Sony Entertainment TV). As Aapa.

2001 *Zindagi Kitni Khoobsoorat Hai* (ETV). As Dadi.

Films

1943 *Shakuntala* (Director: V. Shantaram). As Menaka.
1946 *Dharti Ke Lal* (Director: K.A. Abbas).
Neecha Nagar (Director: Chetan Anand). As Bhabi.
1950 *Afsar* (Director: Chetan Anand).
1953 *Fareb* (Director: Shaheed Latif).
1957 *Paisa* (Director: Prithvi Raj Kapoor).
1967 *The Long Duel* (Director: Ken Annakin). As Devi.
1968 *The Vengeance of She*(Director: Cliff Owen). As Putri.
1969 *The Guru* (Director: James Ivory). As Mastani.
1973 *Tales That Witness Madness* (Director: Freddie Francis). As Malia.
1983 *The Honorary Consul* (Director: John Mackenzie). As Maria.
The Courtesans of Bombay (Director: Ismail Merchant). As Hamida Begum.
1984-85 *Harem* (Director: Arturo Jeoffe). As Affaf.
1985 *The Red Bindi* (Director: Vishnu Mathur). As Maan ji.
1986 *Caravaggio* (Director: Derek Jarman). As Jerusaleme's Grandmother.
Man-Eaters of Kumaon (Director: Alex Kirby). As a hill woman.
1987 *Partition* (Director: Ken McMullen). As Everywoman.
1989 *Manika, Manika* (Director: François Villiers). As the hero's mother.
1991 *Masala* (Director: Krishna Srinivas). As Grandma Tikkou.
1993 *Bhaji on the Beach* (Director: Gurinder Chaddha). As Pushpa.
1994 *Of Two Women* (Director: Nina Singh)
1996 *Hum Panchhi ek Daal ke* (Director: Susheel Nair)
1997 *Tamanna* (Director: Mahesh Bhatt). As Mrs Chopra.
1998 *Dil Se* (Director: Mani Ratnam). As the grandmother.
1999 *Hum Dil De Chuke Sanam* (Director: Sanjay Leela Bhansali). As Dadi.
2001 *The Mystic Masseur* (Director: Ismail Merchant). As Auntie.
Kabhi Khushi Kabhie Gham (Director: Karan Johar). As Dadi.
2002 *Bend It Like Beckham* (Director: Gurinder Chaddha). As Biji.

	Anita and Me (Director: Metin Hüseyin). As Naanima.
	Chalo Ishq Ladaaye (Director: Aziz Sejawal). As Dadi.
2003	*Saaya* (Director: Anurag Basu). As Sister Martha.
	Kal Ho Naa Ho (Director: Nikhil Advani). As a woman of Pakistani origin in New York. (Scenes featuring Segal were deleted in the final cut.)
2004	*Veer-Zaara* (Director: Yash Chopra). As Bebe
2005	*Chicken Tikka Masala* (Director: Hermage Singh Kalirai). As the grandmother.
	The Mistress of Spices (Director: Paul Mayeda Berges). As First Mother.
2007	*Cheeni Kum* (Director: R. Balki). As Mrs Gupta.
	Saawariya (Director: Sanjay Leela Bhansali). As Lilian Ji aka Lilipop.

Advertisement Films

2004	Gobain Glass
2006	Titan Watches
	Leher Snacks
2007	Cadbury Chocolates
2008	Mirinda Cold Drinks

Awards

1998	Padma Shri
2002	Kalidas Samman, Acting
2002	Padma Bhushan
2010	Padma Vibhushan
2012	IIFA Special Award for Cinema

Notes

Act 1, Scene 1: Dance, by Chance

1. Zohra Segal, *Close-Up: memoirs of a life on stage & screen* (New Delhi: Women Unlimited 2010), p. 38.
2. Times of India, *Zohra Segal: the Drama of Life*, 24 August 2003.
3. Joan Erdman with Zohra Segal, *Stages: The Art and Adventures of Zohra Segal* (New Delhi: Kali for Women 1997), p. 13.
4. Ibid.
5. Times of India, op. cit.
6. Segal, *Close-Up*, p. 41.
7. Ibid, p. 47.
8. Ibid, p. 49.
9. Mohan Khokar, *His Dance, His Life: A Portrait of Uday Shankar* (New Delhi: Himalayan Books 1983), p. 13.
10. Ibid, p. 29.
11. Ibid, p. 72.
12. Ibid, p. 38.
13. Ibid, p. 42.
14. Ibid.
15. Ruth K. Abrahams, 2007, 'Uday Shankar: The Early Years, 1900-1938.' *Dance Chronicle* 30(3): 363-426.
16. Mohan Khokar, *His Dance, His Life: A Portrait of Uday Shankar*, p. 56
17. Ibid, p. 161.
18. Ibid.
19. Erdman and Segal, *Stages*, pp. 75-76.
20. Ibid, p. 77.

21. http://www.kalakshetra.in/site/history/
22. Khokar, *His Dance, His Life*, p. 79.
23. Letter dated August 26, 1986, from Uzra to Zohra.
24. Khokar, *His Dance, His Life*, p. 91.
25. Ibid, pp. 91-92.
26. Segal, *Close-Up*, p. 72.
27. Erdman and Segal, *Stages*, p. 81.
28. Ibid, pp. 82-83.
29. Khokar, *His Dance, His Life*, p. 71.
30. Ibid, p. 76.
31. Ibid, p. 77.
32. Erdman and Segal, *Stages*, p. 90.
33. Khokar, *His Dance, His Life*, p. 96.
34. Segal, *Close-Up*, p. 84..

Act 1, Scene 2: The Almora Dance Academy

1. Segal, *Close-Up*.
2. Erdman & Segal, *Stages*, p. 64.
3. Segal, *Close-Up*, p. 56.
4. Hamida Saiduzzafar, *Autobiography 1921-1988* (New Delhi: Trianka, 1996), p. 7.
5. Ibid., p. 61.
6. Segal, *Close-Up*, p. 86.
7. Ibid., pp. 86-87.
8. Khokar, p. 168.
9. Erdman & Segal, *Stages*, op. cit., pp. 96-97.
10. Khokar, op. cit., pp. 169-170.
11. Ibid., p. 163.
12. Erdman & Segal, *Stages*, pp. 95, 98.
13. Segal, *Close-Up*, p. 95.
14. Ibid., p. 95.
15. Erdman & Segal, *Stages*, p. 110.
16. Letter from Uzra to Zohra Segal, dated August 26, 1986/Lahore.
17. Khokar, p. 109.
18. Gertrude Sen to Mohan Khokar, Khokar, p. 112.
19. Ibid., p. 112.
20. Ibid.

21. Segal, *Close-Up*, p. 98.
22. Ibid., p. 103.

Act 2, Scene 1: In the Wings

1. Uma Anand & Ketan Anand, *Chetan Anand: The Poetics of Film* (Mumbai: Himalayan Films—Media Entertainment, 2007), p. 15.
2. Ibid., p. 17.
3. Minnette de Silva, *The Life & Work of an Asian Woman Architect* (Colombo, GEDSANDS Trust, 1998), p. 65.
4. Iffat Fatima & Syeda S. Hameed (eds.) *Bread, Beauty, Revolution: Khwaja Ahmad Abbas 1914-1987*, (New Delhi: K A Abbas Memorial Trust & Tulike Books, 2015), p. 111.
5. Ibid, p. 113.
6. Ibid, p. 116.
7. Kiran Segal, interviewed by Ritu Menon, New Delhi, August 18, 2015.
8. Zohra Segal, *Close-Up*, op.cit., pp. 106-107.
9. For a more detailed discussion of this, see Ruth Vanita, *Dancing With the Nation: Courtesans in Bombay Cinema* (New Delhi: Speaking Tiger, 2017).
10. Segal, *Close-Up*, p. 107.
11. Madhu Jain, *The Kapoors: The First Family of Indian Cinema* (New Delhi: Penguin Boooks India, 2005), pp. 13 & 14)
12. Fatima & Hameed, Bread, Beauty, Revolution, p. 114.
13. Shashi Kapoor with Deepa Gahlot, *The Prithviwallas* (New Delhi: Lustre Press/ Roli Books, 2004), p. 19.
14. Madhu Jain, *The Kapoors*, p. 21.
15. Segal, *Close-Up*, p. 107.
16. Prithviraj and Prithvi Theatres: *Kala Desh ki Seva Mein*, Prithvi Theatre Yearbook, 2007, entries at March 20, 22.
17. Ibid.
18. Ibid, entry March 23, 24, reproducing news clippings.
19. Ibid.
20. Ibid.
21. Segal, *Close-Up*, p. 108.
22. Shashi Kapoor with Deepa Gahlot, *The Prithviwallahs*, p. 24.

23. Shaukat Kaifi, *Portrait of an Actress*, in *Kala Desh ki Seva Mein*, entry dated May 5.
24. Erdman and Segal, *Stages*, p. 125.
25. *Kala Desh ki Seva Mein*, entry dated May 29.
26. Uma Anand-Ketan Anand, *Chetan Anand*, p. 19.
27. Ibid.
28. Ibid, p. 24.
29. Zohra Segal, *Times of India*, July 1997.
30. Kiran Segal, interview by Ritu Menon, August 18, 2015.
31. Erdman and Segal, *Stages*, p. 124.
32. Ibid, p. 125.

Act 2, Scene 2: Onstage with Prithvi

1. Malcolm Darling in *Kala Desh ki Seva Mein*, entry dated April 13.
2. Segal, *Close-Up*, p. 126.
3. *Shri Prithviraj Kapoor Abhinandan Granth* (Bombay: Triveni Rang Manch, 1960).
4. Malini Nair, 'Much before the Partition, Prithviraj Kapoor was warning of its horrors in gut-wrenching plays.' Scroll.in, 15 August 2017
5. *Shri Prithviraj Kapoor Abhinandan Granth* (Bombay: Triveni Rang Manch, 1960).
6. *Kala Desh ki Seva Mein*, entry dated June 11.
7. Erdman and Segal, *Stages*, pp. 135-136.
8. *Kala Desh ki Seva Mein*, entry dated July 20.
9. Shashi Kapoor with Deepa Gahlot, *Prithviwallahs*, p. 39.
10. *Kala Desh ki Seva Mein*, entry dated September 30.
11. https://scroll.in/magazine/847168/much-before-the-partition-prithviraj-kapoor-was-warning-of-its-horrors-in-gut-wrenching-plays
12. *Kala Desh ki Seva Mein*, entry dated September 1.
13. Jai Dayal Kapur, *I Go South with Prithviraj and his Prithvi Theatres* (Bombay: Prithvi Theatres Publication, 1950), p. 45.
14. *Kala Desh ki Seva Mein*, entry dated September 23.
15. Ibid., entry at October 5.
16. Madhu Jain, *The Kapoors*, op.cit., p. 37.
17. *Kala Desh ki Seva Mein*, entry dated December 13.

18. Erdman and Segal, *Stages*, p. 146.
19. Kala Desh ki Seva Menin, entry dated December 31.
20. Ibid, entry dated December 7.
21. Ibid.
22. Erdman and Segal, *Stages*, p. 153.

{FIRST INTERMISSION}

1. Zohra Segal, *Close-Up*, p. 157.
2. Erdman and Segal, *Stages*, p. 167.

Act 3, Scene 1: Rehearsing

1. Zohra Segal, *Close-Up*, p. 182.
2. Naseem Khan, interviewed by Ritu Menon, London, June 14, 2016.
3. Jamila Massey, interviewed by Jonathan Page, London.
4. Renu Setna, interviewed by Jonathan Page, London.
5. Jamila Massey, interview as above.
6. Waris Hussein interviewed by Ritu Menon, London, June 15, 2016.
7. Segal, *Close-Up*, pp. 184-85.
8. http://www.theguardian.com/world/2014/oct15 accessed 5/2/2019
9. Naseem Khan, *Everywhere is Somewhere* (London: Bluemoose Books, 2017), pp. 69, 76.
10. Kiran Segal, interviewed by Ritu Menon, Delhi, January 28, 2018.
11. http://news.bbc.co.uk/1/hi/magazine/4332380.stm, accessed July 29, 2019.
12. Dolly Thakore, interviewed by Ritu Menon, Delhi, September 29, 2019.
13. Waris Hussein, interview as above.
14. Ibid.
15. Renu Setna, interview as above.
16. Kiran Segal, interview as above.
17. Personal communication from Muneeza Shamsie, October 11, 2019.
18. Babar Mumtaz, interviewed by Ritu Menon, London, June 18, 2016.

19. *The Times*, London, March 6, 1967.
20. Prithviraj Kapoor to Zohra Segal, November 17, 1967.
21. Prithviraj Kapoor to Zohra Segal, October 31, 1969.
22. Prithviraj Kapoor to Zohra Segal, June 27, 1969.
23. Segal, *Close-Up*, p. 25.
24. Pavan Segal, interviewed by Ritu Menon, Kuala Lumpur, October 19, 2019.
25. Prithviraj Kapoor to Zohra Segal, November 21, 1968.
26. Kiran Segal, interview as above.

{SECOND INTERMISSION}

1. Kit Williams in a phone conversation with Ritu Menon, December 13, 2019.

Act 3, Scene 2: Breakthrough

1. British Actors' Equity Association, 'Employment of Afro-Asian Artists in the Theatre,' a report, January 1975. All details and figures quoted are taken from this report.
2. Ibid., p. 8.
3. Renu Setna, Interviewed by Jonathan Page, London, September 2015.
4. Ibid.
5. Madhav Sharma, interviewed by Jonathan Page, London, July 28, 2016.
6. Naseem Khan, 'The Arts Britain Ignores: The Arts of Ethnic Minorities in Britain' (London: The Arts Council of Great Britain, Calouste Gulbenkian Foundation and Community Relations Commission, 1976), p. 5.
7. Ibid., p. 155.
8. Naseem Khan, interviewed by Jonathan Page, London, September 2, 2015.
9. Zohra Segal, *Close-Up*, p. 257.
10. Naseem Khan, *Everywhere is Somewhere*, p. 168.
11. Renu Setna, interview as above.
12. Madhav Sharma, interview as above.
13. Erdman and Segal, *Stages*, p. 234.
14. Madhav Sharma, interview as above.

15. Erdman and Segal, *Stages*, pp. 217-18.
16. Kiran Segal, interviewed by Ritu Menon, Delhi, August 13, 2018.
17. Kiran Segal, interview as above.
18. Zohra Segal, *Close-Up*, p. 258.
19. Waris Hussein, interviewed by Ritu Menon, London, June 15, 2016.
20. Gerard Dempsey, *Daily Express*, January 10, 1984.
21. Lou Wakefield, interviewed by Ritu Menon, London, August 13, 2018.
22. Michael Wilmington, 'Caravaggio: A Dialectic of Passions', *LA Times*, September 13, 1986.
23. Tony Pratt, *Daily Mirror*, July 26, 1985.
24. Ian Johnston, http://www.notcoming.com/reviews/partition. Posted on December 7, 2007.
25. Phone conversation with Ken McMullen by Ritu Menon, December 21, 2019.
26. Roshan Seth, interviewed by Ritu Menon, Delhi, September 13, 2018.
27. Ken McMullen, as above.
28. 'Reflections on *Partition*', Ken McMullen in conversation with James Leahy, Second Run DVD, booklet.
29. Erdman and Segal, *Stages*, p. 243.
30. Ibid., pp. 244-45.

Act 4, Scene 1: In Character Again

1. Sudhanva Deshpande, *Halla Bol! The Death and Life of Safdar Hashmi* (New Delhi: Leftword Books, 2019), p. 162.
2. *The Telegraph*, September 2, 1992.
3. *The Pioneer*, May 6, 1992.
4. Lou Wakefield, interviewed by Ritu Menon, London, August 13, 2018.
5. *Daily Mail*, July 3, 1992.
6. As reported in *The News*, London, Bureau, October 9, 1992.
7. *The Hindustan Times*, April 10, 1993.
8. *The Times of India*, January 1993.
9. https://www.theguardian.com/film/2006/Jul/16/features.review1
10. *The Evening Standard*, January 20, 1994.

11. https://inews.co.uk/culture/nikesh-shukla-bhaji-on-the-beach-came-out-25-years-ago-and-nothing-has-changed-276935
12. Gurinder Chadha in a phone conversation with Ritu Menon, January 2, 2020.
13. *The Times of India*, August 24, 2003.

Act 4, Scene 2: The Third Bell

1. Kiran Segal, interviewed by Ritu Menon, Delhi, January 25, 2018.
2. Letter dated December 11, 2000 to Jill Williams.
3. David Tindall in *The Guardian*, March 23, 2001.
4. Philip French, *The Observer*,
5. Letter dated February 14, 2002 to Jill Williams.
6. Letter dated March___ 2002 to Jill Williams.
7. Letter dated December 9, 2003 to Jill Williams.
8. Letter dated February 21, 2004 to Jill Williams.
9. Letter dated April 30, 2004 to Dolly Thakore.
10 Jill Williams, interviewed by Ritu Menon, London, September 29, 2017.
11. Letter dated July 30, 2004 to Jill Williams.
12. Letter dated August 23, 2005 to Dolly Thakore.
13. Letter dated January 8, 2006 to Dolly Thakore.
14. Letter dated December 15, 2006 to Jill Williams.
15. Indira Joshi, interviewed by Jonathan Page, London, June 9, 2016.

Curtain Call

1. *The Sunday Observer*, July 26-August 1, 1992.
2. Erdman and Segal, *Stages*, p. 216.
3. As told to Shreela Ghosh, in *Bazaar*, quoted in Erdman and Segal, *Stages*, p. 262.
4. *The Friday Times*, Lahore, March 11-17, 1993.
5. *The Indian Express*, December 29, 1991.
6. Roshan Seth, interviewed by Ritu Menon, September 2018.
7. Ibid.
8. *TV & Video World*, September 1993.
9. Babar Mumtaz, interviewed by Ritu Menon, as cited.

10. *Economic Times*, March 11, 1992.
11. Madhav Sharma, interviewed by Jonathan Page, as cited.
12. Renu Setna, interviewed by Jonathan Page, as cited.
13. Madhav Sharma, as cited.
14. *TV & Video World*, September 1993.
15. Renu Setna, as cited.
16. Madhav Sharma, as cited.
17. Indira Joshi, interviewed by Jonathan Page, as cited.
18. Shelley King in a phone conversation with Ritu Menon, August 11, 2019.
19. Roshan Seth, interview as cited.
20. *Society*, May 1992.
21. Pavan Segal, interview by Ritu Menon, as cited.
22. Shelley King, as cited.
23. Shreela Ghosh, in *Stages*, op.cit., p. 262.
24. *Sunday Observer*, July 26-August 1, 1992.

ALSO FROM SPEAKING TIGER

ONE FOOT ON THE GROUND

A Life Told Through the Body

Shanta Gokhale

WINNER OF THE CROSSWORD AWARD

'*Filled with humour and candour, [Gokhale's] memoir is a personal and public history of growing up in a progressive world... [This] tale of an ordinary life is extraordinarily told.*'—The Hindu

In this unusual, extraordinary autobiography, Shanta Gokhale—writer, translator, theatre critic and one of India's most illuminating cultural commentators—traces the arc of her life over eight decades through the progress of her body, as it grows, matures and begins to wind down. Starting with her birth in 1939, she recounts her childhood, youth and middle and old age in chapters built around the many elements and processes of the physical self: tonsils and adenoids, breasts and misaligned teeth; childbirth and fluctuating weight, cancer and bunions. And through these memories emerge others, less visible but just as defining: a carefree childhood growing up in a progressive Marathi household in Mumbai; the pleasures, in adolescence, of badminton, Kathak and hairdressing; the warmth of friends and an almost lover in cold, damp England; finding and losing a mate—twice—and bringing up her children as a single parent; the great thrill of her first translation from Marathi into English; nursing her mother, dying of cancer, as she would a baby; surviving cancer herself, and writing her second novel through the recovery.

Told with effortless humour and candour, this is the story of a life full of happiness, heartbreak, wonder and acceptance. It will rank among the finest personal histories written in India.

'*A delightful memoir...* [One Foot on the Ground] *captures a vital moment of social transition and transformation of the Indian woman, from being a set of roles and functions to being a person in her own right, unashamedly and unapologetically.*'—The Book Review